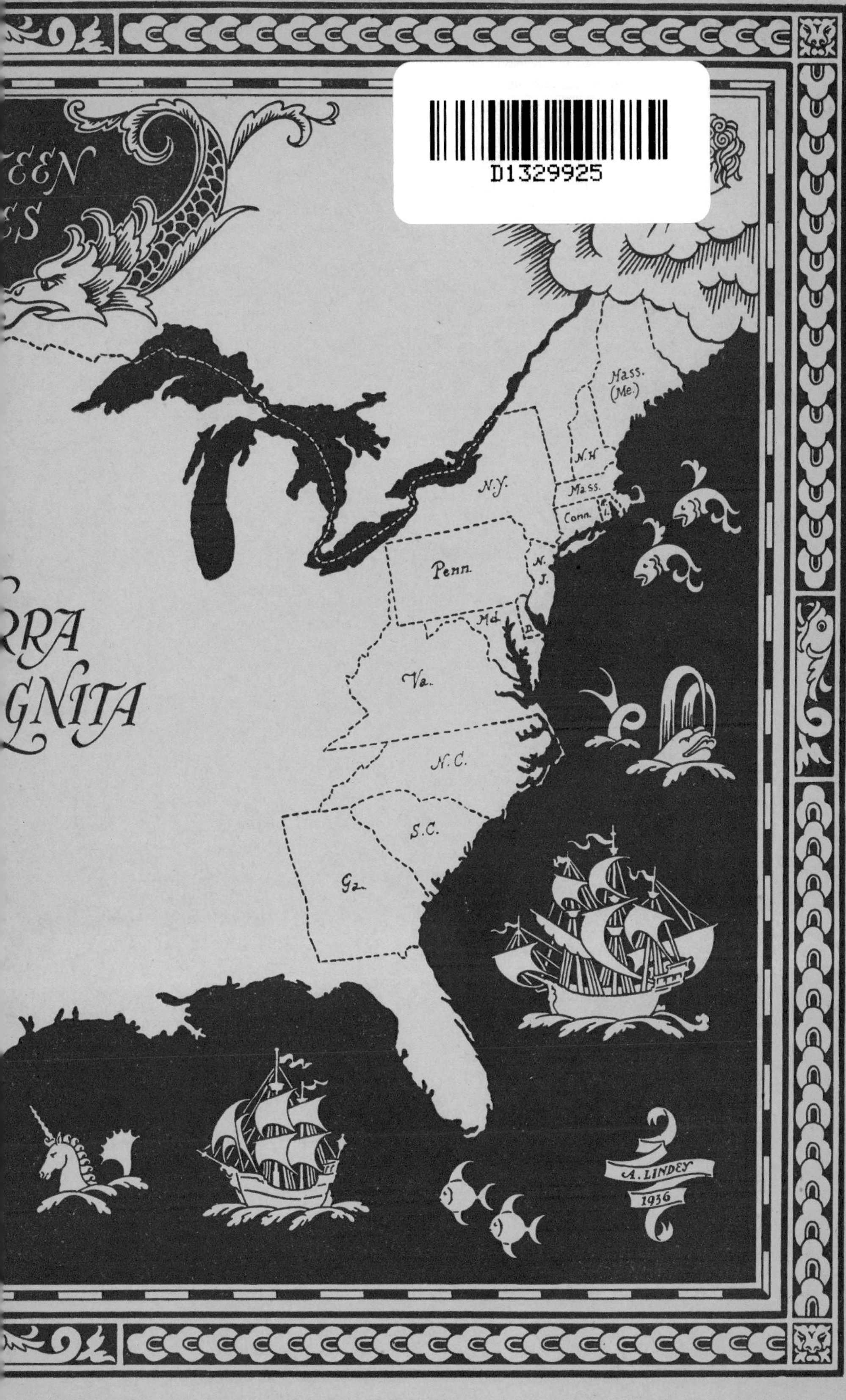
Mass.
(Me.)
N.H
Mass.
Conn.
N.Y.
Penn
N.J.
Md.
Va.
N.C.
S.C.
Ga.
A. LINDEY
1936

THE ULTIMATE POWER

MORRIS L. ERNST

THE
ULTIMATE
POWER

DOUBLEDAY, DORAN & COMPANY, INC.

Garden City, New York

1937

PRINTED AT THE *Country Life Press*, GARDEN CITY, N. Y., U. S. A.

To
HEYWOOD BROUN
who asked
for it.

Contents

INTRODUCTION

I N READING THE GAZETTES of a hundred and fifty years ago I saw a cartoon depicting a lopsided, disjointed barrel. There were thirteen staves, but not a single hoop around them. The staves were all askew. They leaned at disturbing angles. Each stave seemed to prevent its neighbors from standing firm and erect. The cartoonist had written on each stave the name of one of the colonies, and the hoops so badly needed were called "The Constitution." The caption of the picture was "Hoops for the Barrel." That was in 1787.

Now, in 1936, the cartoon should be reprinted with the many additional staves representing the new states. The hoops—our great constitution of 1787—are no longer holding the increased number of staves in line. The staves show signs of cruel depressions. The hoops have been cut or added to on a score of occasions, and still the barrel is less than tight. There are many leaks between the staves.

The chief concern of the nation today must be the prompt examination of the barrel. The placing of the hoops of 1787 around the thirteen staves was a radical change. Since 1787 our advances in the history of nations have been accompanied by an adventurous attitude toward constant change.

I happen to be a member of that exciting profession which has always been the vanguard of the army resisting change. The reason for this attitude is obvious. Those who fear change are those who have amassed wealth and who live, in part or totally, on interest or dividends. Such are the paying clients. In this country more than any other in the world the legislative chambers have always been unduly weighted with members of the Bar. Sitting in those chambers, my profession has continued its advocacy of preserving property with distressing disregard for personal liberty. This disregard is to be expected, for in the struggle for material preservation the personal liberty of those standing in the way never arouses any great amount of sympathy.

Engaged in a recent investigation, I found that 74 per cent of the women working in hotels in New York, catering to the richest sojourners in the world, were earning less than thirteen dollars a week; and only one in ten received more than sixteen dollars a week. My state, New York, through its elected officials, after bitter and well-aired political discussions, decided that the federal government in Washington spoke wisely when it declared that sixteen dollars a week was less than a living, and far less than a saving, wage. It created a forum to determine just what minimum wage should be paid to such women. The Supreme Court of the United States, however, ruled that girls must go back and work for five dollars a week. Not the Court; only some of the judges, but by ill chance more than half of the nine. So the Court as a court wrote a prescription for the women of the land—a prescription of hunger, want and disease.

I look over the American scene. Fabulous wealth, staggering inventive ability, unbelievable energy have brought neither stability nor a decent life for more than a top fringe of the very wealthy. Casting an eye back at the many legislative attempts in aid of a richer life for all, I came to the conclusion that our congressmen, befuddlers and logrollers as they are at times, have consistently had a greater vision than the courts. The pursuit of the last half-century to spread opportunity, to prevent the waste of cutthroat competition, to curtail the abuse of concentration of wealth, has invariably been frustrated by judges.

I look back into the history books, and I find that within thirty years after the nation was formed the wildest myths had been spread about the Founding Fathers and their concept of government. I find almost no literature correctly portraying the struggles of that era and the human foibles and objectives of the men who wrote our Constitution.

George Washington once decided and bluntly said: "Mankind, left to themselves, are unfit for government."

Do we agree with that today? But on just that thesis our government, remote from popular control, was established. Gorham, a wise and influential delegate at the Constitutional Convention, declared: "It cannot be supposed that this vast territory will a hundred and fifty years hence remain one nation." There were then only thirteen states, with a population of less than one half of present New York City. Scarcely a wise prophecy!

This nation and the world have been pressed forward by new sources of energy not within the imagination of any of the farsighted men of 1787. Just over the hill I see the introduction of labor-saving machinery, like the Rust cotton picker, which will cast into irretrievable unemployment many more millions of the citizens of our unplanned society. A few inventions of that sort may devastate all our present economic and political thinking. A nation cannot survive one half employed and one half unemployed.

After reviewing the documents of our Founding Fathers, I think I have found the economic forces which prompted their actions. The identic commercial forces impel present legislators to action. The same use of government to enhance the wealth of the nation impels our present elected officials. But the jurists, sitting like ancient witch doctors remote from the life of the mines and the farms, with words no laymen and few barristers can fathom, hold back the tides of potential prosperity and well-being for all our people.

The Fathers opened the Constitution of 1787 with a replica of the constitution of the Indian Treaty of the Five Nations of 1520 before them. The Indians had written:

"We, the people, to form a union, to establish peace, equity and order . . ."

Those words meant one thing to the Indians of 1520, another to the constitution drafters of 1787, and obviously something quite different to the high judges of 1936.

We can move in one of two ways. Either we can issue new instructions to the judges by amending the Constitution, or the working people of the land will reach for their mass power. It is unreasonable to expect that judges, with eyes glued to heavy tomes, will have the common wisdom to see that they are forcing a revolution. Not even the pace of the last two years in France—so secure, we thought, in 1934 —will impress them. Maybe an amendment enacted with precision and speed will break the tight little bottleneck which the judges have blown and through which progress now filters only as they care to let it pass. Jefferson prophesied: "If this avenue [legislation] be shut off to the call of sufferance it will make itself heard through that of force."

This volume divided itself into ten sections:

1. The background, commercial and social, in the struggle of the thirteen colonies for freedom from England.
2. The task of setting up a new nation determined by the economics of 1787 and colored by the vibrant Founding Fathers.
3. The great document—our constitution.
4. The immediately following agricultural rebellion led by Jefferson against the aristocracy of Hamilton.
5. The capture by the Supreme Court of the function of vetoing legislation.
6. The expansion of production by the use of new sources of energy.
7. The development of three devices created by the Founding Fathers—the presidential veto, the right of states to make compacts, and the power of amending the Constitution.
8. The judicial vetoes of an integrated society so that with all our wealth millions suffer and travel only short distances in the pursuit of happiness.
9. The judges who have held the veto power over democracy.
10. Suggested plans for getting the power back into the hands of the people.

One more word: this volume was not designed for lawyers. After the decision of the Supreme Court vetoing the Agricultural Adjustment Act, John L. Lewis, head of the United Mine Workers, wisely commented: "I am not surprised that none of the four hundred thousand miners understands the Court's opinions, because I know that many thousands of lawyers read it, and each one thought it meant something different." Our present national bewilderment and confusion will not be allayed by the legal mind. I think the time is ripe for the non-lawyers to reassert their earnest disrespect for what lawyers and judges have done to us all.

I wish to thank Eleanor Ernst and Margaret Ernst, and John Craig, of the publisher's editorial staff, for their extensive assistance in the preparation of this book, to whose conclusions they are in no way committed. Also thanks to my partner, Alexander Lindey, for the end-paper design, and to Isabelle Taylor, who compiled the index.

MORRIS L. ERNST.

Nantucket, Mass.
November, 1936.

PART I

We Break from England

THE words of the Constitution, read separately and apart from the decades of resistance to Great Britain, lose their essential content. The machinery established by the Founding Fathers at the Constitutional Convention of 1787 takes on excitement only if we are able to imagine ourselves living on the seaboard of this vast continent then unexplored and literally undiscovered. The commercial struggles and warfare of the thirteen colonies induced a united front, bringing freedom in 1783 and chaos until 1789. The treaty of peace of 1783 by no means insured a nation of thirteen states in America. In the absence of inflation, interstate commercial warfare and boundary disputes, several nations instead of one might have been established.

CHAPTER I

The Rising Sun

THE OLD DOCTOR was gay as usual, but feeble and a trifle shaky on his feet. He had never been known as an orator. In crowds he had always been diffident. And yet, before he rose in that stern but graceful room on Chestnut Street, Philadelphia, that 17th day of September, everyone in the chamber was looking in his direction.

He was very old. Past eighty-one, to be exact. Old enough to be the grandfather of several and the father of all but six of the twoscore men who sat around him in those semicircular rows of mahogany chairs. Near by sat the baby of the gathering, Jonathan Dayton of New Jersey, twenty-seven years old. This hasty-tempered young man sat there as surrogate for his father, elected but not sufficiently interested to attend. Only six men out of the forty-one in the room were over sixty years of age. Six were under thirty-one. The median age was only forty-two.

The average age of the senators of the United States Senate of 1936 was fifty-eight.

No wonder there was an added tinge of deep respect accorded old Dr Benjamin Franklin as he arose to put a final blessing on the last draft of the Constitution of the United States as it came from the pen of the stylist, Gouverneur Morris, to that secret gathering known as the Constitutional Convention of the thirteen colonies.

The Doctor, in a mood such as no other eminent American since then, save only Mr Justice Oliver Wendell Holmes, has ever acquired, glanced for a moment out of the low, large windows and took in the extensive pleasant gar-

3

dens of the Pennsylvania State House—those gardens where the other, more active members of the convention had so often strolled during brief moments of intermission to converse in hushed tones about the problems of this, as many thought it to be, the first written constitution of any nation on this planet.

> *The only running water in even the grandest houses was "a nigger with a bucket." No built-in clothes closets had yet been thought of. At Councillor Carter's plantation, Nomini Hall, a cart and three pair of oxen brought in four loads of wood daily in cold weather (Sunday excepted) for twenty-eight steady fires.*

The chairman's eyes turned toward the Doctor's broad face, topped with straggly gray hair. The chairman's blue eyes, sunk beneath heavy brows, were warmer than usual, for he recalled how, four months earlier, Dr Franklin had been his only competitor for the position of chairman of the gathering. He, George Washington, remembered that Dr Franklin had graciously agreed to nominate him at that time, but, the weather being inclement, the old Doctor could not risk leaving his home.

"Sir," said the six-foot General sitting on the slightly raised dais in a high-backed chair.

"Sir," began the Doctor, gazing, not at Mr Washington, but a few feet above the General's head at the carving which capped the finial arch of the General's chair. "Sir, for four months I have been observing that picture painted on the high arch of your chair. More than anyone in this chamber I have gazed at carvings and paintings of artists of all lands. In the galleries and salons of England and France I have seen innumerable attempts of artists to depict that greatest of planets, the sun. Artists have always found it difficult to distinguish a rising from a setting sun. I have often and often, in the course of these sessions and vicissitudes of my hopes and fears as to its issue, looked at that sun behind the president of this convention without being able to tell whether it was rising or setting. But now at length I have the happiness to know that it is a rising sun and not a setting sun."

He took his seat, his eyes moving along the faces of the other forty members of the convention. He had always known that the Constitution of the United States, about to be signed, was a "jumble of compromises," but just for that reason he was trying to have it go forth to the people as a unanimous report. He knew that many of those present agreed with representative Jonathan Dayton of New Jersey, who called the document an "amphibious monster."

CHAPTER II

One Hundred and Fifty Years Ago

THE CONSTITUTIONAL CONVENTION of the thirteen colonies, sitting in Philadelphia while the regular Congress of the colonies was holding sessions in New York City, had many times needed the gentle touch of the old Doctor to prevent complete disruption.

The call for the gathering had been for May 14, 1787. Only a handful of delegates appeared, and seven states did not have a single delegate present. Not until May 25 was there even a scant quorum, and then from only nine states. There had been no popular imperative demand for a new constitution. One month later, on June 28, Sherman declared, "We are now at a full stop." Dissolution without any results was threatened, when Dr Franklin urged that the delegates "employ the assistance of Heaven." He suggested that a clergyman be hired to bless the deliberations of the delegates. But even on that godly issue no agreement could be reached. Some urged that ministers were charging too much money for even short prayers. Others argued that it would look bad at that late date to invoke Heaven. They feared that if the folks back home ever heard of the belated use of godly advice an inference would be drawn either of irreligiousness at the start or of incapacity without divine guidance after June 28.

But the old Doctor had at least removed some of the tension by his suggestion. Many of the delegates, on the verge of departing for home, decided to wait around a few more days to see if any agreement could be reached.

Of the sixty-two men who technically were delegates,

some were virtually self-appointed, others had been designated by little countryside cliques, none was selected by the people as a whole. Seven of the sixty-two had not even bothered to attend. Of these seven, nonattendance was explained by illness in the family, the excuse that they were too busy, that it was too big a trip or just a waste of time. Of the remaining fifty-five, thirteen had gone home long before the Constitution was agreed upon, several in sheer disgust. Of the forty-two who remained, three—Edmund Randolph of Virginia, Washington's aide-de-camp, George Mason of Virginia, owner of three hundred slaves, and Elbridge Gerry of Massachusetts, one of the signers of the Declaration of Independence—refused on that 17th day of September 1787, when Dr Franklin pointed to the rising sun, to sign the final document.

John Dickinson was absent the final day, but his name appears on the Constitution, he having handed George Read his proxy. Richard Henry Lee gave a ball at Stratford in Virginia, when "the company left the ball quite wearied out" after six days, although the host "intreated them to stay the proposed time."

Only a few of the delegates had known each other previously. Even worldly Franklin had never met Madison until the convention began in May 1787. Patrick Henry, the fiery radical of 1774, adamantly refused to go to the convention because, as he wrote, he "smell't a rat." Thomas Paine, our leading propagandist of all time, the author of America's first best seller (*Common Sense* sold 120,000 copies in three months), had left for Europe to develop his new cantilever bridge. That he distrusted the motives of the framers of the Constitution was only too clear. It is difficult to place him in the struggle between merchants and farmers of that era. Had not Robert Morris been able to hire Paine to write advertising blurbs for the Bank of North America in Philadelphia? Samuel Adams, our first Red, and Thomas Jefferson, who, working eighteen days in the home of a laborer, had written the Declaration of Independence, were far from Philadelphia during those critical days. Not even indirectly did this secret convention feel the influences of these four historic American revolutionaries.

Franklin alone represented the historical continuity of these shores. He had sought to get a job in England as a customs collector under the Stamp Act of 1765. Now, twenty years later, he appreciated man's inability to prophesy the growth of a nation. He had always treated life as an adventure, and he knew the impossibility of charting in mere words a course for future human conduct. He alone of those in the chamber recalled Peter Kalm, the Swedish naturalist, who, a half-century earlier, had predicted the separation of the colonies from England. His memories went back even to hearing his mother, whose father was an indentured servant to one of the group of communal co-operators who had purchased Nantucket Island from the Indians, tell of that very first call of Leisler in 1690 for a convention of the colonies to present grievances to King William III of England.

The old Doctor, with his big gold-headed cane, thought in large terms. He recalled his offer to the historian Gibbon of material for a book to be entitled *The History of the Decline of the British Empire*. Possibly he foresaw that England, suffering its first and only great national defeat—exclusion from half of this continent—would shift its attention, as it did, to new conquests in far-off Australia.

Gibbon may well have envied the literary successes of Dr Franklin, whose Poor Richard's Almanac *continued to sell at the rate of ten thousand copies per year long after the author's death. None of the Fathers was long on spelling. Dictionaries were new—Dr Johnson's, published in 1755, was the only one in English. Burr wrote of a "ballance," George Rogers Clark of the "emence cuntrey," "shugar," "the Mississippy," and generally was "genely." Hamilton wrote of "porc," and even scholar Madison slipped now and then. Chris-*

*tian was sometimes written "X" and then again as
"Y."*

Many of the men in the room had not been born at the
time Dr Franklin attended the Albany convention of 1754;
many were mere hornbook scholars at the time of the Stamp
Act Congress of 1765. Only a few of those present were
old enough to remember those respectful and timid legalistic briefs filed by Daniel Dulany, the great Tory barris-
ter, who beseeched with polite formality that King George
"please give up" some of his power over the colonies, since
taxation without representation was not quite ethical.

From May 14 to September 17 the delegates had worked
with deep concern, tireless energy and complete remote-
ness from any possibility of checking up their day-by-day decisions against the wishes of the people of the land. In a
room 100 × 60, seated in three semicircular rows of seats,
they had deliberated with armed sentries stationed at the
entrances to the building and at the wide double doors of
the chamber. "We, the people" were not to know what was
going on at the convention.

The delegates were sure that if the voters were to get
wind of the convention's quandaries and doubts, no favorable acceptance of the new constitution could be expected.
Of the seventy-nine days spent in arduous labor, twenty-
nine had been under a frightfully hot sun and thirteen were
dismal with rain. Seven hours a day these men worked in
committees and in convention. By ten each night they would
eat dinner and drink their rum. Possibly the prominence of
the delegates led them to believe that they could sense what
the populace wanted. Not until the next winter were they
to be disillusioned on this score. Forty-one of the men had
served in Congress during the Revolution or under the
Articles of Confederation, eight had signed the Declaration
of Independence, and seven had been governors of states.

*One fourth of the signers of the Declaration of Inde-
pendence were "raised in commerce, navigation, and*

contraband." School children were reading of matters worldly as well as moral in The New England Primer. *It taught that:*

> In Adam's Fall
> We sinned All

and

> Zaccheus, he
> Did climb a tree
> Our Lord to see

and

> He who ne'er learns his ABC
> Forever will a blockhead be,
> But he who learns his letters fair
> Shall have a coach to take the air.

Many were active in local or district politics, and during the convention small groups of delegates at taverns and boarding houses worked and played together, thus affording bases, if not for agreement, at least for intelligent understanding of the sectional jealousies which had to be compromised before a new constitution could be written.

Madison, Hamilton, Rutledge, Pinckney, Martin and others made up a friendly but motley crew which lived at the Indian Queen Tavern, two blocks from the convention hall. Small clubs of members met there after their seven hours of quiet, grinding debate, often to dine with George Washington. In fact, the chairman was the leading diner-out. Five nights a week he was away from home; on Saturdays he went to the suburbs, with side trips for trout fishing, playing the horses (losing up to $400 on a single nag in one race), attending Mass at the Romish church and speaking at agricultural (grange) meetings. Gay and amorous dances for the constitution makers were held regularly late at night at O'Eller's, which had fewer bugs than the Sign of the Sorrel Horse, although some delegates preferred the Golden Lion and Yellow Cat for the excellent brew of beer.

Betting on the horses was the exclusive privilege of gentlemen. A court order of 1787 reads:

> James Bullocke, a taylor, having made a race for his mare to
> runn with a horse belonging to Mr Mathew Slader for two
> thousand pounds of tobacco and caske, it being contrary to
> Law for a labourer to make a race, being a sport only for Gen-
> tlemen, is fined for the same 100 pounds of tobacco and caske.

Considering the extensive evening frivolities, it is amaz-
ing that there were no leaks. The press of the day shows
how unaggressive the reporters of 1787 must have been. No
reporter drinking rum or attending a ball was able to dis-
cern what was going on behind those closed doors. Some
few relatives of the New York delegates did gamble in
securities on the strength of the rumors of proposed convention activities, but while delegate Luther Martin was crying
that the convention "was held together by a hair," the press
was announcing the unanimity of the convention. The public
was totally ignorant of the forceful presentation made by
Hugh Williamson of North Carolina, educated at Edinburgh, Utrecht and Philadelphia, when he urged before the
delegates in July that an agreement on important issues was
impossible and that the convention "must soon be at an
end."

The only real danger of destruction of the star-chamber
secrecy of the convention lay in Dr Franklin. With his mug
of ale he became garrulous, and so two or three of the
younger delegates were assigned to attend him every evening to see that this eminent conversationalist did not spill
the beans. All through the convention the delegates were
fearful lest the public, so carefully excluded from all the
debates, should ever know how many sections of the Constitution were carried by a bare majority of one, how much
of the wording was sheer compromise and how often it
looked as if no agreement could ever be reached.

> Mr Elbridge Gerry argued that the clause calling forth
> federal force against a recreant state "ought to be ex-
> pressed so as the people might not understand it, to
> prevent their being alarmed." This idea, however, was
> rejected "on account of its artifice."

The gay old Doctor was a trifle worried because he foresaw the inevitable popular resistance to the new constitution, even in his home colony of Pennsylvania. So violent was the opposition to become in Pennsylvania that no quorum was to be obtained in the state ratification convention until troops were dispatched to arrest and drag in by the "nape of the neck" enough delegates to make a quorum. Franklin knew that, deep down, many of the men in the room were in favor of a monarchy. Only to himself he confided that they, dreaming of monarchy, might be deluded into voting for a partial democracy. On the eve of the convention, John Jay wrote to Washington, "I am told that even respectable characters speak for a monarchial form of government," while Gerry was shouting that the evils of the country "flowed from an excess of democracy." This was reiterated by men like Roger Sherman, shoemaker-jurist of Connecticut, who, in the debates a few days before Franklin rose to look at the sun, declared "People should have as little to do with government as possible." This, although only about 5 per cent of the population voted on any issue, even the acceptance of a constitution.

Approximately 160,000 male persons voted on the Constitution, only 100,000 supporting that revolutionary document. Among William Byrd's portraits in the dining room—earls and dukes in full-bottomed wigs, velvet cloaks and laces—was one of a man of keen, thin visage under a three-cornered hat, merely Mr Waltho, for years clerk of the House of Burgesses. He presented the portrait to Colonel Byrd, "requesting that it should be hung among his peers, for whom he might show his republican contempt by wearing his hat in their presence."

Dr Franklin knew that the Constitution would never be accepted by Rhode Island without a war or economic sanctions. He regretted that the mails were so frightfully slow and uncertain, for with speedier processes of communication Canada might have been the fourteenth colony at the gathering. He appreciated that only a quarter of the people

were able to read and that, in any event, those who were
to vote on the creation of the new nation would not have an
opportunity to read the document before voting for its
acceptance or rejection.

Our youthful Founding Fathers knew how to work as
well as play, though fewer than twenty of the delegates carried the load. Madison never missed a single speech at the
entire convention. Washington, though silent except on two
occasions, was regularly in his high chair. Not so with many
of the others. As near to the close of the convention as September 10, Wilson, known as James the Caledonian, tall
and nearsighted, arose to comment that New York had not
been represented "for a long time past." The average daily
attendance of the delegates at the sessions of our Constitutional Convention was fairly shabby. In fact, the United
States senators of 1936 established a better record. If
attendance is a gauge of deep-seated interest and responsibility, little can be said for the delegates as a whole.

The attendance records show: Constitutional Convention, 73 per cent, omitting entirely the seven delegates who
never even made an appearance in Philadelphia. United
States Senate, 1936, 78 per cent.

In part this may be explained by the lack of convention
salaries, although some of the states compensated their delegates. But most of the men were very rich and could well
afford the time required from their occupations. General
Washington had served all through the war without salary,
although immediately after he surrendered his sword at
Fraunces' Tavern on Broad Street, New York, at the close
of the war, with his usual modesty he filed his detailed expense account for the period of the war. He asked repay-
ment of £14,500, about $75,000, for his out-of-pocket ex-
penses—this not including ordinary food, lodging or servants. Madison had once written: "If I don't get some salary
I'll have to sell a Negro."

*Virginia, as a pension, voted Washington shares of
stock in the Potomac Company and in the James River
Company.*

The gathering remained in session even after brandy-nosed Luther Martin of Maryland had withdrawn because he wanted a national and not a federal government. Even that brilliant roué, Alexander Hamilton, who, while an undergraduate at King's, now Columbia, College, was the author of radical articles urging sedition against Great Britain, had stormed from the convention in disgust, writing to his personal hero, George Washington, that "these men will get nowhere and for me to return will be a sheer waste of time."

But despite all those words of despair, the Doctor appreciated two solidifying forces: two dangers, one from abroad, the other at home. Although the war had been won, England was still a great commercial peril. Against England there was now a united front which prompted most of the colonies to want a strong central government, potent enough to make treaties, to raise taxes for defense, and to cope with the increasing problems of those untouched Western lands, west, north and south of Pittsburgh, that hamlet which by mere chance finally became a part of the state of Pennsylvania instead of the state of Virginia. The English peril created great anxiety among the merchants, who were concerned not only with colonial tariffs against foreign nations, but with irksome and reprisal economics of each colony against its neighbors.

Although many of the delegates had urged that our new government be a replica of that of Great Britain, and although most of those in the room had never consciously thought that the uprising of '76 would lead to more than some home-rule powers vested in the colonies, now that the war was four years behind, everyone was united in avoiding any future foreign economic domination. A new government was needed to fight England in trade and commerce.

The other drive for unity came from economic distress right here at home. The lines of the class struggle, as Madison repeatedly pointed out in the convention, had been clearly drawn—the debtors against the creditors. No one living at that time thought of this problem in terms of

1936, but essentially the struggle was the same. In 1787 banks, or, as they were called, counting houses, had not accumulated vast deposits. The idea of a stock exchange did not take root in this land until more than a decade after the convention disbanded. Only Madison foresaw that at some distant time the man who imported his saddles or ruffled shirts might resell to a retailer. Large-scale retailers, jobbers and manufacturers had not come on the economic scene. Chain stores were embryonic but invisible in the group of trading posts spreading down the banks of the distant navigable streams. Commerce was acutely retarded by the lack of a uniform currency even within a single state.

The first government relief fund was in Boston in 1774, followed later by interstate doles, a flock of sheep being shipped from Wyndham, Connecticut, and 200 barrels of rice from South Carolina.

Spanish dollars flowed freely from Havana, where Spanish troops bought produce from Florida. But all money was scarce, and men were often paid in tobacco, shoes, rum and "ozenbrigs," while women took garters and kerchiefs in barter for toil. When delegate Pierce Butler of South Carolina, vain because of his noble birth, bought himself new lace collars, he paid in gold pistoles; when John Langdon of New Hampshire, who paid the expenses of the New Hampshire delegates to the convention, purchased grog for his servant, he paid with doubloons or Portuguese moidores. Every lad on the street could recognize a "half joe." A great gambling business in arbitrage went on all the time. Each colonist treated money as do people living on the borders of jealous European states today. A dollar was worth six shillings in New England, eight shillings in New York, eight to thirty-two shillings in the Carolinas, five shillings in Georgia and seven shillings, sixpence elsewhere. In western Pennsylvania by 1793 whisky was the circulating medium.

A hairdress for a man was the most expensive single out-

lay of the family. Of course, only a few coveted such luxury:
only those who signed their letters with the word "gentleman" after the name or "Sir" before it. The hairdresser's
charge for white work depended on the currency to be used
by his customer. When Madison bought half a dozen gram-
mars, he paid forty-two shillings in Pennsylvania money,
or thirty-three shillings, sixpence in Virginia coinage. It is
as difficult for us today to think of Portuguese, English and
French coins in general circulation in the colonies as it would
have been for those men of the convention to conceive of
quarters and dollars in a standardized system of coinage
such as we have today.

Against this background of varying media of exchange,
costs had risen violently during and after the war. Salt on
a single day had gone from $2.00 to $5.25 a bushel. Corn
had risen to $50.00 a bushel, and "porc" commanded any
price. Imported goods, of course, exceeded everything else
many hundred per cent.

By 1780 the currency had depreciated one hundred to
one, and even that great old radical, Sam Adams, paid
$2,000 for a suit of clothes. Sailors returning from long
voyages found that money wasn't "worth a continental"
and paraded down the streets in clothes made of the useless
bills. Barbershops were decorated with paper money. As the
delegates were traveling to the convention they found that
shoes cost twenty pounds, milk fifteen shillings a quart,
potatoes ninety shillings a bushel, rum forty-five shillings a
quart and a good cow $1,200.

Not only was the wife of every workman uncertain how
many shillings her husband would be paid by his boss, but
no one could guess what any given quantity of shillings
would buy. If there had been taximeters in the stagecoaches
in 1787 the first drop of the meter would have fluctuated
daily, hitting a high of $106.50 for a single mile. No one
was aware of the myth of a gold standard, but by 1786 the
paper-money proponents had won out in seven colonies.
Away up in New Hampshire mobs attacked the legislature
with placards: "Print paper money and lower the taxes."
To give relief to the debtors, many states passed "stay

laws" tearing wide gashes in the contracts held by the rich creditor class. The farmers' moratorium of 1933 was repeating an American pattern of 150 years before.

When, in Massachusetts, the legislature failed to give relief by moratorium laws, all throughout the state men picked up their rifles. Five hundred men and women gathered in Northampton outside the courthouse and with bludgeons formed into picket lines. In Great Barrington, near the Connecticut and New York boundaries, desperate relatives of imprisoned debtors broke open the jails. Dan Shays symbolized the revolt. Like an early but more vital Coxey he was followed by ragged thousands in his march toward Springfield, Massachusetts, where the muskets and munitions had been stored by the authorities. Dan knew that the government troops had not been paid and would not work much longer without pay. He didn't know, however, until too late, that the rich creditors, hearing of his advance, promptly hired with their own personal funds an army of private sheriffs (like the coal and iron police of Pennsylvania today) to stop Shays and his picket lines.

> *General Knox wrote Washington that the Shaysites believed that the property of the United States had been protected against Great Britain by common action and therefore "ought to be the common property of all." The army was paid $3.00 a month. The first Congress debated whether this ought to be raised to $5.00. Washington, although he was the richest man in the country, had to borrow £600 to cover his cash expenses to New York as president.*

Against this kind of popular movement any single colony was totally impotent. Commerce between colonies was essential for life, and no single community was self-sufficient economically in this land of rising living standards. We can give part credit to the followers of Dan Shays for driving the colonies into a convention that was intended to instill strength into the insipid Articles of Confederation. They aroused the rich creditors into demanding a strong central power to prevent paper-money inflation and to force the courts to put people in jail if they didn't pay their bills.

Some of the local judges were bowing to popular pressure. In many communities the debtor working class was in control of the judicial system by sheer show of violence. The Western land speculators, vocal, as is always the case with entrepreneurs, cried aloud for a new central power so that their acres, bought for resale in small parcels, would be protected, not by their own private and expensive sheriffs, but by nationally paid troops. Every state wanted protection against embargoes and taxes levied on imports by adjacent states. Even if a single colony had been able to stabilize its commerce and finances, competition between states would have destroyed any attempt at a self-contained economy. National control and country-wide regulation were imperative.

Although the forty-two men who remained in Philadelphia were international students of such philosophical concepts as monarchy or democracy, their actions on specific economic problems were uniformly most provincial. Even erudite Madison of Virginia wrote at the time: "Of the affairs of 'Georga' I know as little as of those of Kamchatka," while Butler of South Carolina, born in Ireland, arose to say: "The interests of the Southern and Eastern States are as different as the interests of Russia and Turkey." In the Philadelphia chamber of that summer, Franklin saw not a single American. Randolph, years later, wrote: "You see, I am not really an American. I am a Virginian."

The first president born a citizen of the United States was the eighth—Martin Van Buren, born December 5, 1782, at Kinderhook, New York. On October 15, 1797, all foreign silver coin except the Spanish dollar ceased to be legal tender. "Had the law been strictly obeyed, three-fourths of the population of the country would, on that day, have been reduced to the necessity of barter." And so the order was evaded, ignored and countermanded. Foreign coins continued in circulation until 1857.

Strangers to one another, the delegates were products of civilizations strikingly different one from the other. The barriers of tedious and hazardous travel and lack of communication were further raised by varieties of language used in the several colonies. Pennsylvania was one-third German. As late as 1821 General Archibald McNeil said he was the first man elected to Congress from his district in the interior of North Carolina who had not canvassed in Gaelic. As late as 1859, President Taylor's message to Congress was printed, 15,000 copies in English, 5,000 in German. Two Supreme Court judges selected Reading, Pennsylvania, for hanging out their law shingles mainly because of their knowledge of German.

But even if a single language had been in use, the means of communicating from one colony to another were meager and too expensive, except for the very richest, to discover how others were living and what the people a few hundred miles away really wanted from the new government.

The old Doctor, while postmaster thirty years earlier—in 1758—had admitted newspapers to the mails, and shortly thereafter had cut down the delivery time between Boston and Philadelphia from six to three weeks in good weather. The cost of letters by 1787 had been reduced at the seventy-five scattered post offices to about the cost of telegrams to-day. Postage was always paid on delivery, or on a charge account, and thus you saved money if the mail was stolen, as often happened, en route. Much mail was hijacked. Seldom did Jefferson or Madison write important letters to each other except in private and ever-changing codes.

There are now about 50,000 post offices and 1,800,000 miles of post roads as against 1,800 miles in 1787. Friction matches were first made forty years later. Noah Webster called the workers "poor porpoises."

Between New York and Philadelphia, by 1787, there was Mersereau's "flying machine" mail and passenger service, wind and weather permitting; in the summer letters could make the trip in two days, but in winter no mail was guaranteed in less than four days. On most roads tolls were paid, the highways being blocked by spiked rods or pikes. These were, upon sufficient payment, turned aside to allow vehicles to pass and to give us the origin of the word *turn-pike*. Between Boston and New York mail traveled only three times a week, and letters from Gloucester reached Georgia sometimes in less than four weeks.

> *William Byrd collected at Westover more than four thousand books in half a dozen languages. Byrd's exceptional library was the greatest, not only in Virginia, but in all the colonies, except that of John Adams, which was equally extensive and varied. But most jurors could not read, and few could write their own names.*

Considering these barriers of space and time, how could the New Hampshire delegates dream that the Virginia delegates thought the biggest problem in the Constitutional Convention was the control of navigation on the Mississippi? The delegates from Connecticut never understood why South Carolina was worried about the need for Negroes, while Virginia was breeding Negroes for resale. The insistence of Massachusetts that the treaty of peace with England be held up until the right to cure and dry fish caught off Newfoundland had been clarified, was unintelligible to uninformed delegates from Georgia.

Although few in number, newspapers were closely followed. The letter columns, full of anonymous communications, were read by the delegates at the convention whenever local mail came to Philadelphia. Since the treaty of peace in 1783, many more newspapers had sprung up. The forty-three papers which served the Revolution seldom got more than fifty miles away from the printing plants. But the pamphleteers were increasingly effective. In those days there were no newspapers such as we have today, with boiler-plate editorials, entire articles stereotyped for public propaganda. A hand press, a printer's devil and a printer with a cause were the ingredients of the battle for freedom of the press.

But in 1787 the ninety-three newspapers, surviving by sale of copies rather than by advertising, had integrity of a type and a zeal which make a comparison with our two thousand dailies of 1936 quite odious, even though the circulation of the most successful paper of 1787 was not over one thousand copies per issue.

The American institution of the family rag bag was started after the Revolution because of a rag famine and the need for paper for newspapers.

The delegates at the convention sensed public reactions not so much through the press as through the pulpits. Ever since Dr Mayhew of Martha's Vineyard had been credited with starting the Rebellion, ministers were deep in national politics. It is amusing to note how many men and women think of Dr Harry Emerson Fosdick or Father Coughlin as modern divines who, with novelty, have found that the social welfare of the people lies outside as well as inside of ecclesiastical frontiers. Minister Hart of Charleston in 1773 had been fairly cute when, during a sermon against dancing, he digressed in favor of complete independence from England. On the other hand, down South most of the clergy, except the Presbyterians, were only lukewarm in favor of a national government. The Presbyterians, however, who through intolerance against the Baptists had accomplished Madison's conversion into a liberal, were by 1787 as ready to set up a national government which was to take them in as they had been ready previously to pull down one that was to shut them out. Madison wrote: "I do not know of a more shameful contrast than might be found between the Presbyterian memorials on the latter and former occasions." The main drive against the delegates from the clergy was for the establishment of a religion sanctioned and, what was more important, financed by the State. But the bitterness and jealousies between innumerable religious groups minimized the force of this pressure. Although no state religion was adopted, and although we have been taught that religious freedom was implicit in the Constitution, it took decades before an Episcopalian from Virginia enjoyed in Connecticut the same rights as a Congregationalist in that state.

There was no Catholic presidential nominee until 1872 —Charles O'Conor of New York; but two members of the Constitutional Convention were Catholic.

The delegates were all male. They listened to clergy, read the gazettes, but were also mindful of the feminist movement then evident in sporadic episodes of dramatic violence. Although women took no part directly in politics, Mrs Bingham of Philadelphia set her table nightly for the aristocrats of the colonies. At her board, behind those newly planted citron trees, all the styles of Paris were emulated. At the houses of women like Mrs Bingham the aristocracy of Europe was being aped and monarchy was devoutly desired. But in the countryside, feminine leaders of democracy had appeared without fanfare or organizations, but with single-purposed hates. The newspapers of 1787 addressed clarion calls to the ladies:

It is the duty of the American ladies in a particular manner to interest themselves in the success of the measures that are now pursuing by the Federal Convention for the happiness of America. They can retain their rank as rational beings only in a free government. In a monarchy (to which the present anarchy in America, if not restrained, must soon lead us) they will be considered as valuable members of society only as they are capable of being mothers of soldiers who are the pillars of crowned heads. It is in their power, by their influence over their husbands, brothers, and sons . . .

These feminine democrats remembered effective and violent Catherine Schuyler, who, single-handed, had burned down acres of rich full crops before the advance of the Tory troops. The same women who in 1776 had refused to make love to men other than those loyal to the cause of independence, were now outside of the convention waiting to learn if their men would be protected by a new bill of rights.

Against this confused and inarticulate background of home distress and foreign commercial perils, a handful of

youngsters prepared a constitution for presentation to the
voters of the colonies. It was to lay down a rule of communal living. To interpret the Constitution—whether on the
English theory of judges incapable of declaring acts unconstitutional, or on the unaccepted theory of judges nullify-
ing any act of Congress—a few highest judges of the land
were needed.

How were these sages to be picked? Elected by the people, selected by the senators, appointed by the president?
Should there be three, ten or thirty? No delegate had
any great faith in any particular formula to satisfy this
quandary.

Once more Dr Franklin, our first civilized American,
arose from his chair to address the delegates. Everyone
knew that the Supreme Court judges would not be very busy.
They would ride circuit, holding court wherever a problem
called them. In January they might go to Saybrook, Connecticut, to determine who owned the conquered pirate ship
recently captured by a New Bedford fisherman. In July they
would hold court on the boundary line of South Carolina
and Georgia to decide just which river or mountain ridge
the state line should follow in accordance with the old royal
charters.

This was the sphere of the Court. And still the old Doctor
wanted to be sure the best legal minds of the country were
to be applied to these all-important controversies.

He suggested: Let the members of the legal profession
select the Supreme Court justices. Will not the members of
the Bar (far fewer in number than the number of lawyers
in Chicago today) select the leaders of the profession so as
to remove the leaders from competition, in order to divide
up their practice among those not so selected?

Such was the casual but realistic approach of Dr Franklin
to that portion of the Constitution which in 1936 gives us
so much concern.

With a last-week rush of changes and compromises, the
convention adjourned. General Washington was eager to
get back to his vast estates, which covered a territory so
extensive that he had to travel seven hundred miles to en-

circle them. With a last glance at the two large fireplaces on either side of the General's chair, where hundreds of logs had kept the Framers warm during the chill of the last few days, the forty-one men filed out of the building. Outside of the hall the cobbles had been torn up and replaced with dirt so that the noise of the horses' hoofs and of raw wooden wheels would not disturb the silence within.

Dr Franklin left the chamber with a side remark to General Washington, asking that much thought be given to the official title of the president of the United States. Washington answered that he preferred "His High Mightiness, the President of the United States and Protector of Their Liberties."

CHAPTER III

The Barrel Staves

THE FORTY-TWO DELEGATES represented thirteen distinct republics, each vast in size but tiny in population. A total population of about three million was distributed equally between the North and the South. In 1787 there were fewer than five men, women and children to the square mile. In this same territory there live today over fifty-five million people, or over forty persons per square mile. Few Indians were left east of the Alleghanies. The six leading cities of 1787 were:

Philadelphia	42,000
New York	33,000
Boston	18,000
Charleston	16,000
Baltimore	13,000
Newport	10,000

There were over 500,000 Negroes, with twenty slaves for each one hundred white persons.

The pleasant wooded coast from Maine to Georgia contained fewer inhabitants than now live in the city of Chicago alone. The thirteen colonies had an average per state of less than the population of Richmond, Virginia, today. The inhabitants of Puerto Rico in 1936 exceed in numbers the total population of eight of the thirteen colonies of 1787.

With this sparse population dotting the Eastern coast, each colony was virtually isolated from its neighbors. The travel-time distance from New Brunswick, New Jersey, to Atlanta, Georgia, was far greater than from Kansas City to London, England, today. There were few roads fit for travel, and only the very wealthy visited away from home.

So long as Virginians never came into contact with Rhode Islanders there was no reason to expect to find uniformity of culture. Even the market places of commerce were narrowly confined. Seldom did trade practices extend with uniformity for a radius of more than five or ten miles. If a community wanted to suppress "regrating"—that is, the buying of corn and selling it again in the same market —the definition of *market* usually referred to sales within ten miles from the place of purchase. Whereas every colonist up and down the land was familiar with the universal governmental control of "common victualers," common "hoymen" (carriers by water) were unknown in the South, and in Delaware no one heard of the Northern practice of "smoak money," a tax on common ovens.

Not only were the controls of occupations and commerce different in each section of the land, but the very dress and clothing varied as greatly as do the top hat, white tie and tails of the rich today from the overalls and cap of the workers. In 1787, however, this variation in dress distinguished not only aristocrats from workers but the Eastern shore from what was known as the Far West—that is, about a hundred miles west of the Atlantic Ocean. The wealthy Easterner wore small clothes, silk stockings, pumps with buckles, heavily powdered hair and cocked hat. The well-turned-out Westerner wore a wool hat, blue linsey-woolsey hunting shirt with a cape, a belt with a gaily colored fringe, deerskin or linsey pantaloons, moccasins and shoe-packs of tanned leather. In winter a striped linsey vest and white blanket coat were added.

Few of the delegates at the convention had any intimate knowledge of the mores of any colony but his own. There was scant literature, other than letters written in painful longhand, to describe a Georgia rice plantation to a Cape Cod glassblower. A Connecticut tidewaiter was in total ignorance of the sporty racing meets of the wealthy farmers of Williamsburg, Virginia.

The Virginia Council in State heard arguments in the first breach-of-promise case on this continent. The

*lonely lover was the Reverend Greville Pooley, whose
fair Cicely Jordan, widow of Captain Samuel Jordan,
had jilted him in favor of William Farrar. That jilting
was the order of the day is clear from the rule of court
that a third offense was punishable by both corporal
punishment and a fine.*

In the brilliant debates of the delegates, current facts
about the state of industry or education or transportation
in any single colony were seldom mentioned. Although they
argued at length the merits of the Helvetian form of government and though, at times, the Massachusetts system of
selecting judges was casually mentioned, never once did any
delegate refer in his arguments to local rates of duties, the
effects of local embargoes, specific shortage or surplus of
colonial labor, or the condition of the schools.

The time it took man to communicate with man hedged
each colony within tight frontiers and deep internal currents
of human behavior. Under such circumstances, suspicion of
alien ways—and alien meant fifty miles away—forced business competition into insolent moods of bitter reprisal. The
facts about the economy of one colony never seemed per-
tinent to the resolution of the problems of the neighboring
state.

Naturally delegates were not unaware of the values of
European trade, but they never felt that we were at all dependent on England for trade and commerce. It may rather
be said that the Caribbean Islands were the focal point for
the vision of these trading delegates. American geography
at that time had its main foreign accent in the Barbadoes,
because news sailed and did not fly. During the days of the
convention the press of the colonies featured the hurricanes
at Martinique with stories of the six hundred homes
destroyed and the fifteen hundred persons who perished.
Nothing happening in Europe seemed quite so important.

A careful reading of the debates at the convention will
leave the reader in total darkness as to the land to be
governed or the condition and welfare of the people to be
ruled. Many of the delegates were no doubt fully informed

about the living conditions in their home cities or colonies, but they must have considered it a waste of time to try to predicate a theory of government on the widely varying statistical and factual material which such expositions would have disclosed.

A unified government was imperative. It was accepted by all that the thirteen colonies had recently had a great common enemy—Great Britain—and that each in its own way had had a century of violent and revolutionary background. Each state was developing an economy based on its own sea or soil.

As these delegates carried on the thrilling debates of 1787 we can only give meaning to those discussions if we keep in mind the industrial background of each separate republic and the century of violent rejection of the rule of England whenever the Crown stood in the way of what the people wanted at any particular time. Up and down the coast there was never a decade during the eighteenth century when one or more of the colonies was not ejecting a governor, confiscating the lands of the King's representatives, or getting rich by sending forth troops to fight for the Crown.

Since this persistent pattern of military resistance ran up and down the coast without any concerted action of any two adjacent colonies at any one time, it will be well to look briefly at each colony without regard to its territorial location.

The delegates were spokesmen for separate colonies, but represented two different cultures categorically set forth in Jefferson's letter to Chastellux when he wrote:

While I am on this subject, I will give you my idea of the characters of the several states:

In the North they are	*In the South they are*
cool	fiery
sober	voluptuary
laborious	indolent
persevering	unsteady
independent	independent

[*In the North they are—Con.*]

jealous of their liberties, and
   just to those of others

interested
chicaning
superstitious and hypocritical in
   their religion

[*In the South they are—Con.*]

zealous for their own liberties,
   but trampling on those of
   others
generous
candid
without attachment or preten-
   sions to any religion but that
   of the heart

GEORGIA

*Small patches of the Georgia forests had been cleared
by 1787 for the beginnings of cotton and tobacco planting, but the corn and peanut crops of that state are of
later date.*

Georgia, in the far South, was scarcely a single colony.
Colonized as a buffer state against Spanish invasion into
South Carolina, Georgia housed an internal fight so keen
that at one time it had two legislatures and two executives.
The revolutionary group which had come from Dorchester,
Massachusetts, to settle in St John's Parish gave the state a
nonindigenous pattern.

Only five of the twelve parishes of the state sent delegates to the Provincial Congress of January 1775, but
Georgia was nevertheless strong for unification. Motivated
by the Spanish peril, it voted unanimously for the ratification of the Constitution. By 1793 its ardor had abated and,
after the Supreme Court of the United States had rendered
a decision in favor of South Carolina and against Georgia,
the Georgia legislature debated an act decreeing that any
agent of enforcement sent by the Supreme Court "would
suffer death without benefit of clergy."

If you think our constitution grew gently and without
great points of passing pressure, bear in mind that we required this arrogant defiance of the Supreme Court to
produce the Eleventh Amendment to the federal constitution.

SOUTH CAROLINA

*The Port of Charleston and high-grade cotton produc-
tion supplemented the South Carolina staple of rice. As
rice had replaced indigo, so cotton manufacture has replaced rice in the state economy. Tobacco and peanuts
are also exports.*

South Carolina, unlike North Carolina, was long accus-
tomed to having its own way. As early as 1765 its delegates
took the arduous five-week trip up North by scow and ferry
and horse to attend the Stamp Act Congress at New York.
By June 1775, before the Declaration of Independence, a
self-organized revolutionary council of safety formed an
extralegal provincial congress, drove out the governor and
took over the power.

In its rice swamps thousands of Negro slaves died each
season. During the period of the Constitutional Convention,
South Carolina had a shortage of slave labor while other
Southern states were breeding and importing slaves at such
a pace that the suggestion was offered to plow under every
fifth black man. Black men were quoted like tobacco and
sugar on the auction blocks and at the market places—so
many English pounds sterling per pound of blood and flesh.

In this interstate business competition, South Carolina
cared little if the value of slaves dropped in other states. Its
desire for a federal government stemmed in part from a
need of more cheap labor.

NORTH CAROLINA

*North Carolina's basic commodities were naval stores,
cotton and tobacco. Today it leads the states in mica,
and exports peanuts, grains, manufactured textiles.*

Between the years 1674 and 1712 North Carolina, with
two major uprisings and many minor revolts, drove out six
different colonial governors. The weakness of the powers of
the governor in 1936 is traceable to these early revolts.

In that territory, for the first century the largest town had fewer than one thousand people. There were practically no roads passable during the entire year. This rebellious countryside, fearful of any outside influences or controls, at one time opposed by a vote of two to one the new constitution of the United States of America, although it is now quite clear that few, if any, copies of the proposed constitution were ever seen by anyone in the state save only the delegates to the state convention. Many inhabitants of this territory never heard of George Washington or of the Revolution until long after the treaty of peace. The rebellion of 1776 was, to many, just another ordinary rebellion to which North Carolinians were so well adjusted.

VIRGINIA

Out of 3,172,444 persons in the United States in 1790, 697,624 were slaves and 563,699 were slaveholders, reports the first census. Virginia was at the time a slave-breeding state, with tobacco planting and ship-building as complementary pursuits. Today its greatly reduced territory also grows corn and manufactures textiles and paper.

In 1740 there were more blacks than whites in Virginia. Naturally she dumped her excess property—Negroes—on the foreign soil of other states. By 1790 one out of every six families in all the colonies held slaves. But the eyes of all Virginians were turned, via tobacco and not Negroes, toward the Mississippi. Like many other colonies it claimed land "to the South Sea," wherever that might be. In 1785, two years before the convention, Madison wrote:

What a metamorphosis would the liberal policy of France work in a little time on the Island of New Orleans! It would be to her a fund of as much real wealth as Potosi has been of imaginary wealth to Spain. It would become the Grand Cairo of the New World.

Looking to the west, the historic families on the coast feared the courageous newcomers who migrated from

Pennsylvania and other lands into western Virginia. These fears grew eventually into hatred, so that the rich planters of the seaboard despised those radical sympathizers, Jefferson and Patrick Henry, even more than they did the British.

But the land was rich, full of phosphates and nitrates. Not yet had unplanned, rugged, personal agriculture sapped the soil. In those days we had a soil that could outcompete the soils of all other continents then discovered. No one foresaw that the next century of land prostitution would require a governmental Tennessee Valley project which, through legumes and grass fertilization, might gradually rebuild that earth until it could once again bear simple natural growth like trees.

The revolution of the colonies from Great Britain was inevitable; but, just as the Russian Revolution took on the color of a Lenin and a Trotsky, so did our first revolution gather its peculiar pigment from three Virginians—George Washington, James Madison and Thomas Jefferson. Madison, all during this period, preached the population theories of Malthus twenty years before Malthus wrote his famous work. Blue-eyed Madison was weak of voice but secure in judgment. Jefferson, born to the purple, hater of Blackstone, lover of Coke, favoring Locke over Rousseau, seldom looking people in the face, had a genius which was denied to the colonies during the drafting of our constitution, but which was later to be commandeered at the turn of the century to bring about the second and perhaps more important revolution of the United States.

This man Jefferson, while subtly foreseeing our judicial tribulations of the twentieth century, was busy reading that astonishing essay published by Condorcet, the French mathematician, entitled: "On the Application of the Laws of Probability to Plurality Decisions," an essay which endeavored to supply mathematical formulae to explain the later five-to-four Supreme Court decisions.

George Washington, rich bon vivant, quiet and unassuming, is one of the few men in history who could have been king or dictator but truly preferred the leisure and dances of his own home at Mount Vernon on the Potomac.

Under such influences, long before Lexington, the Virginia House of Burgesses, under the leadership of fiery and still radical Patrick Henry, not dismayed by the gubernatorial disbanding of its meeting in the capitol at Williamsburg, went off along the Duke of Gloucester Street to Raleigh Tavern to start resolving. Years later these manifestoes of 1769 encouraged other colonies to a similar show of courage. In North Carolina the militia, entering Mecklenburg County on May 31, 1775, wrote a declaration of independence based on the Raleigh Tavern manifestoes, to be in turn redrafted into our July 4th Declaration of Independence.

MARYLAND

In colonial days Maryland was the garden spot of America, famed for its hardwoods and beautiful women. Today it subsists on clothing manufacture and truck gardening.

In 1682 Maryland reluctantly gave over to Pennsylvania what is now the state of Delaware. Sixty years before the Constitution was drafted, the inhabitants of Maryland forced a surrender from their governor of the sole right to initiate legislation. Maryland, the best-governed of the colonies, not much bothered by British troops, unconcerned about the Revolution, instructed its delegates not to vote at the Congress for independence from Great Britain. Thus did that state turn its back on our July 4th celebration.

DELAWARE

The state with the smallest population in 1787 is today the home of Du Pont munitions and cellophane. It continues to be a food-raising state and to chastise its criminals at the whipping post.

The estate of Lord de la Ware, united with Pennsylvania in 1693, procured a separate legislature a decade later,

though the governor of Pennsylvania was its chief executive
until the start of the Revolutionary War. For ninety years
the boundary dispute with Maryland increased the jealousies
between these two future states. These frontiers were most
indefinite, seldom charted, and by no means determined by
economic factors. Delaware first became really well known
to all colonists through its Blue Hens Regiment, which never
failed to carry gamecocks right up to the battle front for
the evening entertainment of the ragged and valiant troops.
In 1781 she hurt the Union far more by refusing to join in
the embargo on Great Britain than she helped it with those
fighting cocks. But she became rich by not joining in the embargo.

PENNSYLVANIA

*The original printing industry and grain-naval-stores
export of Pennsylvania have yielded to coal, steel, glass
and textile manufacture. Border warfare between belligerent Scotch-Irish and harassed Indians was a
primary pursuit which no longer prevails.*

Pennsylvania's fame arose from that metropolis Philadelphia, which until 1790 was much more populous and gay
than New York City, though not so festive as Annapolis,
the Deauville of early America. And still this seat of the
Constitutional Convention had in 1776 decided that the
Declaration of Independence was premature. So deep was
the affection for England that the new state, instead of confiscating the lands of the governor and his heirs, as was
done elsewhere, actually paid them £120,000 and some lands
in return for the seized properties. As late as January 1783,
Pennsylvania citizens seized a cargo of supplies which had
arrived for the British and German prisoners, even though
these goods carried passports from the highest command,
General Washington. Thus did they snap their fingers at
the simplest attempts at joint action.

NEW JERSEY

*New Jersey was a "barrel tapped at both ends by New
York and Philadelphia." Its trade in naval stores has
turned into oil refining. Textile manufacture has replaced grain production, but New Jersey fruit remains
a leading commodity.*

New Jersey was really more than one state for many
years. Legislatures met alternately at Burlington and at
Perth Amboy until 1790. Eastern New Jersey, settled by
Long Islanders, was Puritan, while western New Jersey was
Quaker. A split was avoided only by shifting the capital between May 26 and July 2, 1776, so that the second provincial congress met in rotation at Burlington, Trenton and
New Brunswick. On July 3, 1776, the new state constitution
was published as law, without any prior submission to the
people. This was a sample of our many unconstitutional
revolutionary constitutions.

NEW YORK

*New York's colonial shipping and fur trade no longer
monopolize the attention of that state. Wall Street
finance and women's clothing manufacture supplement
the port activity.*

One hundred years before the Stamp Act was imposed by
Great Britain in 1768, and two hundred years before the
nickel or five-cent piece was authorized, shrewd Frederick
Phillipse, the first American banker, cornered the market in
wampum in New York City. He buried several hogsheads
of these shells to force those who had to use this medium of
exchange in New Amsterdam to purchase wampum from
him at a higher price.

New York, on the one hand, balanced its budget by confiscating millions of dollars' worth of property of loyalists, and at the same time refused to send delegates to the Second Continental Congress. A coup d'état with a rump illegal assembly was needed in May 1775, after the news of the Battle of Lexington, to force New York to join in the independence movement. Of course New York City was unique in that it was subject to the British fleet, and the northern part of the state was like a different colony, due to the raids of the Iroquois and other Indians who sided with the foreign rulers against the local inhabitants. In June 1776 the New York provincial congress refused to instruct its delegates for independence; though a new assembly, after hearing the false rumors spread against Washington, reversed that position. Only one of New York's delegates remained to sign the new constitution in Philadelphia, and the state, slow to vote ratification, did so by the slimmest possible vote and then only after the pressure of news of New Hampshire's and Virginia's acceptance.

CONNECTICUT

The heavily wooded state of Connecticut built ships and fed New York until it discovered its industrial propensities, today leading the nation in hat and typewriter manufacture. Its capital has become the insurance center of the country.

The early constitution of Connecticut provided that the "Judicial Laws of God as they were declared by Moses" should constitute a rule for all courts. Maybe that was as clear a guide as the present weasel words, *due process,* under which our courts are now operating. Such mandate did not, however, bespeak kindliness in the courts. Throughout the colonies there were more than one hundred crimes which were punishable by death; in Connecticut even the tender offence of concealing a Quaker carried the death sentence.

Connecticut edged deep into Rhode Island, while New York claimed all of Connecticut up to the Connecticut River.

Up to 1786 Connecticut claimed the western reserve as far out as the land now called Ohio. But within its conceded boundaries Connecticut generally played a lone hand, even refusing in 1782 to send agents to discuss with the Pennsylvanians mutual tariff problems. In the contested frontiers of what is now Connecticut, ministers were not allowed to enter parishes other than their own, except at the copper mines at Simsbury, converted into a stinking military prison during the Revolution. How little the state of Connecticut was willing to join with others is seen by the act of the general assembly which resolved with infinite certainty that the incorporation of state troops into a federal army will always, forever and a day, "be utterly subversive of the rights and liberties of the people." In 1780 the population was 200,000; 40,797 were males over twenty years of age, but only 3,477 voted.

RHODE ISLAND

The great rum-running state, whose retail merchants had bled an aroused patronage in the days of currency depreciation, today manufactures textiles and jewelry in law-abiding fashion.

Rhode Island was always the Peck's Bad Boy of the group. Started by refugees from Massachusetts, the current morality encouraged the swapping of rum for slaves in the West Indies. In 1764 the Sugar Act destroyed this business. This tiny territory established a wholesome dependence of the judiciary on the legislature, a democratic process substantially maintained until 1860. Judges lived and held their positions in constant fear of the elected legislators. Rhode Island saw fit to send no delegate to the Constitutional Convention of 1787 in Philadelphia, and not until the Senate of the United States, in 1790, considered a measure threatening Rhode Island with economic isolation, did Rhode Island come into the Union—begrudgingly, at that, and only by a margin of two votes.

MASSACHUSETTS

*Fishing and shipbuilding were always primary employ-
ments. The first China packet returned from the Orient
in 1790, heralding the great maritime era of Massachusetts. But these are insignificant concerns of the
great manufacturing state today.*

The people of Boston from early times lived in their own
homes, while New Yorkers and Philadelphians rented
houses. At the time of the Constitutional Congress this small
city had eighteen churches, a hundred and thirty-five streets,
eighteen courthouses, thirty distilleries, eight sugar houses
and two breweries.

Home-loving Massachusetts nurtured a fighting population. In 1702 it sent troops against Jamaica; in 1709 it
helped England kill Canadian colonists; in 1740 it warred
against Cartagena; and shortly after 1745 it was paid
£183,000 by the Crown for fighting the French at Lewis-
burg. It used this sum to retire two million dollars of depreciated currency.

Despite Sam Adams and that other wealthy radical, John
Hancock, Massachusetts was basically antinationalist. It
held on to Maine until 1820; and in 1813, when the United
States floated a war liberty-loan bond issue, Massachusetts,
rich and populous, subscribed a scant $75,000, while
Pennsylvania helped the nation by purchasing seven million
dollars' worth of those very bonds.

In 1814 Massachusetts led the secessionist groups which
headed up at that Hartford convention for dissolution of
the baby union. Had there been a single dramatic and
popular personality at that convention, the map of this
continent might today be printed in many colors instead of
in a single shade. At any rate it must be recalled that the
seditious, though unmolested, Hartford meeting proposed
the adoption, for the nation as a whole, of that rule of
government found so salutary in New Hampshire, a general

election every seven years to reconsider the revision of our too rigid federal constitution.

NEW HAMPSHIRE

The Granite State was run by a single family—the Wentworths—up to the Revolution. When that Tory clan was dispossessed, the state settled down to dairying, agriculture and later textile, shoe and paper manufacture on its own water power.

New Hampshire, with the same government from 1699 to 1741, had no revolutionary background; but it was nevertheless the first to pronounce political independence from Great Britain. Before 1692 it had tried to establish a provincial authority; it then merged with Massachusetts in a temporary union; and then for decades Massachusetts and New Hampshire both laid taxes on the same towns and villages, and many a man was arrested or had his business destroyed by such territorial tax competition. Frontiers between states grew at random or were created without evident rhyme or reason. The concept of city planning of today was never applied to those more important units called states.

CANADA

The fur trade which was so advantageously pursued by the coureurs du bois *was the only important industry of Canada, the northern colony.*

No one should forget the Fourteenth Colony. If the ruts in the roads had been a trifle less deep, if the turnpikes had permitted quicker travel, the thirteen red and white stripes of our first national emblem might have numbered fourteen.

No one knew just where Canada began or ended. The Pennsylvanians had claimed parts of Canada. Vermont and Canada are described by contemporary historians as being the same territory. The projected Vermont-Canadian canal created great excitement long before Vermont was in the

Union. By 1774 Canada, inhabited by 100,000 persons thinly spread (Quebec and Montreal had populations of only six hundred each), had received memorials from the assemblies of the thirteen colonies to join with them.

The ban on marriages between English Protestants and French Catholics had not only divided the Canadian colonists into two groups speaking different languages, but had also created an artificial birth control. England had been more lenient to the colony of Canada than to the southern thirteen. But the complete separation of Canada from the United States of today did not exist up to the end of the eighteenth century. The appointment of the former chief justice of New York, a native of New York, William Smith, to be a chief justice of Canada indicated a governmental kinship. The very boundary line between Canada and Massachusetts was undetermined for decades. For twenty years Vermont flirted first with Canada and then with one or more of the thirteen colonies for a merger. Canada was no more alien to Vermont than was New Hampshire. As late as October 24, 1783, the governor of Canada reported to Lord North that negotiations were under way between Vermont and Canada; and that Vermont had indicated that it "must be annexed to Canada or become mistress of it."

In the following year Quebec, over the opposition of the French Canadians, petitioned Great Britain for a free constitution. By 1790 Vermont negotiated in London for recognition as an independent separate state or nation. Ethan Allen and his boys treated with Canada as a threat to New York, from which they wanted freedom. In 1791 Vermont joined the United States, thus settling the New York–New Hampshire boundary dispute.

Still, if the Vermont farm boys before Bunker Hill had not taken Ticonderoga and Crown Point, the regimental aspects of the Revolution might have been changed, with the Canadians sending delegates to the Constitutional Convention.

In area, in boundaries, in population, in manners, in appearance, in industry, in farming, these British colonies were not only each unlike the other, but totally unlike the seaboard states and their people today. Their very alphabet was different; they had the use of an additional letter which we do not even recognize today—the Anglo-Saxon "thorn," representing our sound "th."

In our busy persistent struggle for wealth during the century and a half after 1787, little attention was paid to our past, so that today a false myth of colonial solidarity has been accepted in our literature and our schooling. Never have thirteen more jealous, more alien governmental groups been represented in a single chamber to consider creating a new government.

Perils within and without dictated a choice between starvation and a national government. Playing on these thirteen distinct individual states were forces which compromised them into a single nation.

The cartoonists of 1787 enjoyed the metaphor of thirteen barrel staves without a single hoop. But the hoop was to be welded in part on the battlefields and later in the bitter struggles of intercolonial commercial warfare.

CHAPTER IV

We Fight England and Then Ourselves

Each of the colonies had been developed under the same form of imperialism—they had the unifying influence of a single mother country whose purposes and methods of control of distant possessions were unique in the world of the seventeenth and eighteenth centuries. To understand our development up to 1787 it must be recalled that France, Spain and England carried on their imperialistic expansions with strikingly different techniques.

The French on this continent did not clear the forests but preferred a life of the woods as huntsmen and trappers. The Spanish, who came before the English and remained on our soil after the British had been driven out, worked through conquest rather than through colonization. The English, on the other hand, colonized with a clear eye toward the wealth of trade. Not only did they supply the colonists with manufactured goods and raw materials, but they insisted that most articles which the colonists needed must first go to England and then be reshipped in British bottoms to America. On every article the British merchants and shippers expected and made a handsome profit.

The colonists, in turn, with a pleasing irony, learned how to gather sizable profits out of the French and Indian wars. The fruits of capitalizing such British expansion first came into full bloom during the Seven Years' War against France, when many of the colonies sent out their troops to fight with the British and at the same time dispatched their ships to sell supplies to the French in the French islands. Any loyalties to the king or ideals that may have existed about not killing human beings were fully submerged by helping both sides at war, provided only that each contestant paid a

42

high enough price. The colonial governors residing in this desolate land, not only for honor, permitted such national sabotage to prolong the French war, falsely excusing to the Crown the departure of colonial trading vessels on the slim hope that French troops of war were being exchanged.

The patronage left in the hands of many and oft-changing colonial governors resulted in anything but a unified pattern even in a single colony. The turnover of governors spelled constant shifts in the favored groups. But not until 1688 was there any significant animosity toward the distant controls of the British Crown, no matter how irritated the colonists may have been on recurring occasions at the representatives sent over by the kings. In that year England itself went through its own revolution, which might well have produced a written constitution had not the aristocrats in power wanted to disguise the fact that there even was a revolution. Gradually the million people in the thirteen colonies were encouraged to resent the acts of the British Throne. The rebellion in the homeland made such heretofore seditious attitudes seem practical and possible.

These were harsh, cruel days. The insane were chastised; thousands had been murdered by the State for a crime called witchcraft; prisons stank so that no one walked on the side of the pike where the prisons stood; one fourth of all deaths were from tuberculosis; water was dangerous to drink; few families reached maturity entire; and frequently "less than half survived the ordeals of baptism, contagion and sitting for hours on end in ice-cold churches every Sunday."

Only one half of the population grew to reach the age of seventeen, as compared to two thirds today. The few who passed sixteen had developed immunities which permitted those rare cases of great vitality in old age which history books record.

"More medicine," says MacMaster's History of the People of the United States, *"was then taken every year by the well than is now taken in the same space of time by the sick."* During the yellow-fever epidemic of 1793 in Philadelphia, New York asked that coaches

cease running from the southern city, but business was good and the coach companies refused. By 1936 as many as 10 per cent of the farmhouses have water piped into a bathroom.

Despite the shocking mortality record the population of the fourteen English colonies doubled every twenty years up to 1787; but the Alleghany Mountains, near the seaboard, slowed up the western march. In 1770 Detroit was a grazing land for French Canadians with three hundred shacks for homes. It was not until twenty years after the Constitution was adopted that Michigan had a population of four thousand people. By 1840, however, Michigan grew to 212,000. But no one realized that the United States was on the path of a westward world migration until the famous London correspondent of the New York *Tribune*, Karl Marx, pointed it out in the 1850s. That mountain range slowed up our western march and helped in the early years to solidify the colonies, thus explaining in part the unity of the English-speaking colonies in the northern, as compared to the still separate Spanish nations in the southern, continent of America. A decade after the Constitution was adopted the steamboat further solidified the nation, but in the middle of the nineteenth century it would have disintegrated had it not been for the development of the railroad.

By 1750, to the east of the mountain ranges several hundred families had pegged out vast landholdings within the vague frontiers of these colonies. The soil was the great source of income and wealth. Industry in the form we see it today had not begun. The four great inventions of the latter part of the eighteenth century had not commenced to change our world economics. The spinning jenny of Hargreaves, the water frame of Arkwright, the mule of Crompton and the power loom of Cartwright were to make new history, but until 1800 our life was primarily wedded to the sea and the soil.

Capital was so scarce that it was most often raised by lotteries, especially for public improvements. Jeffer-

*son's estate was saved from bankruptcy by a national
lottery. A century later ten million bicycles were traveling our roads.*

The Church, for centuries preaching the ungodliness of
possessing wealth, had indirectly encouraged the accumulations of great fortunes by a few. The wary rich in our
colonies were aided by the clergy who preached the beauty
of poverty for the masses of man. The rich capitalized this
doctrine. The ecclesiastical establishments, as Madison repeatedly pointed out, increased class warfare, encouraged
"ignorance and corruption" and, when necessary, inspired
the upper classes to use the lower classes to protect them
against English legislative interference. When Madison
wrote: "To their eternal infamy the clergy can furnish their
quota of imps," he was preaching much more than the plea
of Jefferson, that nonatheist endower of churches who urged
the separation of State and Church. Nine of the thirteen
colonies carried established government churches, some at
times supported by a complete monopoly of taxes. That we
should have created a church-free state in the eighteenth
century such as France could not attain until the twentieth,
is still one of our great contributions to history, even though
not until 1833 did Catholics acquire political equality in the
United States, and even though today children of religious
groups are jailed for refusal to salute the flag, an act which
violates their religious mandate against bowing to a graven
image.

Up to the middle of the eighteenth century Great Britain
used the colonies as a consumer outlet for home-made goods.
Colonies spelled profit to England through controlled trade.
The shift of British imperialism from a trade-profit device
to a taxation and trade-profit mechanism brought on the
trouble. In 1754 the then young Dr Franklin first politely
voiced a protest to paying both ways. In that year England
proposed to reimburse itself for its colonial advances by a
parliamentary tax to be imposed on the colonists. The feeble
answer of the colonists to this tax program was the meeting
of delegates at Albany and the Doctor's suggestion that

such a tax was "unconstitutional, unjust and impolitic." So long as the mother country raised the cost of living here by increased charges concealed in the cost of shipping and goods, we were comparatively unconcerned with the amount of wealth created by us to be shipped to absentee owners abroad.

Matters slumbered for about a decade, until 1763, because England wanted to make peace with the Indians in order to control the fur trade. Animal skins were more important than red skins. In the next year a Sugar Act was imposed by Great Britain to increase its revenue by reducing the vast amount of smuggling carried on at all ports by all colonies. By 1765 hard times had hit the northern colonies. England controlled us through an inarticulate and unimaginative Council of Trade and Plantations, which title in itself indicates the mood of Parliament's attitude.

By November 1, 1765, a consumer boycott against Great Britain was in full swing. Although New York was loudest in protest, it was slowest in the movement for concerted action. Before New Year's Day of 1766, market places for the sale of home-made goods had been opened in six cities of more than eight thousand population—Philadelphia, New York, Boston, Charleston, Baltimore and Newport.

At this time the trip from Philadelphia to New York took three days but cost only $6.50 for transportation, lodging and meals. Three hundred and twenty acres of land were sold for an eighth of a dollar per acre. Real-estate speculators were inducing inspection of lands by free transportation in "boats 40 feet long with 20 pairs of oar."

In 1765 the first sensitive relationship between the public and the troops, which precedes every revolution, arose. British troops were billeted in private homes, and the common people started to grumble. On June 10, 1768, wine from Madeira was being smuggled into New York, and when the custom officials were offered a bribe by our righteous New York wine merchants, the King's officials refused the bribe and were thrown into a cabin until the wine was landed. The New York wine party set the pace for the later, more publicized, Boston Tea Party.

Then there was a brief respite from agitation because the upper classes became fearful that the lower classes had been aroused too much. A wine merchant cannot openly violate a tariff law without encouraging his workers to pick some other law for defiance. Energetic minorities had gone too far to please the rich merchants and the landowners. Peaceful methods were to be pursued from now on. By 1770 lists of merchants who continued to import from Great Britain contrary to boycott agreements were published in many colonies. The first unofficial American straw ballot was taken in 1770, when, out of fifteen hundred questionnaires sent out, three hundred showed a desire to continue the boycott on goods in addition to tea.

New York City put a fine of $25.00 on the planting of any new tree except in front of a church; too much forestation had to be prevented. Slaves preferred wives on different plantations as affording occasions for going abroad and exempting them on holidays from a share of the little calls to which those at home were liable. Americans deplored the use of finger bowls, which they said in England entailed washing hands, rinsing mouths, rubbing gums and squirting water back into the bowls.

On November 17, 1772, Samuel Adams of Boston organized a secret left-wing movement, set up in cell formation much like the antifascist organizations in Italy, Germany and Hungary today. By 1774 each state had a secret committee. Then the youth of the land took a lead in the situation. Less than two thousand young scattered secret committee members set the pace for the revolt. Committees of Correspondence were organized in many towns and villages. The use of cipher in all letters of the committees added to the sense of revolutionary solidarity.

On September 5, 1774, on a call from Massachusetts, the

First Continental Congress met at Philadelphia. Twelve colonies, all but Georgia and Canada, were represented by fifty-five delegates. Seven of the twelve delegations were chosen irregularly, not by regular assemblies but by revolutionary conventions called by local self-constituted committees. In Massachusetts, Rhode Island and Connecticut, which by that time were dominated by the Reds, delegates were selected by the regular assemblies.

In most districts less than a hundredth part of the people turned out to vote. There was no semblance of democracy. In one place two men met, and the one appointed the other the official delegate. In North Carolina there was so little interest that eight of the fifty-four districts sent no representatives. In Long Island most districts were opposed to sending delegates. One third of the delegates were Whigs and one third were Tories, according to Sam Adams' appraisal. Some historical continuity was evident in the assemblage, however, because one delegate had been at the Albany congress and eight had been at the Stamp Act Congress.

But nothing happened save polite talk of protest. Efforts at conciliation with the Crown were discussed, and the envy and jealousy of each colony toward the others became more and more pronounced.

Ice cut off all northern communication for six weeks. The leaders of the American Revolution were in their forties, as compared to the leaders of the French Revolution, who were in their thirties. The bullets for the Battle of Brandywine were wadded with pages torn from an edition of Fox's Book of Martyrs.

On May 10, 1775, one month after the Battle of Lexington, the Second Congress was audaciously organized, although no one has ever explained the process of telepathy by which Ethan Allen on that same May 10, 1775, took Fort Ticonderoga in the name of the Great Jehovah and the uncreated Second Continental Congress. After fifty-two days of argument a continental association was decided on. The entire drive was for a boycott. This was to be an

economic war only. The turn in the tide took place historically, as it always does, at the precise moment when men
and women, unafraid of British troops, jeered at them with
insulting names such as "hireling," "informer," "redcoat"
or "mercenary." Anonymous threatening signs appeared on
the streets.

And still the colonists were as a whole loyal British subjects. This was to be only a sympathetic strike, with the
radicals in the saddle supporting the businessmen. Joseph
Galloway of Pennsylvania, with the aid of respectable John
Jay of New York, represented the liberals and drooled along
for days about a plan for a new union of England and the
colonies.

The legal powers of this gathering were early questioned,
but our Founding Fathers, being practical men, promptly
agreed with Edmund Randolph of Virginia, who was sec-
onded by Alexander Hamilton of New York, that we need
not be "scrupulous on the point of power." Thus were legalisms discarded.

*At this time sugar was already selling at $4.00 a pound,
linen at $20.00 a yard and flour at $500.00 a barrel.
The rich prewar group in Boston held the monopoly
of duck for army tents. It cost $40.00 to cross the Ap-
pomattox River.*

Meanwhile in England much sympathy was flowing to the
colonists. Under the Earl of Chatham and Edmund Burke
the desire for liberty at home, coupled with the animosity
against King George and his second-rate politicians, encouraged open support of our cause. Nevertheless, and even
after the redcoats had killed many of our boys and stolen
our food, we did not want to separate from England. We
were far from thinking in terms of an independent nation.
In August 1775 the British Parliament was so secure that
it refused to hear our lawyer, John Dickinson of Delaware,
present a polite memorial for the remedy of our grievances.

In May 1775 John Adams wrote home that the Congress

was so divided that every important step was opposed and killed by bare majorities. This though the war was on.

> *Milk delivery in bottles was not made until a hundred years after this time. Soap was chopped out of large hunks. No bathrooms, no pencils, no rakes, no overshoes were extant. Girls were not admitted to schools until fifty years later.*

Later in the same month Congress mildly recommended to the colonists the establishing of new governments where old ones had fallen. Connecticut and Rhode Island replied that their old charters required only the deletion of the King's name. That's all they thought vital. South Carolina did not revise its royal constitution until July 1776, and Massachusetts waited another two years. But Connecticut declared itself a republic which "shall forever be and remain a free sovereign and independent state." Sam Adams then arose to say: "Is not America already independent? Why not declare it?" This was a novel and revolutionary concept. A committee was appointed in June to consider the subject. After eighteen days the committee of one conservative, William Livingston, and four radicals, Thomas Jefferson, Benjamin Franklin, John Adams and Roger Sherman, made its report—the Declaration of Independence.

> *The leading spy was the Reverend John Vardill, assistant minister of Trinity Church in New York; Copley and Trumbull, noted American painters, deserted to live in England.*

Fifty-six men signed that document written by Jefferson, who had deftly twisted Locke's philosophy for protection of property into protection of liberty. Of the fifty-six, eight were rich merchants, twenty-five were leading lawyers and six were doctors. There were no galleries, no mobs waiting to hear the report. It took weeks before any substantial part of the populace ever knew of the Declaration. It was twenty-nine days before Charleston got the news from Philadelphia. Thus our first united indignation was expressed in the Jefferson manifesto, containing no blueprint for a united government. And yet three years later, in 1779, Joseph Galloway of Pennsylvania told Parliament that "many more than four fifths of the people would prefer a union with Great Britain upon constitutional principles to that of independence."

CHAPTER V

The War Is On

IN THE MEANWHILE the war went on. It was a contest of skirmishes instead of battles. There being no centralization of power, there could not be any military concentration.

Adams had nominated George Washington for commander-in-chief of the army to placate the Southern colonies. Washington wisely realized that his choice was due to the "partiality of Congress to join to a political motive." By December 1776 Congress, unable to get money from the colonies, in complete jitters named George Washington dictator for six months, giving him power to raise troops, collect supplies and punish offenders. It *did* happen here! But while he and his troops froze at Valley Forge, the Pennsylvania farmers were selling their farm produce to the British army at high prices and great profit.

All through the war most of the judges, executives and capitalists were loyal to the British. Whole brigades of our troops in confusion deserted to the British lines. Great efforts were required to get forty thousand privates out of three million people. One state offered each volunteer a bounty "of a healthy sound Negro between the ages of ten and thirty, or sixty pounds in gold and silver." This was our first recorded war bonus. Many people did not care which side won.

In 1783 half pay for life to soldiers for sacrificing themselves for seven years, making themselves unfit for occupations, was proposed. Many objected to the stigmatized word "pensions," urging that "those who had lent their blood to the public receive an annuity just as those who had lent their money." Later on, technical lawyers were to object to even half pay for the army, as the pay was voted before the Confederation and by a vote of fewer than seven states.

> *Shortly after the war the bonus army at Newburgh-on-the-Hudson threatened to take over the government if they did not get the lands and money long promised. Washington had to go to address the men, and the gazettes report how "he left the men in tears." In the administration of President Hoover a similar bonus army scared the President into locking the White House gates after storing up ample munitions on the ground floor.*

Not until 1777 did Congress agree on Articles of Confederation to be sent to the states for ratification. Even these articles, according to Professor Beard, "were wrung from reluctant delegates in the Congress and their still more reluctant states."

The entire power now vested in the president, the Congress and the courts was placed in one body—the Congress. Each state was to have one vote, and delegates were to be paid by their own states. The Congress was to handle diplomatic matters, declare and wage war, negotiate peace, coin money, control the Indian affairs, establish a post office and control the army and the navy. It was also to establish courts to try felonies and cases arising at sea. One other important provision declared that each state must recognize the laws and court decisions of every other state.

There was no power to tax. There was no responsible executive to run the government. After 1778 it was difficult to get a quorum of the states. In 1780 Madison came forward with two practical suggestions to meet the emergency—commandeering of all commodities to anticipate peacetime revenues; and liberating the Negroes so as to reinforce enlisted white soldiers.

> *Virginia grants license for a lottery to raise £2,000 for Mr Maury's school. Two men of the same family are growing into prominence—Thomas Jefferson, the*

great-grandson, and John Marshall, the great-great-grandson, of William Randolph and Mary Isham.

At the close of the war our forces had dwindled to less than one third of the original number, and the British number had doubled, General Sir William Howe having three thousand loyalists with him at Philadelphia and nine hundred with him on his trip from Boston to Halifax.

That the war was carried on at all is still a governmental miracle. Congress had no money and no power to get any. The whole sum contributed to the public treasury from May 14, 1781, to January 1, 1783, amounted to $300,000 less than expenses, the differences being made up by notes of financiers, mainly Robert Morris and George Clymer. Compulsory taxation was clearly impossible because the cause of the war was so intimately identified with resistance to taxation by England.

Seven states were needed for action in Congress on any question, and seldom more than nine were present. It would have been difficult to set up a less efficient government.

By 1782 the debts were no less than fifty million dollars. Hamilton proposed state scrip with equalization by negotiations between states, much like one of our 1933 bank-holiday plans. Virginia paid taxes to the national treasury in tobacco because it had no money. The proposed 5 per cent impost was a failure and in fact was unanimously rejected in the legislature of Rhode Island. "The states are every day giving proof that separate regulations are more likely to set them by the ears than to attain the common object," declared a sober delegate to the Congress.

Matters grew still more complicated. As in Chicago in 1930, salaries of government employees were not paid. Far outside of the admitted constitutional powers of the Confederation, a national bank was organized to meet the task of feeding the army.

Between 1775 and 1779 Congress issued 240 million and the states 210 million of paper credits. Congress made 55 million dollars by paper credit operations through inflated currency. Madison had been rejected in marriage by William Floyd's daughter.

The Confederation was in danger of breaking up, but it held together in part because the Southern states feared that the Eastern states would become too powerful at sea, leaving the Southern states opulent but weak.

In December 1782 Sam Adams introduced a gentleman from Canada as a person who could negotiate the union of that province with the Confederation, if the Confederation would only stick together a little longer. In that year Congress begged for eight million dollars but was given only $430,031 by the states. An export tax on fifteen million dollars of shipments was estimated to bring in $750,000 of revenue, but only a fraction of that amount was received by the Congress. All kinds of taxes were proposed—even a 2½ per cent rental tax on houses leasing for more than twenty dollars a month. A 10 per cent tax on lawyers' fees was actually enacted. For months there were two treasurers, both appointed by a majority vote of Congress. Then there followed a control committee of thirteen; then a treasury board of five, three of whom were chosen from outside of Congress. The election of a secretary of Congress was the order of business for months without a vote being taken. Meanwhile John Francis Mercer and others threatened to use everything in their power "to destroy the existence of the Congress if plans went through for a fixed permanent revenue."

By February 21, 1783, Randolph got letters indicating that Washington's influence was rapidly declining in the army. The unpaid soldiers formed a bonus army, marched on Philadelphia and actually scared the Congress into moving up to Princeton. One of our early mutinies.

Jefferson writes a long letter on the equatorial diameter of the earth in comparison to the polar diameter. Meanwhile Mrs Bingham, to be heard of later, curses around the house and orders wallpaper copied after patterns at the Vatican, while two thousand slaves are

*sold on the auction block in New York City. Labor is
so scarce that British prisoners hire themselves out on
bond from their employers for their return.*

Robert Morris, the treasurer, wrote: "Talking to the
states is like preaching to the dead." Congress remained
impotent, and Morris resigned rather than "be the minister
of injustice." The government broke down not only in revenue but in its control of commerce. In foreign affairs European nations were doubtful of the endurance of a unified
nation and considered dealing separately with each of the
thirteen states.

But eight years of running troops up and down the coast
brought English popular opinion to the point of peace.

CHAPTER VI

In Search of a Hoop

IN AUGUST 1782 a close vote was reported in the British cabinet on the subject of Peace. Jay, Adams, Franklin and Laurens were our negotiators in Paris. When this news reached New York there occurred a terrible break in the commodity market, to be repeated when word of King George's letter of December 5, 1782, intimating possible peace, leaked out. Merchants had large stocks of merchandise on their shelves, and peace would bring ruin to the middleman, though cheaper goods to consumers. A treaty of peace was finally approved in Parliament by only thirteen votes, having been defeated on the first ballot by sixteen votes. Signed at Versailles September 3, 1783, it contained, in addition to English abandonment of colonial soil, three features, of vital significance at the time, but, because of changed conditions, no more than slightly amusing today.

1. No provision was made for return of the $40,000,000 of property confiscated by the colonies. In fact we never did give any of it back, but subdivided the large-sized estates and sold them in small acreage on the installment plan—a kind of resettlement administration. Congress agreed merely to recommend the return of confiscated property. This it did without enthusiasm and to slight avail. Acquisition by confiscation was accepted and enjoyed. The properties so taken without compensation were not the lands and riches of unknown aliens, but often of lifetime neighbors and friends. We were greedy. We also insisted that Great Britain leave here all the Negroes it had captured or acquired by desertions from our forces.

2. Great stress was laid on the rights to fish on the Newfoundland Banks. This important economic issue of the

Revolution was considered essential for any real development of the United States.

3. The Mississippi was to remain open for our navigation.

Congress, of course, was more than anxious for peace. The delegates were paid, if at all, by the colonial legislatures. No money was left to continue the government. In the past fourteen months less than half a million dollars, paper money at that, had been paid into the treasury, not enough to meet the interest on foreign debts; $4,500,000 of paper fiat money was outstanding. We owed $70,000,000 in addition—with no revenue in sight to pay interest or principal. All operations of a centrally managed government were benumbed by lack of funds.

Franklin explains:

> This Currency as we manage it is a wonderful Machine. It performs its office when we issue it; it pays and clothes troops and provides victuals and Ammunition; and when we are obliged to issue a Quantity excessive, it pays itself off by Depreciation.

Only Hamilton saw the possibility of uniform taxes and tariffs during all this time when the states refused to live up to Congress' request for funds. The states should not destroy each other. Connecticut, for example, as a national defiance, was taxing imports from Massachusetts at a higher rate than those from Great Britain. As facile Elbridge Gerry said:

> At the beginning of the war we possessed more than Roman virtue. It appears to me it is now the reverse. We have more land and stock jobbers than any place on earth.

Private profit was invigorating the need for a planned national political economy. Adams was pleading:

> The Confederation is to make us one individual only. It is to form us like separate parcels of metal into one common mass.

First and foremost was the need of a strong central government powerful enough to meet the direst problem of the day. The most important need was for national arrangements to prevent cutthroat competition between different states. There could be no enforceable tax program if commerce remained at a standstill owing to unregulated interstate commerce. The obvious weapons of such mercantile warfare at that time were colonial embargoes and state tariff walls. The second most important need was a potent power to tax: money was needed centrally to run a national government. A national government could not survive if it had to rely on state gratuities and voluntary contributions. Collateral to these problems was a third object: the necessity of defining boundaries of the states in geographical terms. Taxes could not be equitably levied by a national government, and interstate trade could not be wisely regulated unless the boundaries of each state were staked out with precision. The subdividing of Virginia, pleas from a new province called Mayne, recognition of Vermont, were much-discussed territorial dilemmas. The final need was for a central power with the capacity to make treaties and deal with foreign powers. This was essential for maintenance of trade and peace.

Whisky was unknown in the East, north of Baltimore. Women shopped for amens, amblets, duffils, dowlas, and fearnaughts.

Lord Sheffield's new economic policy in Great Britain worried the colonists, for it aimed at destruction of our shipping and it emphasized the weakness of separate states:

Parliament should endeavor to divert the whole Anglo-American Trade to British bottoms. America cannot retaliate. It will not be an easy matter to bring the American States to act as a nation. They are not to be feared as such by us. . . . We might as reasonably dread the effects of a combination among the German as among the American States.

Great Britain intended to force the colonies to compete against each other to the destruction of all except Great Britain.

After the peace treaty of 1783 many of the courageous fighters of the Revolution showed signs of despair.

Madison, writing to Monroe in 1786, urged haste of action in these words:

The question whether it be possible and worth while to preserve the union of the states must be speedily decided some way or other.

At about this time he received a letter from a member of Congress:

The truth is we have not a government to wield and correct. . . . We have only four states now on the floor.

In 1785 the legislature of Rhode Island, which later played such a stubborn, lone hand, instructed her delegates to Congress that the United States in Congress assembled should be exclusively empowered to regulate trade and commerce of the respective states and citizens thereof with each other. In May of the same year delegate Monroe reported to a committee of Congress:

The United States in Congress assembled is to have the sole and exclusive right and power of regulating trade of the states . . .

Professor Charles A. Beard points out the utter inability of merchants, moneylenders, discharged soldiers holding government securities, loyalists with claims to their own properties, and planters with uncollected bills to do business in a rapidly fluctuating currency, because of rival state courts, absence of commercial treaties, and uncertain values for Western lands. For all people it was a critical period, as had been that which brought on the Revolution.

The drive to strengthen the Articles of Confederation was frustrated in part because many delegates hoped that a delay in fixing up the government "would bring the government into disgrace and pave the way for a form of government more congenial with monarchial or aristocratical predilections." An American king or dictator seemed more than likely.

During all this time Congress was ineffectual. The Articles were inflexible—unanimous vote of all colonies was required for even the slightest amendment. Any change passed by fewer than thirteen states would be unconstitutional.

Hamilton was soon to write: "No amendment to the confederation leaving the states in possession of their sovereignty could possibly answer the purpose." He and others realized that if the "Federal powers were limited at all the rivalship of the states would gradually subvert it." He pointed with erudition to historical examples in Persia, the Holy Roman Empire, and the revolts produced under the delegated powers to satraps and proconsuls.

Many appreciated that the increased sense of unison developed during the war had, as soon as the state governments were formed, evaporated midst jealousies and local ambitions.

Prophesied a pamphleteer under the name of Agrippa:

> The idea of an uncompounded republick, on an average one thousand miles in length, and eight hundred in breadth, and containing six millions of white inhabitants all reduced to the same standard of morals and habits, and of laws, is in itself an absurdity, and contrary to the whole experience of mankind.

This fear of regimentation (1787) was probably not read by many people because the post was so overburdened that newspapers were often crowded out of the postbags, although they were often only a double sheet.

When New York discriminated against Connecticut merchants, Connecticut retaliated with a boycott entailing a large fine for any man found dealing with the state to the south.

Virginia was the focal point of our political philosophy. In addition to dreaming, it acted. When the tobacco of North Carolina started to flood the Virginia market places, embargoes were voted. Economic reprisals then became popular up and down the coast. Virginia had to protect her exports: tobacco $800,000, wheat $50,000, iron $35,000, Indian corn $25,000, deer and other skins $25,000. It was high time some body was assembled to discuss the flow of commerce between the states. If Congress would not act someone else should.

Not discouraged by the vast extent of the country, as was Hamilton, or by the tremendous number of inhabitants, as was Gerry, Virginia, desiring economic uniformity between the states, started us on our way to an unconstitutional constitution to handle interstate commerce.

George Washington utters these stirring words:

I do not conceive we can exist long as a nation without lodging somewhere a power which pervades the whole union in as energetic a manner as the authority of the state government extends over the several states.

CHAPTER VII

Our Interstate Commerce Convention

Most americans, if asked about the formation of the United States, report: We fought the British. We drove them out. We adopted a declaration of independence and a constitution.

Such a statement is a decided oversimplification of history. The span of years between our declaration of independence and the formation of a nation was the equivalent of three presidential terms of office. An amount of time elapsed such as ran from the death of Harding until 1937.

Moreover, four full years passed between the signing of the treaty of peace at Paris in 1783 and the drafting of the Constitution. But what is still more important—a fact consistently overlooked by the judges of the Supreme Court of the United States in most of the decisions since 1900—is that after the English were sent back home there was no spontaneous comradeship between the colonies tending toward a single nation. In fact, as soon as the redcoats sailed away the union of interests arising out of self-defense were dissipated, and during the period of 1783 to 1787 new pressures had to become powerful enough to convince the separate colonies to unite against a new common enemy—this time domestic and not foreign. Each colony became an active enemy against every other colony. Our constitution became necessary as a means of regulating interstate commerce.

Much of our interstate commercial warfare was tied up with the seas. Ships, the vehicle of our cohesion in the absence of usable roads, were also the medium of disintegration. Shippers, fishermen, cooperage artisans, whalers, white mast cutters, were competing for coastwise, export and import business. The war had cost the colonists $15,000,000 in trade, not to count several hundred thousand dollars of depreciation in ships. Luckily John Adams, one of the American peace negotiators in Paris, was close to industry and appreciated the importance of trade and commerce and fought for protective clauses in the peace treaty. He knew that over four thousand men in Massachusetts alone sailed the 665 fishing ships which set out from Massachusetts each year. During the war military exemption had been granted to men experienced in shipbuilding, salt business and cooperage trades. Nantucket, neutral during the Revolution, sent out 120 ships of 33,000 tons on its coastwise trade with twenty-five whalers sailing to the African coast for oil, ambergris, and whalebones for ladies' stays. The codfish business engaged ten thousand men and was valued at two million dollars annually.

Although some of the colonies came to informal agreements on tariff rates against British wares in these years of business depression, such compacts were more often violated than enforced. The gross quantity of interstate shipment of raw materials and finished goods was not very large in proportion to the total production of food and goods; nevertheless, local merchants and manufacturers brought severe pressure on each colonial assembly to create tariff walls against the threatened import of goods from other colonies.

After the war, capital had followed the loyalists back to England. The densely populated North and the sparsely populated South both felt the economic destruction of the revolution. Navigation restrictions immediately applied by Great Britain called for retaliation by the states. The colonial commercial attack was at first directed against Great Britain by means of a sort of Gandhi civil boycott on English goods. Soon, however, tariffs were imposed by each state at varying rates and on different commodities to prevent foreign dumping. Each colony promptly learned that British competition was less destructive than the intercolonial trade rivalries. Each colony created import tariffs against every other. Products, ships, merchants of adjacent states became the objects of state regulations and imposts. The technique of economic warfare, developed in the struggle against Great Britain, was easily applied at interstate borders.

The guests who frequented the drawing rooms at the turn of the century were expected to sing or play. The flute (on which Washington performed), the guitar, and the harpsichord were the instruments in vogue. No one played the violin—Lord Chesterfield had pronounced it ungenteel.

Separate colonial restrictions on exports were also generally in vogue. These laws affected many common wares such as hides, tar, iron and lumber. The regulation of interstate commerce by each colony covered in the main the raw materials—the necessities of life. Manufacture was, of course, very limited. Lack of currency, scarcity of labor, absence of capital, difficulties of transport and the novelty of the newly invented machines permitted the handicrafts to be supreme until after the turn of the century. The interstate flow of raw materials was therefore doubly important. In 1775 Philadelphia experimented with textile production under Samuel Wetherell, but not until 1790 did Samuel Slater, in Pawtucket, Rhode Island, set up the first of those devilish mechanical inventions which were to amaze, irritate and eventually disemploy the workers.

Not till the Constitution was ratified was John Fitch to run his steamboat on the Delaware, or Nicholas J. Roosevelt to use a steam engine to saw timber. The oil industry was limited to snake and skunk oils for internal use; lubricants still came from whale oil or tallow. The astounding number of thirty-one iron forges existed in New England by 1776. The paper mills located on the coast were soon to be shifted by Isaiah Thomas, publisher of the *Massachusetts Spy,* to the far west near the Berkshire Hills. Meat packing was unheard of until 1811.

Industry was still sedentary and noiseless. Wooden pegs were used in shoemaking until 1800, although tanneries and bootmakers flourished in Lynn, Massachusetts, as early as 1630.

Industrial centers were in their infancy: Lancaster for furnaces, Germantown for textiles, Trenton for mechanical devices; but what manufacturing industry there was existed primarily for local markets. The modern factory was as yet unconceived on this continent.

It took nine farmers in 1783, working such hours as today would seem impossible, to raise enough food to support ten people. In 1936 each working farmer raises enough produce to support twelve people. Four fifths of the population had to stick to agriculture in order to survive, even though wages were only fifty to seventy-five cents a day in the North and farm slaves were sold for life from a hundred to two hundred dollars a head in the South.

The coastwise trade among the thirteen colonies was about 185,000 tons out of a total of 660,000 tons clearing from and entering American ports annually. As soon as intensified production developed, the coastwise trade grew by leaps and bounds. Across inland colonial boundary lines the flow of raw materials was ever increasing.

In cotton textiles there was already a comparatively wide market, although only eight mills existed by 1805. To manufacture such cotton goods, Southern farmers were planting, growing, exhausting the land; and then deserting the sterile fields to move further inland. A very low grade of sheep supplied each housewife with wool for her frame. She washed it, carded it, and stretched it *on tenterhooks* herself to make the family's clothing.

What manufacturing industry there was outside of homes could be found near streams and waterfalls. Innumerable tiny factories were under government domination. Employees' wages were artificially stabilized by ordinances designed to prevent competing for artisans, and government-controlled guilds were small replicas of our present chambers of commerce. Most of the colonies had legalized price fixing of long lists of commodities. Nearly every business was limited by a licensing system.

All running waters and the businesses of all those who used them were of vital public concern. Water, whether navigable or not, was important; it was power. Mills using water wheels for power were regarded as something quite remote from unconditional private property. To foster such mills, New York put fees on all vessels, while Delaware and New York competitively lowered their port duties to entice navigation away from each other. The public interest was so acute that most colonies encouraged by bounties the development of running waters.

In the use of farm and stream the states collided in the flow of commerce. Bitterly they fought against each other.

New Jersey endeavored at one time to cripple New York by taxing the Sandy Hook lighthouse in New York Harbor the immense sum of $1,800 per annum. Connecticut bore down on New York industry from the north by a boycott on New York goods with a substantial fine for each violation.

Delaware has consistently underbid the other states in one form of business—incorporating new companies. In January 1929 it organized companies with par-value stock of 245 million dollars, and no-par-value stock of 85 million shares.

We had learned from England the governmental domination of business. We had been brought up on the theory of regulation—common herdsmen, common wine taverns, common chirurgeons, common bakers, common glass houses, common lightmen. Such was the common-law practice of England that on July 4, 1776, England not only permitted all kinds of regulation and price fixing, but such regulation had been the practice for centuries past. As far back as 1351 the control of the labor market was fixed in England by rigid laws. Blackstone, the great legal educator of our Founding Fathers, states without a dissenting reference the common-law rule of apprenticeship requiring seven years of service on threat of "forfeiture of forty shillings by the month." The colonists all knew of the regulations in England which provided a five-hundred-pound fine for "transporting and seducing English artists to settle abroad." As late as 1776 the city of Chester, England, passed an ordinance—based on custom—that no one but a freeman of the city "could keep open shop and exercise the trade of grocer" within that city.

The statesmen and leading officeholders in each colony had been brought up under a common practice and law which called for governmental regulation of business. But separate colonial power to fix prices, to permit persons or companies to do business, to prevent the rise of wages soon proved to be of little benefit in any district if adjacent colonies continued to dump, undersell or smuggle labor or goods across the border.

Up and down the coast economic warfare continued. Each colony by duties or other device tried to entice foreign trade from other more popular ports.

Adams was very much worried about the commercially backward states, calling America "a great unwieldy body like a large fleet sailing under convoy. The fleetest sailors must wait for the dullest and slowest. Like a coach and six the swiftest horses must be slackened and the slowest quickened that all may keep an even pace."

The population of the thirteen colonies was less in 1787 than the number of employees used on railroads and transportation in the United States in 1936.

Madison had a slight premonition of a small segment of the clash of the twentieth century. Others spoke of commercial jealousies between North and South, but this student of economics knew that "in all countries the mass of people became sooner or later divided mainly into the class which raises food and raw materials and the class which provides clothing and the other necessaries and conveniences of life." He talked in realistic terms the underlying philosophy of the Agricultural Adjustment Act of the Roosevelt administration, the equalization of income of those who produce from the soil and those who manufacture articles. He knew that the farmers' ability to buy pants and shoes depended directly on the price that city folk paid for wheat and corn.

Each year Madison would write to some one of his friends that he hoped the contest between South and North would end and that the manufacturers would be able to swim "without the bladders [tariffs] which have supported them." Virginia corn should flow without restraints to Massachusetts, New Jersey vegetables to Georgia, and New England rum to the Carolinas. While Madison watched the crude production of hoes in Carolina, nails in Philadelphia, tow cloth in Connecticut, he never dreamed of electricity and our modern forms of power.

Jealousies grew not only north and south, but east and west as well. Letters published in the newspapers bitterly criticized "those westerners," those "foreigners" who might well go back where they came from if they didn't like our land!

But all sections of the people were outwardly united through fear of the announced policy of Great Britain to destroy any attempt at union of the thirteen colonies. England's best interests were to be served not only by monopolizing our trade, but also by effecting a breach in our confederacy.

One of the early American statements of economic principles, "The Witherspoon Resolution of 1781," had indicated the trend:

It is indispensably necessary that the United States and Congress assembled should be vested with a right of superintending the commercial regulations of every State, that none may take place which shall be partial or contrary to the common interests.

At a Philadelphia town meeting in June 1785, the need for a national planned economy was repeated in a resolution which read:

. . . that relief from the oppression under which the American trade and manufactures languish could spring only from the grant to Congress of full constitutional powers over the commerce of the United States.

Colonial records disclose similar sentiments in every colony.

Early in 1786 a letter, received by Jefferson from an important Virginian, reads:

If anything should reconcile Virginia to the idea of giving Congress a power over trade it will be that this power will annoy Great Britain against whom the animosities of our citizens are still strong.

For ten years Virginia had been at loggerheads with Maryland over the commercial rights to the Potomac. During the war, in 1777, these two states had appointed commissioners to try to work out an amicable intercolonial trade agreement. No settlement could be reached. The negotiations dragged on. No industrial leader appeared on the scene with enough strength to force an agreement. Adams was to write:

Remember, democracy never lasts long. It soon wastes, exhausts and murders itself. There never was a democracy that did not commit suicide.

At length, in 1785, at Washington's home at Mount Vernon, the leaders of political action of Virginia proposed that Pennsylvania be invited into the conference. Maryland, nationally minded on commercial matters at that time, then suggested that Delaware also be asked to sit in at the gathering. Gradually the hope of commercial interstate peace developed. All the colonies were invited to send delegates to meet at Annapolis on September 11, 1786.

Although unemployment was increasing and business was at a standstill, Annapolis of 1786 continued to be a gay city. The rich planters came there for the society season. Hence, it seemed logical to choose it for a convention on interstate commerce; everyone being in agreement that it would be imprudent to meet in the neighborhood of Congress, then sitting in New York City.

Although the idea of such a meeting seemed to be generally favored, only five states bothered to attend. When the delegates gathered, Maryland, to the surprise of everyone present, had not sent a single representative.

Virginia, the prime mover toward a commercial national planned economy, would have remained unco-

operative and opposed to union if Congress had not
withdrawn from Spain the previously granted twenty-
five-year rights to the Mississippi.

Monroe had guessed quite incorrectly when, writing to
Madison on September 3, 1786, he said he expected "the
emissaries of foreign countries to be on the ground at Annapolis."

Not only did the foreign potentates disappoint, but even
the few emissaries of states who did appear thought it fruit-
less to work out a national agreement unless more states
were represented. The delegates present did not even represent contiguous colonies. The meeting was a fizzle. Madison
was to write to Jefferson that the break-up of the Committee of the States at Annapolis

proceeded *partly from irritations among the committee, partly from*
dislike to the place of their session, and *partly from an impatience to*
get home, which prevailed over *their regard for their private char-*
acters, as well as for *their public duty.*

Hamilton who, with Washington, thought "a radical
cure" must be found, sat down on a Maryland veranda one
cool evening to write that subtle and cautious invitation for
another interstate-commerce meeting to be held in the following year, May 14, 1787, at Philadelphia. This invitation
was approved by a minority of the colonies—only five of
the thirteen were present at Annapolis. In fact the colonies
as such did not do the inviting. The call was sent by the delegates from the five colonies assembled at the ineffective Annapolis convention. It was nevertheless forwarded to the
United States Congress and to the states.

The sole purpose of this new proposed Philadelphia convention, according to the call, was to "revise the Articles of
Confederation." There was no intention to free commerce
from restrictions but rather to impose uniform equitable
restrictions. Hamilton knew that such revision would be
lawful and within the agreement of the Confederation only
if three definite requirements were met:

1. Each and every one of the thirteen colonies must ap-

prove any changes agreed upon. We were operating under the unanimity rule, with each state, large or small, casting one vote.

2. There must be *amendment* only, not a scrapping in entirety of the old document. Any suggestion of rewriting the Articles of Confederation would have met the opposition of Congress and a rejection by all the states.

3. Submission to and acceptance by the separate states must be procured through the separate thirteen legislatures. This was the only known method of procuring changes in our basic laws. Never had there been even a suggestion of putting amendments to the people for a vote. Any such device would have been thought a short circuiting of state authorities.

We shall see how the great Constitutional Convention acted in utter disregard of all the known and recognized rules of government, how it violated every constitutional provision of the Articles of Confederation to which each of the thirteen colonies had been bound for a decade.

PART II

We Form a Nation

THIRTEEN *rebellious colonies broke away from the mother country. The organization of a new nation was still a great problem. The war began in 1775 and ended in 1783. The conflicts of peace slowly developed a cohesion which the common hatreds of war had been unable to arouse. The year 1787 was the great one in our history. The Constitutional Convention of that year developed our constitution. No other gathering of men in the history of the world has ever done such an effective job. On the philosophy of that instrument we have built our nation.*

The deliberations and personalities of the delegates, the compromises, and the structure of government which was conceived have rarely been told except in legalistic fashion for lawyers or in deceptive cherry-tree style for children. Out of the human fears and hopes of the delegates there was established a national pattern, dictated by the same basic disruptive influence which is defeating this nation today.

CHAPTER VIII

The Gathering

A HARD WINTER OF SUFFERING elapsed between the break-up of the Annapolis convention and the date set for the Philadelphia conference. Unemployment increased between September 1786 and May 1787. Another year or two without a united plan and many thought that either the colonies would send out troops against each other or a monarchy would arise.

The changes to be made in the Articles of Confederation had not been discussed in any of the colonies. Some of the gazettes urged a federal or national control of business and commerce, the power to make treaties and the need for congressional powers to levy taxes.

The form the amendments were to take would depend on the delegates sent from the various colonies. Would they be rich or poor, creditors or debtors, employers or workers, city folk or farmers, democrats or monarchists? No proposed amendments had been offered by any colony in advance of that momentous May 14, 1787.

The delegates gathered slowly, state by state. Some were sent by governors convinced of the emergency of the situation; others because a state felt it important to have full representation. In many instances it was found difficult or impossible to persuade men of high qualifications to take the arduous trip. Some of the delegates attended because it was thought fashionable to be at a gathering with the famous men of the day—Washington, Dickinson and Franklin.

Geographically the delegates came only from coastal towns. Twelve were of New England birth; twelve from the middle states; twenty-one from the South; and eight, born abroad, were what we would call immigrants. The ages ran from Dayton, twenty-seven, to Franklin, eighty-one. The median age was forty-two.

Of political experience there was ample:

41 had served in Congress
26 in state legislatures
14 as state judges or attorneys
13 in state constitutional conventions
 7 as governors

As a group they were rich and prosperous. Only two were what might be called poor; ten were of moderate means, and the rest were more affluent. They represented property and possessions. They were the people who used yard-square napkins and drank from crystal goblets instead of from pewter mugs. They were one and all creditors. Cheap money was ruining their fortunes.

Forty were holders of government securities, either national or colonial. These securities took the place of the entire list of stocks and bonds now dealt in on the stock exchange.

24 were the leading creditors of their communities.
15 were slaveholders.
14 were owners, though not occupiers, of Western lands.
11 had substantial shipping or manufacturing interests.

In this body it was natural that lawyers should predominate, although many practiced several callings.

Lawyers	28
Planters and landowners	9
Financiers	6
Merchants and shippers	4
Doctors	4
Manufacturers	1
Public officials	4

In those days, when only the rich could acquire education, when few men and practically no women were taught to read and write, these delegates were peculiarly cut off from

the general citizenry by their exceptional educational backgrounds. Twenty-six had studied at Princeton, William and
Mary, Harvard, Yale, King's and Pennsylvania. Eleven
had been educated either entirely at British universities or
had gone there from the American colleges. Seven had private tutors in their homes. Seven had achieved only a
grammar-school training.

Their studies, often carried on in Latin, consisted primarily of discussions on the nature of liberty, ethics and
justice. Their textbooks were similar to those used in the
scholastic universities of the Old World.

Many, growing up on wealthy estates, had always been
waited on by servants. After going to school and college
they returned to the old homesteads as the only available
aspirants for seats in the upper legislative chambers. Education for the eldest son was a privilege inherited from the
father along with the future control of the estate, which
passed in feudal fashion to the eldest son by the strictest
laws of entail.

The majority of the members were of the established
state religions. Anglicanism was as much the badge of aristocracy as it is in Great Britain today:

15 Episcopalian
10 Presbyterian
 9 Congregationalist
 3 Quaker
 2 Catholic
 1 Methodist
 1 Huguenot
14 unrecorded, but none known to be ungodly.

Virginia's delegation, the outstanding state group, organized itself into the first American legislative caucus. That
delegation consisted of:

George Washington, aged fifty-five, less provincial than
most men of his day, having seen much of our country.

James Madison, aged thirty-seven, whom Washington
called the Father of the Constitution.

George Mason, aged sixty-two, aspired to Patrick

Henry's title—"The People's Champion" and refused to sign the Constitution because it contained no bill of rights. He was never sure that his vast Potomac and Western real estate would not depreciate in value if a strong national government were created.

George Wythe, aged sixty-one, who, after ten years of dissipation, became the law teacher of two presidents and one chief justice of the Supreme Court.

Edmund Randolph, aged thirty-four, a Jeffersonian despite aristocratic heritage, who induced George Washington to attend the gathering.

John Blair, aged fifty-five, a conservative with training as delegate to two state conventions, privy councillor and judge.

James McClurg, a medico, forty-one, a stopgap appointment as the last member of the delegation.

The Pennsylvania delegation, acting as host, was the largest. Besides Franklin it included two lawyers and five merchants. Only two were natives of the state. The lawyers were one Scot and the other Yankee. James Wilson was the leader of the American Bar. Jared Ingersoll was later to face Hamilton in important Supreme Court cases. Robert Morris, well known for the arms contract his firm of Willing & Morris had made with the secret committee of the Continental Congress, lined up with Hamilton in support of a monarchy, always confident that a republic could not survive if the senators and congressmen were not appointed for life, if every worker over twenty-one years of age was allowed to vote, and if the president's veto power were not absolute and final. Gouverneur Morris, no relation of Robert, was opposed to Western influence, favored senators for life and a president elected by the people. The other important delegate was James Wilson, later to be a judge of the United States Supreme Court and arrested for debt while riding circuit.

From May 14 until May 25 not enough delegates had presented their credentials to form a quorum and proceed to business.

Even after May 25 the attendance was most irregular. Delegates came and went. Some arrived late. Some left early. Much of the confusion in the voting can be traced to the casual appearances and departures of those drafting the great document. On the opening day, for example, the roll call showed:

State	No. of delegates
Massachusetts	1
New York	2
New Jersey	3
Pennsylvania	4
Delaware	2
Virginia	7
North Carolina	4
South Carolina	4
Georgia	1

Total states, 9; total delegates, 28. Four states were absent, less than half the delegates were present.

On the 28th day of May a delegate appeared from Connecticut, another from Delaware, two more from Massachusetts, one from Maryland and four more from Pennsylvania. Even these arrivals brought the number of states represented up to only eleven and the delegates to a total of only thirty-seven.

In order to proceed, the Fathers provided that:

A House to do business shall consist of the deputies of not less than seven states, and all questions shall be decided by the greatest number of these which shall be fully represented and by a less number than seven may adjourn from day to day.

The delegates were the outstanding products of the culture, education and financial prosperity of the times. Their earnestness and devotion to the monumental task which confronted them is evident in every word spoken at the meetings. The forty-two who attended with something like regularity delivered a series of debates and discussions which have seldom been equaled in a convention of men.

Someone painstaking enough to count them records that Gouverneur Morris made 173 speeches; Wilson,

168; Madison, 161; Sherman, 138; Mason, 136; and Gerry, 119. Washington made one address.

Who Selected These Delegates?

How did these gentlemen happen to be chosen for this historic task? As a starting point two conditions of the day must be recalled. The choice of all delegates was once removed from the electorate. They were picked by legislators. In the second place, difficult as it may be to appreciate the fact, the truth is that, even if the delegates had been selected by the people, less than a fifth of the adult males were entitled to vote at any election.

Let us look first at the restrictions upon voting. If similar restrictions existed today, the popular vote for president in 1932 would have been less than 5,000,000, instead of 38,000,000. If we had today such a severe limitation on democracy, the unemployed, all people on relief, the entire lower East Side of New York City, the Loop of Chicago and all the people below Canal Street in New Orleans would be disenfranchised, in addition to the Negroes who have such a limited vote today. The test for voting was wealth, and the requirements were modeled on those in England, where to represent a county one had to have a substantial income.

In Massachusetts every voter had to have some income from investments and an estate of at least sixty pounds. In Connecticut until 1845 the right to vote was conditioned either on an income from landownership or on the possession of at least forty pounds of personal property. But once the required standard of voting was attained there were ample rewards. Arthur Train writes in his family chronicle, *Puritan's Progress:*

The townsmen rotated in public office much as they do now in the rural districts of Maine and Massachusetts, where the theory obtains that every voter ought to have his whack at the taxes. . . . As an officeholder Samuel Train, Sr, seems to have been a sort of hardy perennial, for he was in turn surveyor, fence-viewer, "wardin," constable, and selectman, and as soon as one term ended he started in on another. His favorite office was that of constable, but although his salary as such amounted to only twenty shillings per annum, he made a fairly good thing out of his perquisites and fees for "warning town meetings" at four shillings each, "making rates" (usually spelled "rats") and "carrying paupers out of town."

The New Jersey constitution provided that

all inhabitants who are worth fifty pounds proclamation money clear estate in the same shall be entitled to vote for representatives in Council Chamber.

In Delaware, to vote for your legislator who picked your convention delegate, you had to abide by the constitution of 1734 which generously extended democracy so that you could vote if you owned

50 acres of land, with 12 acres cleared and improved, or otherwise worth 40 pounds of lawful money.

Pennsylvania suffrage was more liberal; but New York, except for freemen in Albany who received special voting latitudes, permitted but a tiny percentage of males of good behavior and over the age of twenty-one to vote at any election.

The Maryland property qualifications were fifty acres or thirty pounds, thus reflecting the realty-market changes as one traveled south. Virginia, by its new constitution, provided a qualification of twenty-five acres of improved or fifty acres of unimproved lands except for certain artisans in Norfolk and Williamsburg, who, through strong pressure groups, had procured access to the ballot boxes.

At an earlier date the alternative of a town lot with a house was offered in Virginia as a qualification. It was reported that one Thomas Payne, owner of part of a lot

purchased of one Mary Almond for the value of ten shillings and a small House about 4 and a half Feet Pitch, 4 or 5 Feet long, and two or two and a Half Feet wide, floored or laid with Plank in the midst of its Height, to put Milkpans or such things on, and that he had the same removed in a cart, with one Horse, with the Assistance of 7 or 8 men, and placed on his said Lot, on purpose (as he acknowledges) to qualify himself to vote at that election.

North Carolina, as in some other colonies, had rights of voting dependent not only on wealth but upon the importance of the office to be voted for. To vote for a state senator required fifty acres, but voting for an assemblyman was granted to all freemen who paid "public taxes."

The South Carolina law contained an urban point of view. Voting in the country was possible if you owned fifty acres and in towns if you owned a town lot or paid taxes equal to those on fifty acres of land. The ownership of slaves was a concomitant to the electoral franchise in the South.

Georgia, desiring to develop mechanics, permitted voting on proof of owning ten pounds or being of a mechanical trade.

Without further analysis it must be evident that the voters were the rich, the affluent, the small minority of the public.

At no time in our entire national history, with all our great annual income and basic wealth, could more than a trifling proportion of the population have qualified under such property qualifications.

Not only was the selection of the delegates vested in the wealthy upper class, but the great majority of inhabitants had no stake in government. Nor was there any organized effort to spread the franchise or to establish a real democracy.

But that is only a part of the aristocratic process which underlay the selection of delegates to this great convention. In practically every state, even if the franchise had been widely democratic as it is today, the voters could not have selected any but the large property owners and the rich.

In South Carolina, by its constitution of 1778, no one could take a seat in the colonial senate unless he possessed in his parish at least two hundred pounds free of debt. A nonresident needed seven hundred pounds clear of debt to qualify as a senatorial candidate. Such provisions limited the candidates in some parishes to fewer than five or six possibilities. Thus the son of a rich man was by his wealth alone automatically called into public service.

In New Jersey every member of the upper house had to

own at least one hundred pounds of proclamation money, or real or personal property in the same county. New York senatorial seats were cheap. One hundred pounds was enough to qualify. In New Hampshire and elsewhere only Protestants were admitted to upper houses. Massachusetts kept a constant check on its legislators. Even if upon election you had the required number of pounds, you might later lose your seat should the value of your assets shrink below the minimum set by the law.

To hold an office which entitled you to vote for a delegate to the convention, you had to meet such property qualifications in practically all the states, while in some states special restrictions such as religious denominations were added to the tests for wealth. The Anglican minority had been disestablished only recently in the South, and not till 1755 was there an Act of Toleration in Virginia. Taxes were paid to the Congregational Church in the New England States in 1787, and as late as 1833 in Massachusetts.

Some who are not in favor of our American experiment with democracy, agreeing with the Hamiltonian theory of aristocratic rule, may attribute the high degree of intelligence at the Constitutional Convention to these very limitations. But irrespective of possible conclusions as to whether the United States should or should not abandon its democratic attempt, it is clear that the delegates to the convention represented the rich creditor group and were selected by state legislators who held their seats only after meeting relatively high financial tests, and who, in turn, were elected by a negligible proportion of the male adult population, which males in turn were the rich, the investors and rarely if ever the workers of the land.

This volume is not the proper place for lengthy biographical sketches of the great Fifty-five Delegates, but short profiles of those who attended and of a few who were not delegates will give more vital meaning to the debates, the compromises and the form of government which they thought they had established.

CHAPTER IX

The Founding Fathers

Profiles of the Fifty-five

Note: Asterisks indicate that delegates whose names are so marked
did not vote in favor of the Constitution.

ABRAHAM BALDWIN, Georgia, aged thirty-three at time of
the Convention. (1754–1807)
Born at Guilford, Connecticut, son of well-to-do blacksmith, educated at Yale, licensed minister and law teacher
at Yale. Chaplain in army. Good talker, industrious but not
ambitious except for money. Educated six brothers and sis-
ters by speculating in government securities. Serene, benign,
died without an enemy. Violently in favor of United States
senators being elected on basis of property only.

RICHARD BASSETT, Delaware, forty-two. (1745–1815)
He deserted his family. His father was a tavern keeper.
Adopted and educated by lawyer Lawton. Though a captain
in the army, was enthusiastic about religion. A man of plain
sense and modest enough to hold his tongue. Very rich—
owner of three homes, including Bohemia Tavern.

GUNNING BEDFORD, JR, Delaware, forty. (1747–1812)
Presbyterian, born in Philadelphia, lived in Dover and
Wilmington, Delaware. Came from family of large landowners. Princeton education. Fluent, impetuous, irrepressi-
ble. Tall, stout and handsome. Irritated at French manner-
isms. Owner of bonds but not a very large profiteer on national economic distress.

JOHN BLAIR, Virginia, fifty-five. (1732–1800)

Educated at William and Mary, and Middle Temple, London. Poor until he inherited money in 1743. Was granted only 100,000 acres of land in 1745 and felt that he had not been fairly treated. Father was acting governor of Virginia. He was a jurist of imposing stature, noble forehead and hair with a red tinge. Patriot but no orator. Large dealer in government securities on inside tips but had reputation as blameless of disposition, pious and possessed of great benevolence and goodness of heart. A member of the Supreme Court bench for seven years—1789–96.

WILLIAM BLOUNT, North Carolina, thirty-eight. (1749–1800)

Of noble descent with large estate, paymaster in Revolution, did not debate in convention and signed only in order to try to make the vote unanimous. Speculator with success in Western lands. Became governor of "The Territory of the United States South of the Ohio." First senator from the new state of Tennessee, thus continuing his life task of officeholding. Later expelled for plotting with Spain, which increased his popularity at home. Believed private profit not incompatible with discharge of his governmental administrative duties.

DAVID BREARLY, North Carolina, forty-two. (1745–90)

Active Episcopalian, inherited large estate from grandfather; law education at Princeton, twice married. A joiner-member of the Society of the Cincinnati, Masons, etc. Supreme Court justice. Had small security holdings of government issues, attended convention regularly and most active in opposition to proportional representation in House of Congress. Wanted the president chosen by joint ballot of senators and congressmen but not by the people.

JACOB BROOM, Delaware, thirty-five. (1752–1810)

A man of many businesses—cotton mills, insurance, real estate. His father was of gentry though a blacksmith.

Cheerful in private, knew his limitations well enough not to talk at the convention. Urged nine-year terms for senators, life tenure for president and thought Constitution would surely fail because Congress was not finally granted the absolute power to veto all state legislation which it did not approve.

PIERCE BUTLER, South Carolina, forty-three. (1744–1822)
Planter and politician, born in Ireland of noble birth, which he never could forget. Ambitious, dictatorial and easy at making enemies. Large slaveholder, director of United States Bank, profited greatly by new central government's refinancing of separate colonies. To him the Senate was forever to represent wealth and thus create a strong, enduring nation. One of the leading conservatives. The present Supreme Court justice of the same name is not a relative of this delegate.

DANIEL CARROLL, Maryland, fifty-seven. (1730–96)
Inherited large estate and business, educated in Flanders, favored protective tariff, popular election of president, and opposed to pay for congressmen. Held many government securities. Active real-estate operator. The capitol was built on his land. Man of force, sufficient to overcome popular prejudice against his Catholic faith.

GEORGE CLYMER, Pennsylvania, forty-eight. (1739–1813)
Three generations of merchants on both sides. In addition he inherited the wealth of his guardian, in whose library he was educated. Continental treasurer, seldom speaking, diffident and retiring. Spoke ill of none. He arbitraged with great success between continental currency and specie.

*WILLIAM R. DAVIE, North Carolina, thirty-one. (1756–1820)
Born in Cumberland, England, adopted by minister in England, educated at Museum College and at Princeton. Officer in Revolution, he favored strong central government

with Senate based on property holdings. He was tall and elegant, with a mellow voice and a flowing style which enraptured his audiences. Close friend and legal adviser of the proprietors of his colony, from which connection he profited greatly. Against all forms of popular elections of congressmen or senators.

JONATHAN DAYTON, New Jersey, twenty-seven. (1760–1824)

Businessman of the first family of the town. His father, owner of the general store, upon being selected to go to the Philadelphia convention, turned over his seat at the convention to this hasty-tempered son. Dayton, Sr, was too busy at his counters, and also wanted to get his nuisance son out of the way. Dayton, Jr, the youngster of the convention, was a gay blade. Notorious for inside speculation in lands, bonds and currency. His gambling in such governmental issues ran up to as much as $82,000 on one item. Thought it proper for officeholder to capitalize on inside information.

JOHN DICKINSON, Delaware, fifty-five. (1732–1808)

Quaker lawyer and statesman. Educated at Middle Temple. Born of established family and married rich girl. Long the leader of group desiring peaceful settlement with Great Britain, voting against Declaration of Independence. Said by a contemporary to have acted like a dutiful child. He had been governor of both Delaware and Pennsylvania. A monarchist in Constitutional Convention, favoring high property qualifications for voters. As a member of Stamp Act Congress and other bodies wrote many important documents including Declaration of Rights, Petition to the King, Address to Inhabitants of Quebec. His book, *Letters of a Farmer,* still easy and delightful reading. He was an able, sincere, nervous and cautious Bourbon. His contemporaries held him to be a sorry orator and a "piddling genius." Urged a vital national government with a feeble executive. His indebtedness to Robert Morris led many to suspicions as to his votes. An important figure in later years in opposition to John Adams.

*OLIVER ELLSWORTH, Connecticut, forty-two. (1745–1807)

Law and theology student at Princeton and tutor at Yale. He was a gentleman of substance. Became a leader at the Bar. Amassed tremendous fortune. He and his family held securities which have been thought to have influenced his behavior at Congress. He did not sign the Constitution. He became chief justice of the Supreme Court, holding that office for the four years, 1796–1800, and later chief justice of the Connecticut Supreme Court.

WILLIAM FEW, Georgia, thirty-nine. (1748–1828)

Born in Maryland; moved to North Carolina and then to Georgia. Shifted from farming to law. His Quaker family failed at tobacco planting. Gathered education from itinerant teachers and vast reading. His rough background made him socially insecure. He was tall, grave, slender, pious and benevolent. Though a land commissioner, dealt extensively in Yazoo lands and government securities.

THOMAS FITZSIMMONS, Pennsylvania, forty-six. (1741–1811)

Catholic. Born in Ireland. Merchant shipper; married daughter of wealthy merchant. Very practical man who speculated in lands jointly with Robert Morris. In the convention he was for a powerful central government, limitation of voting rights, protective tariff and potent taxing powers.

BENJAMIN FRANKLIN, Pennsylvania, eighty-one. (1706–90)

He was the *enfant terrible* of his day. A realist supreme. Although doubting the wisdom of many sections of the Constitution, he was philosopher enough to know that compromises were necessary and that later generations could "easily amend the errors" of the convention. Sophisticated through his amorous and political training in European capitals as well as in the colonies, at the convention he was looked upon as the peacemaker. His *Poor Richard,* selling over 10,000 copies a year during his life, had made him a popular hero.

In 1787 he was so near death and so well prepared for that event, no pettiness entered into his emotions or thoughts. Mentally alert, he followed the activities of these youngsters, ever ready to send over a speech of conciliation to be read in case he felt the meetings might break up in chaos. No ordinary pride in his own sketch of the Articles of Confederation of July 21, 1775, prevented him from accepting other people's experimental formulas.

When Gerry arose to say, "The evils we experience flow from the excess of democracy. The people do not want virtue but are the dupes of pretended patriots," Franklin observed that although few of the wealthy had richly paneled houses most of the people who grew our food lived in hovels.

When Rutledge declared, on July 16, "Had we not better keep the government up a little longer hoping that another Convention will supply our omissions than abandon everything to hazard?" the old Doctor, arising with a supporting arm of the nearest seated delegate, maneuvered the talk so that no issue could be drawn between defeat and victory. Although he wrote none of the words of the instrument, without his tolerance to an ever-changing environment for man the battle between the thirteen nations might have ended in an utterly different fashion.

*ELBRIDGE GERRY, Massachusetts, forty-three. (1744–1811)

Merchant, shipper, son of a sea captain. Harvard graduate, he married the daughter of a New York merchant. He was a spare, dapper, pleasant little fellow. One of the leading conservatives and a hesitating, laborious speaker. For a strong government in theory, his positions in the convention were often inconsistent. Owner of Western lands, which no doubt colored his thinking on territorial-expansion and state-vote questions. Often he would argue that commercial and moneyed interests would be more secure in the state legislatures than in the people. He was even afraid of elections by districts "because the people could not be brought to one place for that purpose, frauds would result, and small states would form one district with a large one." Refused to sign the Constitution because he feared civil war in Massachusetts. While governor of Massachusetts the counties were juggled for election purposes, giving us the term *gerrymander*. He owned government securities yielding $3,500 income.

NICHOLAS GILMAN, New Hampshire, thirty-two. (1755–1814)

Bachelor, army man. Of no real consequence but trailed along all his life with important people. Made no contribution to any part of our history except to irritate his associates by his vanity. He was nicknamed "Congress Gilman." Without realizing the social implications he advised his state, New Hampshire, to buy up government securities at depreciated value so as to cash in with a final 700 per cent profit due to the Hamilton debt-assumption program.

NATHANIEL GORHAM, Massachusetts, forty-nine. (1738–90)

Merchant of distinguished but uneducated English ancestry. Educated as apprentice. More sense than ability. Went broke in Western land speculations. In convention urged Supreme Court judges be appointed by president and thought the country too big to be a single nation. The vastness of the thirteen colonies bewildered him, and he considered the advisability of forming several separate nations.

ALEXANDER HAMILTON, New York, thirty. (1757–1804)

Born in Leeward Islands. A bastard. King's College, 1773. Married a daughter of General Philip Schuyler. Although not active at the convention, his control of the Annapolis meeting was of great historical importance. Conceited, able, daring, he was convivial only with the social élite. Leading American orator until Clay and Webster. With reddish hair and blue eyes he looked Scottish. He never consulted. He never conciliated. He was forever fighting his lowly birth. The only man of the era who avowedly wanted to become the American king or dictator. His fascistic brain never comprehended the forces for democracy behind Thomas Jefferson, whom he feared and detested. His amorous adventures, which led him to much public calumny, were essentially no different from those of his group, but his arrogance in this field of adventure made him blind to public opinion. The first American to urge a planned national economy. As a member of the first cabinet he urged a national economic control, with assistance to any and every business which the national government thought wise to encourage. To him the economy of the nation was not to be throttled by artificial state lines. His great part in our history was his leading of the conservative forces, favoring an aristocratic nondemocratic government, against the forces asking the extension of democracy and the broadening of electorate powers, later to be led by Jefferson.

*WILLIAM C. HOUSTON, New Jersey, forty-one. (1746–88)

Teacher of mathematics and law. Born in North Carolina, educated at College of New Jersey and at Poplar Tent Academy. Married a granddaughter of John Dickinson. Left Constitutional Convention early, probably after first ten days. Although active in committee of safety, Annapolis convention and other preliminary colonial gatherings, he was primarily interested in business deals—Western lands —and later in promoting Fitch's steamboat.

*WILLIAM HOUSTOUN, Georgia, thirty-two. (1755–1833)

Lawyer of good family with education in Great Britain. A contemporary writes: "Nature seems to have done more for his corporeal than his mental powers. His person is striking but his mind very little improved with useful or elegant knowledge." Dropped in at the convention for about three weeks. Had a pleasant time but got bored and went away.

JARED INGERSOLL, Pennsylvania, thirty-eight. (1749–1822)

Ablest lawyer at Philadelphia Bar. His grandfather was a Massachusetts Bay colonist, and his father was London agent for Connecticut merchants. He spoke well and with modesty. Represented Georgia in the famous Chisholm case in the Supreme Court of the United States. Georgia lost the case. Later matched wits with Hamilton before the Supreme Court. He was a strong Federalist with a notorious speculator for a father-in-law.

DANIEL OF ST THOMAS JENIFER, Maryland, sixty-four. (1723–90)

Son of a doctor, he became a public servant, general officeholder, collector of taxes, etc. Bachelor. Friend of Washington, with whom he went on dancing parties. Extensive real-estate operator. He was good-humored but silent. Played a minor part in convention. His greatest heat developed on question of length of terms of congressmen. Thought three-year term essential for continuance of nation.

WILLIAM SAMUEL JOHNSON, Connecticut, sixty. (1727–1819)

One of the best educated at the convention. Studied at Yale and Harvard; a Doctor of Laws at Oxford. Father was a Church of England minister. Later he became President of King's (Columbia) College. Having been London agent for Connecticut, when war came he "could not conscientiously take up arms against England." Attended convention regularly, persistently argued for strong central government. Pleasing personality, conciliatory temper, he was the friend of all the Southern delegates. In the final committee on style he urged his pet phrase, "in law and equity." His two wives both died of smallpox. His son speculated in government issues intensively for himself and for his father.

RUFUS KING, Massachusetts, thirty-two. (1755–1827)

Born in Maine (then Massachusetts) of a sea captain-farmer-lumberman. Educated at Harvard and married the daughter of the president of the New York Chamber of Commerce. Opposed to slavery, and, although he started with a small state point of view, was one of the few who obviously was convinced by the debates. He was handsome, able, possessed great personal charm and was very popular with Philadelphia damsels. As a speaker he was engaging, with ease and dignity, though often rude to his allies. How far his voting was determined by his holdings of bank stocks and securities is difficult to say.

JOHN LANGDON, New Hampshire, forty-six. (1741–1819)
Merchant and shipper after grammar-school education and experience at sea. Early in life he accumulated a large fortune and graciously paid the cost of a brigade at the Battle of Bennington and the expenses of the delegates from New Hampshire at the Constitutional Convention. With charm he courted popularity. At one time governor of his state. He never disguised his republican tendencies. He and his brother were two of the largest creditors of the United States. Often advised his state, New Hampshire, to play the market in government securities.

*JOHN LANSING, New York, thirty-two. (1754–1829 [?])
The mystery man of his time. After studying law, this descendant of an old Dutch family was active in the army with Schuyler and then mayor of Albany. A contemporary said of him at the convention, "His legal knowledge is not extensive nor his education a good one." In December 1829 he went to New York City on business relating to Columbia College. Left his hotel at nine o'clock in the evening to post some letters on the Albany boat at the foot of Cortlandt Street. Never returned. No trace ever found. Held considerable securities of the United States government. Family profited also. Attended convention only six weeks, and did no talking because he "had a hisitation in his speech." He really favored the continuance of the feeble Articles of Confederation.

WILLIAM LIVINGSTON, New Jersey, sixty-four. (1723–96)
Born at Albany, New York, this gentleman farmer and lawyer was educated with missionaries among the Mohawks, and at Yale. Married a daughter of large land-

owner. In the convention he urged the New Jersey plan.
Was later very effective in gaining ratification for the Constitution. He was nicknamed "The Whipping Post." He
was tall, slender, graceless and petulant. Although possessing a dry wit, he spoke "rather to indulge a sportiveness of
wit than a strength of thinking." Eleven times governor.
He died before he cashed in on the rise of his government
securities, but his son increased the family fortune thereby.

*JAMES McCLURG, Virginia, forty-one. (1746–1823)
Doctor. Son of superintendent of Hampton Hospital.
Educated at William and Mary, Edinburgh, Paris and London. Surgeon in the war, medical leader of his state but
without public political experience. He favored life tenure
for the president and federal veto power of all state legislation. Spoke twice in convention without success. Director
of United States Bank, owned over $26,000 of Virginia cer-
tificates and speculated in federal securities.

JAMES McHENRY, Maryland, thirty-four. (1753–1816)
Doctor, born in Ireland, immigrating here when eighteen.
Educated in Dublin, Ireland, Newark Academy and with
the famous Dr Benjamin Rush. Doctor in the war, he was
secretary at times to Washington and Lafayette. No marked
ability in any field—oratory, medicine or legislation. Conservative, he trailed successfully on successes of others. In
convention he said, "I distrust my own judgment especially
as it is opposed to the opinion of a majority of gentlemen
whose abilities and patriotism are of the first case." He was
for a high protective tariff and was in his early life devoted
to Hamilton.

JAMES MADISON, Virginia, thirty-seven. (1750–1836)
Graduated from Princeton when the 115 students were
"all of them in American cloth." He had the most complete
and correct knowledge of the affairs of the colonies of any
man in the Union. Slender, retiring, usually in black, he was
the scholar in politics. In 1783 he commenced the study of

law so "as to live as little as possible on the earning of his slaves." His family land grant, dating back to 1653, had not insured him any substantial income, so we find him speculating in lands with Monroe (who died in poverty), borrowing from his friend Haym Solomon, and dealing in tobacco at the Liverpool markets in 1785 through his agent, James Maury. He never quite liked New Englanders but was by all odds the most internationally minded (in the sense of thirteen separate nations) of all those present. He was the main pillar at the convention.

Madison was the only one at the convention who was allowed to take full notes of the speeches and votes. He never missed a single speech. An indefatigable worker, he went from the convention to his room to grasp his quill pen for hours on end to rewrite his daily notes, which in 1837 were sold by his widow to the government for $30,000.

His contributions to this gathering cannot be estimated in any few words. In the caucus of Virginia delegates which met daily for two or three hours to form "a proper correspondence of sentiments" he was the quiet stabilizer. In the historical discussions on the floor he was the one who would quote from Grotius and Locke and Malthus.

In the few discussions indicating historical tendencies of the future he, more clearly than others, appreciated that other countries rivaled us in manufactures, "but we may be said to have a monopoly in agriculture."

He foresaw the economic warfare of the future in the simple terms of his day when the round wheel, the ratchet and the press were the exciting contemporary vehicles for increasing man's power over inanimate things. In discussing a planned economy shortly after the close of the convention he pointed a clear danger signal for the United States of 1936:

But laying aside the illustrations of these causes, so well known to all nations, where cities, companies, or opulent individuals engross the business from others, by having had an uninterrupted possession of it, or by the extent of their capitals being able to destroy a competition, let us proceed to examine what ought to be our conduct on this principle, upon the present occasion. Suppose two commercial cities, one possessed of enormous capitals and long habits of business, whilst the other is possessed of superior natural advantages, but without that course of business and chain of connections which the other has: is it possible, in the nature of things, that the latter city should carry on a successful competition with the former?

While preaching such gospels he would exchange lengthy letters with his friend Jefferson on the relative position of the kidney in different species of weasels, and then proceed with basic observations on economy:

Let the lands be shared among them [the people] ever so wisely, and let them be supplied with laborers ever so plentifully; as there must be a great surplus of subsistence, there will also remain a great surplus of inhabitants, a greater by far than will be employed in clothing both themselves and those who feed them, and in administering to both, every other necessary and even comfort of life. What is to be done with this surplus? Hitherto we have seen them distributed into manufacturers of superfluities, idle proprietors of productive land, domestics, soldiers, merchants, mariners, and a few other less numerous classes.

In the convention struggles he always saw the class struggle. Again and again he would ask, "What are the different classes of legislators but advocates and parties to the causes which they determine?" and remark "The causes of factions cannot be removed. . . . We know from experience that neither moral nor religious motives can be relied upon as an adequate control."

Feeling confident that the document prepared in 1787 in Philadelphia would be subjected to periodic revisions, he was determined, in view of the great part he had borne in its origin and adoption, to prefer a seat in the House of Representatives—"as least exposing me to the imputation of selfish views."

His brilliant contribution to the Constitution was soon to be discredited because he never fitted comfortably into the task of running our nation while at war (1812), and the composite of the affection felt for him at this time scarcely reflects the high admiration and respect tendered him at the convention.

At his death one hundred slaves gathered in true grief at his grave.

*ALEXANDER MARTIN, North Carolina, forty-seven. (1740–1807)

A planter, merchant and public official. Although he was born in New Jersey and educated at Princeton, his affiliations were with North Carolina, where he was a slaveholder and a politician of eminence. He was unmarried and a Presbyterian. He had served in the state senate, in the Continental Congress, and as the governor who dealt with the Regulators of the backwoods. Although he had been dismissed for cowardice while fighting with Washington, he made his political comeback with the ease of a Tammany sachem. He was never credited with great oratory or genius, but is known rather as a parliamentarian who knew how to follow the tide of popular opinion. He left the convention at the end of August, not signing the Constitution.

*LUTHER MARTIN, Maryland, thirty-nine. (1748–1826)

Luther Martin was the one spokesman of the debtor cause in the convention. Albert C. Beveridge describes him as "of medium height, broad-shouldered, near-sighted, absent-minded, shabbily attired, harsh of voice . . . with a face crimsoned by the brandy which he continually imbibed." The state of his health we learn from a patent-medicine testimonial in which Martin recorded that Dr Hamilton's Elixir had cured him of "a painful and troublesome aflection of the breast, accompanied with soreness and obstructed and difficult breathing." Considering the peculiarities of his temperament, it is not surprising that his marriage to the daughter of a pioneer-soldier was unhappy.

Martin's father had been a farmer in New Brunswick, New Jersey, and had afforded him an education at Princeton. Because of his legal acumen he was elected to the Continental Congress and was given the job of prosecuting the loyalists of Maryland as attorney general of the state. His law practice brought him £1,000 a year, and he owned six slaves and a few thousand dollars' worth of government

securities, but his intemperance and improvidence kept him
sympathetic to debtors. As an orator he was boring, but
thorough in his argument and able to draw on a vast memory. In the convention he opposed slavery and walked out
on September 4 to show his disapproval of a strong central
government. Early a friend of Aaron Burr, later his counsel
in the famous treason trial, he was a firm democrat and
Anti-Federalist. Relentless in his opposition to the new constitution.

*GEORGE MASON, Virginia, sixty-two. (1725–92)
Lawyer and planter, born on the Potomac, brought up by
a wealthy guardian, married twice, once to a lady of large
estate. Outstanding aristocratic liberal opposed to slavery
and centralization, although responsible for having the central government operate on people instead of states. He
rivaled Patrick Henry as people's champion, calling Washington "that damned young surveyor." Madison thought
him the greatest debater of the period. Owned three hundred slaves, treasurer of Ohio Company and other Western
land companies. His fight for Bill of Rights made possible
the first ten amendments to the Constitution. He urged
secrecy and no recording of votes in order to keep proceedings flexible. He refused to sign Constitution because he
feared the judicial powers. "He devoted his life to manag-
ing large estates," including his own, which covered more
than five thousand acres of good lands.

*JOHN FRANCIS MERCER, Maryland, twenty-eight. (1759–
1821)
Born in Virginia of one of the great American landown-
ing families. Educated at William and Mary and studied
law under Jefferson. Married wife with estates. Fought
under Lee and Lafayette. Democracy was a religion to this
fighter, intriguer and agitator. He detested Hamilton and
adored Jefferson. Consistently he opposed strong central
government because he feared that it would be controlled
by those who wanted a monarchy. Opposed ratification of
the Constitution. Owned only a few securities and only six

slaves, and opposed all property qualifications for voting
and officeholding.

THOMAS MIFFLIN, Pennsylvania, forty-three. (1744–
1800)

Educated at Quaker school, College of Philadelphia, and
in Europe. Married the daughter of Robert Morris. An
extremist in Revolution. Later president of Continental
Congress, mixed up in Conway Cabal against Washington
but retained friendship with the General. Handsome, well
dressed, careless about money—died penniless. High-
protective-tariff advocate. A French ambassador wrote of
him:

Former President General of Congress, speaker of Assembly, an
avowed and proven friend of France. Very popular and possessed of
an astonishing influence over that hundred-headed monster called the
People. A good lawyer, a good officer, a good patriot and an agreea-
ble personality.

GOUVERNEUR MORRIS, Pennsylvania, thirty-five. (1752–
1816)

His father was the Second Lord of the Manor, and his
mother was a loyalist. King's College graduate, 1768. His
business was that of commercial agent. Most frequent
speaker at convention, he was sharp, audacious with a graceful humor. His college theses had been on "Wit and Beauty"
and "Love." Assistant to Robert Morris and married to a
Randolph, he was consistently an aristocrat. Originated
decimal coinage system, urged the building of the Erie
Canal, favored strong national government, opposed the
Catholic Act, and although fearful of abolition of slavery
was anxious to do something about that "investment and
labor problem." Reputedly the only man who was daring
enough to welcome Washington with a slap on the back.

His most important utterances were for true unification
to permit a national economic entity:

This country must be united. If persuasion does not unite it, the sword
will. . . . State attachments and state importance have been the

bane of the country. We cannot annihilate but we may perhaps take out the teeth of the serpents.

Died an unhappy death, having opposed the War of 1812 and lent his influence to the disunion movement in the North.

ROBERT MORRIS, Pennsylvania, fifty-three. (1734–1806)

Merchant and financier, born in Liverpool, immigrant to Maryland at the age of thirteen. Father an exporter of tobacco. He married a close friend of Martha Washington. Active during Revolution and in fact dictator of finances during a part of the war. Established the important Bank of North America. Never spoke in the convention, although his speech "was adequate." He was large, blond and pleasantly impressive. A leading aristocrat and one of the most outspoken in favor of monarchy. Had no use for the riffraff which democracy would develop. Reputed to be Washington's closest friend at the convention. Although of inestimable service to the colonies as a financial giant during the twenty years preceding the Constitution, he nevertheless made "neat sums" by selling arms to the colonists during the Revolution. In his time he was constantly suspected —and probably correctly so—of making personal profits out of personal tradings between Robert Morris, an individual, with Robert Morris, representing the United States. Although it is now clear he did so transact his affairs, it must be admitted that he filled a great need of that day. He wangled our finances through the days of inflation, foreign borrowings, overdrafts and barter for taxes. Within a decade after the convention he became involved in land speculations in Washington and spent over three years in jail.

WILLIAM PATERSON, New Jersey, forty-two. (1745–1806)

Born in Antrim County, Ireland, of a peddler, tin-merchant father. Educated at New Jersey College (Princeton) and married twice. In the convention he introduced the famous New Jersey, or small-states, plan. Showed surprising knowledge in debates and "never spoke but when he understood his subject well." Modest but fiery individual. Able lawyer of the nonlegalistic type. A justice of the Supreme Court of the United States—1793–1806.

*WILLIAM LEIGH PIERCE, Georgia, forty-seven. (1740–89)
Merchant and banker. Place of birth in dispute. He left the convention before July 1 for business reasons. Not of great wealth and prayed for a job as collector of revenues. His Savannah banking house was William Pierce & Company. His only contribution to the convention consisted of the entertaining notes he made on the personalities of the convention. Once some papers of the star-chamber proceedings were found and handed to Washington. Not a delegate claimed them. Pierce returned to his lodgings at the Indian Queen greatly worried, only to find his copy securely in his coat pocket. His report of this episode stamped him as a potential fiction writer.

CHARLES PINCKNEY, South Carolina, thirty. (1757–1824)
His father was a wealthy lawyer and planter. The family lands were confiscated as "damnable loyalist possessions." Married a daughter of a "merchant prince" according to a local gazetteer. At twenty he was a member of the Continental Congress and at thirty governor of his state. Superficially brilliant, his great conversational powers made him an important person at the convention, though his "iridescent genius offended some whilst dazzling others." His vanity was such that he later believed that he had written the federal constitution. Owned fifty-two slaves and $14,000 in government issues.

CHARLES COTESWORTH PINCKNEY, South Carolina, forty-one. (1746–1825)
Lawyer, son of chief justice of the province. His mother was the famous woman planter who developed indigo. Educated at Oxford under Blackstone, with courses in science in France. Married twice. President of the Society of the Cincinnati. In convention—for slavery, for high property

qualifications for voting and officeholding, against religious qualifications for office. Genial, liberal and charming, illustrating the virtues of the class to which he belonged. Owned forty-five slaves and securities of both the 3 per cent and 6 per cent government issues. Ambassador to France, author of "Millions for defence but not one cent for tribute," which he replied to Talleyrand when that gentleman demanded $240,000 before he would begin peace negotiations.

*EDMUND RANDOLPH, Virginia, thirty-four. (1753–1813)

His father was a king's attorney, joining the loyalists. His mother was the daughter of a king's attorney. Edmund was educated at William and Mary, studied law with his father and married the daughter of the state treasurer. Most popular Virginian after Patrick Henry, whom he succeeded as governor in 1786. Striking manners and harmonious voice, portly, nearly six feet tall, handsome. In the convention he led the battle for a plural executive. "We need more than one president at a time." He favored powerful national government and opposed the slave trade, although he then owned over two hundred slaves. Refused to sign the Constitution as not republican enough, but finally voted for ratification. In the convention he appears as a Jeffersonian, but weak and vacillating. Although usually in debt he did gamble with $14,000 worth of government securities.

GEORGE READ, Delaware, fifty-four (1733–98)

Educated in academy in New London, Pennsylvania, married a minister's daughter. His father was a founder of Charleston, his mother the daughter of a Welsh planter. Signer of Declaration of Independence, attended Annapolis convention, and at one time president of Delaware. In the Constitutional Convention fought for small states. But he urged that we must all look beyond the continuance of state governments because a national government "must soon of necessity swallow all of them up." He was cautious like his close friend Dickinson. Shortsighted, tall, well dressed. Respected as a moralist. Director in Bank of North America, holding several thousand Continentals, while mother had still greater holdings.

JOHN RUTLEDGE, South Carolina, forty-eight. (1739–1800)

Father a doctor, mother independently rich. Educated by tutors and at Middle Temple. Active at Stamp Act Congress and urged self-government for colonies without leaving British Empire. He vetoed, as governor, his state constitution as being "too democratic," and in convention he favored seats in Congress based on wealth, urged legitimacy of slave trade, and early saw fortune to be made out of federal assumption of all debts. Arch aristocrat and devoted leader of the eighteenth-century South Carolina attitudes. At one time was dictator of South Carolina. With great wealth, he owned twenty-six slaves, though not a planter. Went insane toward end of his life. Was the second chief justice of the Supreme Court of the United States—1796–1800.

ROGER SHERMAN, Connecticut, sixty-six. (1721–93)

From shoemaker to jurist. Born in Massachusetts of farmer stock, early self-educated, with an honorary M.A. from Yale. Tall and awkward, he irritated many at the convention by his "vulgarisms and New England cant." Long career of public activity in committees of safety, mayor of New Haven, etc. One of the few self-made men at the convention, he was industrious and active. Not a big speculator in government issues, owning only $8,000 worth.

RICHARD DOBBS SPAIGHT, North Carolina, twenty-nine. (1758–1802)

Educated at Glasgow, his mother was a sister of the governor of North Carolina, his father was a King's counsel. As a planter he held extensive acres, owning seventy-one slaves. Later governor of his state. Of no importance at Constitutional Convention, although a man of some shrewdness. He died in a duel with his successor in Congress.

*Caleb Strong, Massachusetts, forty-two (1745–1819)

Of "good connections," with Harvard education, he was called from convention by illness in his family. Tall, angular, solid, he was a hesitating speaker. Sympathetic to the rural districts. Although of considerable wealth he picked up several thousand pounds' worth of government securities in May 1787 at about ten cents on the dollar and cashed in at par in September 1791. A neat turn in the market, his friends called it.

George Washington, Virginia, fifty-five. (1732–99)

Educated by a local sexton, he married to 15,000 acres, 30,000 francs and several hundred slaves. In 1758 at the age of twenty-six "he was elected to the House of Burgesses of Virginia after standing treat to the voters, a prodigious quantity of punch, brandy, beer and cider royal." He was the richest man in the United States, leaving over $530,000 in his will and providing that his slaves be emancipated on death of his wife.

He was the final stabilizing personality of the period, an excellent presiding officer, for he seldom spoke other than to recognize someone who wanted the floor.

Having been a man of action, he was truly anxious in 1787 to lead a less strenuous life and had to be begged into coming to the convention.

Two years later he took his famous trip over the Northern colonies. Then with his aide-de-camp, private secretary, six servants, nine horses and luggage wagon he went as far north as Kittery (now Maine, then Massachusetts), omitting of course Rhode Island and Vermont, not wishing to visit those states which had not yet joined our nation. The Southern tour took him over 1,880 miles, which he covered in less than three months.

At the convention, in that chair a trifle higher than those of the other delegates, he sat with dignity. Awkward, with the big hands of a horse breaker, with legs usually crossed, everyone felt his modesty and total lack of personal ambition.

His extreme reserve mixed with asperity of temper later

added to that decline in his popularity which led in his own
cherished Virginia to a toast at a large dinner, "to the
speedy death of George Washington." But in 1787 he was
respected by all.

That he did not want to be the king or dictator of this
land is one of the dramatic flukes of history. The setting
was ripe—the rivalry between the states invited it. Later,
through his naïveté, his friend Alexander Hamilton was to
wheedle the General, then president, in that direction. But
during that summer of 1787 in Philadelphia he was a silent
moderator, making only one speech but joining with small
groups many evenings to prepare the material for the following day's sessions.

Little can we imagine how easily an indiscreet chairman
could have closed the convention almost any day. Delaware
was interested only by her weakness and not materially by
the credits of her citizens; Maryland, never being in the
seat of war, found her citizens opposed to central government taxation powers; while the Carolinas favored union
only because of the maritime superiority of the Eastern
states.

Looking down on the economic confusing and conflicting
impulses, Washington wanted more than a compromise:

My wish is that the convention may adopt no temporizing expedient
but probe the defects of the Constitution to the bottom and provide
a radical cure whether they are agreed to or not.

HUGH WILLIAMSON, North Carolina, fifty-two. (1735–
     1819)

Doctor and merchant, educated at College of Philadelphia, Edinburgh and Utrecht. His father was a trades-
man of Dublin, Ireland. Hugh became a preacher, professor, merchant, doctor and politician. He was eccentric,
hard to know. A friend at the convention wrote, "In his
manners there is a strong trait of a gentleman." All during
the war he traded in commodities and Western lands.
Picked up a few thousand dollars' worth of government
issues at ten cents on the dollar.

JAMES WILSON, Pennsylvania, forty-five. (1742–98)

Born in St Andrews, Scotland, came to New York in
1763 and Philadelphia in 1766. Educated at St Andrews
and Glasgow and then at Edinburgh with John Dickinson.
Within a decade made himself important. Signed Declaration of Independence, became Indian commissioner, advocate general for France, director of Bank of North America.
He was called James the Caledonian. Tall, large-featured,
he wore thick glasses. He had the respect of all, but the
affection of few. He favored centralized government,
popular election of senators and representatives, but an appointed president and judiciary. Many think him the most
important man in the convention next to Madison. He was
a student of revolutions. Active in big business, such as
Insurance Company of North America, Georgia Land Company—and finally mixed up in numerous speculation land-
fraud cases. Was a member of the Supreme Court bench for
the last decade of his life.

*GEORGE WYTHE, Virginia, sixty-one. (1726–1806)

Educated by mother and later at William and Mary, he
became the leading law teacher of his day. He taught Jefferson, Marshall, Monroe, Clay and many other thinkers of
that period. He indicates the first break in our legal thinking from the "witchcraft law" of Blackstone. In a quiet way
influential at convention, although Pierce possibly points to
his shortcoming: "Yet from his too favorable opinion of
men, he is no great politician." Emancipated his slaves and
supported them. Regular in attendance at convention. Opposed to slavery. Died from mysterious poisoning at the
age of eighty.

*ROBERT YATES, New York, forty-nine. (1738–1807)

Studied law with Livingston and later became chief justice
of Supreme Court of New York. Widely known for series
of anti-British articles written under the name of "Rough
Hewer." Left the Constitutional Convention about July 10.
He opposed ratification. Strong anti-Federalist. One of the
few poor men at the gathering. He opposed the pernicious

implications of those who were determining national policies, and embarrassed his colleague Hamilton by resisting all change in the Articles of Confederation. Nevertheless he did not resist buying and selling state or federal securities for small profits.

CHAPTER X

The Absent Fathers

THERE ARE SEVERAL additional names of great Americans of the period generally associated with our new constitution. At Philadelphia we find Washington and Madison; but Jefferson, John Adams, Sam Adams, Patrick Henry, Tom Paine and many other of our early celebrities were left out of the gathering for one reason or another. Falsely, our histories have coupled these names with the making of the Constitution. It was their very absence that colored the document as it was finally reported to the people.

JOHN ADAMS OF MASSACHUSETTS

John Adams was some thirteen years younger than his distant cousin Samuel and, unlike the elder revolutionary, his legal reputation kept pace with his political advancement all his life. Writes his grandson:

Not tall, scarcely exceeding middle height, but of a stout, well-knit frame denoting vigor and long life, yet as he grew old inclining more and more to corpulence. His head was large and round, with a wide forehead and expanded brows. His eye was mild and benignant, perhaps even humorous, when he was free from emotion, but when excited, it fully expressed the vehemence of spirit that stirred within.

His family had been farmers and Harvard men before him, and his wife, Abigail Smith (a minister's daughter), figures as prominently in the feminine history of America as he in the masculine. His law practice grew slowly at first, but his time was fully occupied with minor public office and newspaper writings. He made his name for all time by defending first the soldiers who had fired into the crowd to make the "Boston Massacre" and then the patriot cause

of Hancock's sloop *Liberty*. Soon thereafter he refused a
bribe of office, the job of the King's advocate general. Instead he joined the General Court, the Continental Congress, became chief justice of Massachusetts and served on
the committee for drafting a declaration of independence.
Jefferson describes him as "the pillar of its support on the
floor of Congress, its ablest advocate and defender against
the multifarious assaults it encountered."

He served on the board of war and in the Massachusetts
convention, but spent most of his time abroad negotiating
loans from Holland and arranging, with Jay and Franklin,
the peace treaty. Although he was in England at the time
of the convention, the first volume of his *Defense of the
Constitutions of the United States of America* came out in
1787 and may have been read by the Framers.

His subsequent vice-presidency—"the most insignificant
office that ever the invention of man contrived or his
imagination conceived"—and his presidency are too well
known to be recorded here. Madison, on January 10, 1801,
wrote about Adams:

I would not wish to discourage any attentions which friendship,
prudence or benevolence may suggest in his behalf, but . . . I find
him infinitely sunk in the estimation of all parties.

SAMUEL ADAMS OF MASSACHUSETTS AND THE U. S.

At the age of sixty-five, the bald-headed Adams had failed
of election to the convention, along with his friend Hancock. Yet he had been the leader of the state through the
Revolution. For his M.A. at Harvard he had defended the
thesis: "Whether it be lawful to resist the Supreme Magistrate if the Commonwealth cannot otherwise be preserved."
His skill as a drafter and pamphleteer had kept the controversy with England alive even in the years of little
economic friction. When resentment was at its height, he
had started the Committees of Correspondence and of
Safety which had constituted the ministry of propaganda
for the war years. "I doubt whether there is a greater incendiary in the King's dominions or a man of greater
malignity of heart," warned Governor Hutchison.

No other American ever was such a bad businessman and such a good politician. Although he had inherited an estate and a brewery business from his father, his fortune was soon dissipated. His house became run down. His business failed. He was £8,000 in arrears as a tax collector. But he, who had stood fifth in the social roster of his class of twenty-two at Harvard, did not lack bounteous friends or public office. His steady job as clerk of the Massachusetts assembly assured his family sustenance.

Adams had had a hand in the drafting of the Suffolk Resolves and the Articles of Confederation. He played second fiddle to Hancock in popularity in the state and was defeated for the new Congress by Fisher Ames.

In spite of his absence from the convention of 1787, the Constitution would not have been adopted without his support. He was the leader in conceiving a national rather than a state citizenship.

Christopher Gadsden of South Carolina

This aged radical "feared leaders more than he feared Tories." He himself had led the radicals of South Carolina throughout the Revolution. He had served thirty years in the state assembly, represented the state in the Stamp Act Congress and the Continental Congress, had been an officer of distinction in the war, served ten months' imprisonment, and was principally to be credited with the achievement of the state constitution. His following among the skilled mechanics of Charleston had fallen off, because he had pronounced against the confiscation of loyalist property, and he had been shelved into the vice-presidency by the Rutledge group of conservatives.

At sixty-three Gadsden turned Federalist, supporting ratification of the Constitution in his state, and later campaigning for Adams in 1800. His conservatism was coincident with his completion of the thousand-foot wharf which he, as a merchant of means, had been building. His rash temperament and religious zeal may further explain his change in politics.

JOHN HANCOCK OF MASSACHUSETTS

Hancock's career was made upon his adoption by a rich uncle, a merchant. His father had been a minister, and he was sent as a matter of course to Boston Latin School and Harvard. Having inherited an estate of £70,000, and pursuing a profession of smuggling, considered legitimate by the merchants of the time, Hancock's popularity with the colony was immeasurably heightened by the case of his ship *Liberty,* which was harassed by the King's officers and harried in the King's courts. James Truslow Adams' appraisal of him reads:

His wealth, judiciously expended among the people, and his espousal of the American side of the controversy had made him immensely popular with those who did not work with him so closely as to perceive that his mind was of mediocre quality.

He was the richest New Englander on the patriot side.

Allied with Samuel Adams, he became president of the Provincial Congress, a member of the General Court, a signer of the Declaration of Independence, a framer of the state constitution, and governor uninterruptedly thereafter —except for a judicious leave of office during Shays' rebellion. He failed of election to the position of commander-in-chief of the colonial army and to the Constitutional Convention, but he supported ratification in Massachusetts when tempted with national office and when chosen to introduce the popular amendments.

He allowed his vanity to become more apparent than most men's. He had written his name so large and clear on the Declaration of Independence that George III could see it without his glasses; and at another time he made a gift to Harvard, of books worth £500, insisting that the present be generally made known as his.

PATRICK HENRY OF VIRGINIA

Here was a Virginia frontiersman who had come of good family. His father was a planter from Aberdeen, a man of education, a magistrate, a colonel of militia, a vestryman, and a loyalist in the fray. He had married the daughter of a small planter. The young red-headed Patrick had picked up an education from his father and a minister uncle. His first marriage brought him a dowry of six slaves and six hundred bad acres. Despite parental and matrimonial assistance, Henry failed twice as a shopkeeper and once as a farmer.

Taking to the law as a last resort, he found his reputation made overnight by the Parson's Cause, a case in which he reversed public opinion by his eloquence alone. Between the ages of twenty-four and twenty-eight he took part in 1,185 lawsuits and proceeded into politics as the people's champion. He led the frontier faction in the House of Burgesses, on the committee of correspondence, in the Virginia convention, and the state legislature—favoring slavery, the restoration of the loyalists (because the new country needed citizens) and the payment of taxes to all churches impartially. Richard Henry Lee was his political ally and Jefferson his political guide. His leadership of the state was due more to eloquence than to administration. The "Caesar had his Brutus," "Give me liberty or give me death," and "one heart, one mind" speeches, rather than his public office or legal practice, gave Henry his place in American history.

Henry's life story is packed with colorful items. It was he who sent George Rogers Clark on his expedition to the West. He refused six major public offices—a convention seat, senator, secretary of state, chief justice of the new Supreme Court, governor, and envoy to France. Although no friend of Washington at the time, he supplied him with evidence of a cabal against him. As a colonial rebel, Henry had at first befriended Washington; then, with growing suspicions of the North, he had opposed ratification of the Constitution and had sent two Anti-Federalist senators to Congress; but by 1798, as his great wealth and legal reputation weaned him to conservatism, he gave his approval to Washington's administration and would have been an assured Federalist voter had he lived until the election of 1800.

THOMAS JEFFERSON OF VIRGINIA

Jefferson was abroad at the time of the convention, and his point of view was sorely missed in the Philadelphia assembly. He never made a "proper" speech in his life, but he had injected himself into American civilization through his personal contacts and writings. He wrote many of the colonial messages to the King, the Declaration of Independence, *A Summary View of the Rights of British America,* parts of the Virginia constitution, the Kentucky Resolves, the Ordinance of 1784, and *Notes on Virginia* (a scientific record).

The tall, loose-jointed man with sandy hair, freckles and a red face was a product of the Virginia frontier. His father, a surveyor by profession, had made the first accurate map of Virginia. The elder Jefferson was a magistrate, a colonel, and a member of the House of Burgesses who had married into the Randolph family and had left to his son an estate of some two thousand acres. His son had received the best education of the time at the hands of local ministers, at William and Mary College, and under the legal tutelage of George Wythe. Jefferson spent few years in the law, preferring to perform his duties as a public official and a planter. He advanced naturally from local magistrate to the House of Burgesses, to the Continental Congress, to the Virginia convention, to France as American minister, to governor of the state, to Congress, to the cabinet as secretary of state, to the vice-presidency, and finally the presidency. His career was further perpetuated through the administrations of Madison and Monroe.

Jefferson expounded an agrarian philosophy. Cheap land was the basis of his thought. He opposed navies, manufacturing interests, and urbanization—cities he saw as "sores upon the body politic." He campaigned for free churches, free land, gradual emancipation of slaves, and free state education. "I have sworn upon the altar of God eternal hostility against every form of tyranny over the mind of man." He had even seen the justice of the Massachusetts revolt of Daniel Shays.

It is seldom realized that Jefferson had, before the Con-

federation, returned to his scientific, agricultural and philosophical studies. The death of his wife drove him back into
public life in 1782.

In spite of his large fortune, he was often harried by
debt. Receiving five thousand acres from his father-in-law,
he had increased his estate to ten thousand acres, with two
hundred slaves. He had an average income of £300, which
was large for the time, but the debts which came with the
lands he acquired and from public office totaled $20,000
when he left the presidency. The sale of his library to the
Library of Congress and a national subscription of $16,500
just before his death eased his affairs somewhat.

Jefferson "lacked a sense of humor, and hated the sight
of blood." By 1787 he had sown the seeds of a party and
was in that year sending back from the Old World books,
architectural plans, new plants and political ideas which
were to color every phase of American life. He endowed
churches.

WILLIE JONES OF NORTH CAROLINA

Willie Jones refused to come to the convention because
he thought the cause of liberty was getting along very well
without any changes or amendments. He was a North
Carolina planter and merchant of forty-six. His father, a
Welshman, was attorney for Lord Granville and had sent
Willie (pronounced Wylie) to Eton in England and then
to the Continent. Having married a girl of good family and
inherited a large fortune, the young planter was able to
indulge a taste for gay society, hunting, racing, cards and
lavish entertainment.

In spite of his aristocratic life at home, Jones had picked
up democratic notions on his travels. Gifted as a politician,
he became a leader of the local committee of safety, the
Provincial Congress, the state constitutional convention,
and the new House of Commons. Although named a radical
in the history books, he aided the campaign against the
Regulators of the frontier. He prevailed upon the state
convention to refuse ratification of the Constitution and to

propose twenty-six amendments—a bill of rights without which, he believed, no government would be democratic.

THOMAS PAINE OF ENGLAND, FRANCE AND THE COLONIES

A stateless journalist of fifty, Paine had served a long apprenticeship for revolution. He was the son of a Quaker corset maker and an Anglican lady of good birth. His formal education ended in grammar school, but by dint of wide reading "he achieved what was rare in Europe at the time, an education strictly confined to contemporaneous matters. No conservatism, no evaluating discipline stood between his temperament and his times." In England he had been a corset maker, seaman, teacher, tobacconist and grocer, finding that he could only make ends meet as an exciseman. When he was fired a second time from his excise job for collective-bargaining activities (he organized the excisemen and lobbied for them at Parliament), he started off for America with letters of introduction to Dr Franklin.

Franklin launched him in colonial journalism, to the lasting credit of the good Doctor. In 1776 *Common Sense,* a two-shilling pamphlet of forty-seven pages, was published, and so exactly did it express the inarticulate thoughts of the rebellious colonials that it sold 500,000 copies. In a very short period every American had read it or heard tell of it. It "worked a powerful change in the mind of men," said Washington.

And again at an opportune time Paine's words, in a series of articles called "The Crisis," cried encouragement to the rebels: "These are the times that try men's souls." His lucid and clarion style made him a welcome ally. New York gave him a loyalist farm and £500. He served as secretary to the Continental Congress until an indiscreet use of government information necessitated his removal to the clerkship of the Pennsylvania assembly. He contributed from his personal moneys to the troops and made a trip of solicitation to France, recovering only his bare expenses.

Paine has been maligned for atheism and immorality. He had separated from his second wife before leaving England, but his life was a singularly chaste one. The last of his writ-

ings, *The Age of Reason,* shows him to be what today
would be called an ethical culturist or a Unitarian. Paine
"seems always to have been careless about his personal appearance, and age and ostracism made him in his last years
a trifle unlovely."

From America he returned to England before the Constitutional Convention was called, there to erect the iron
bridge which he had invented and to answer, by the publication of *The Rights of Man* in 1791, Burke's attack on the
French Revolution. William Blake hurried him out of England when his book was suppressed by the authorities, but
his participation in the Paris convention was no more fortu-
nate. Imprisoned there, together with all foreigners, he was
spared a trial and released through the intervention of
James Monroe, the American minister.

The man whom Theodore Roosevelt was to describe as
"a filthy little atheist" was the friend of the great liberals of
three nations. He admitted that the masses were apt to be
fools, but this reflection did not quench his humanitarianism.
"His success as a writer sustained his self-confidence, while
his failure at everything else supplied him with an abund-
ance of grievances."

This great internationalist was born in England in 1737
and died in New York in 1809. Ten years later his body
was carried back to England.

PART III

The Document

THE *Constitution developed from the discussion of four divergent plans, the demand for four great powers and the construction of three great equal departments. After a provision for later improvements and amendments was added, it was presented to the people for adoption. Despite popular opinion of today the colonists of 1787 came very near to rejecting all of the labors of the delegates. But finally, on April 30, 1789—thirteen years after the Declaration of Independence—the states were sufficiently united into one nation to elect a president of these United States.*

CHAPTER XI

The Four Plans

THERE HAS NEVER BEEN a convention in the recorded history of man which proceeded with such dignity. There was no attempt to filibuster. No offensive expressions were employed. No records were taken of individual votes, for as King and Mason pointed out, "a record of the opinions of the members would be an obstacle to a change" and would "furnish handles to the adversaries of the Result of the Meeting."

Not until 1792 did Senator Griswold spit in the face of Senator Lyon in the House Chamber—Our first congressional combat.

No member was allowed to speak twice on the same subject until every other delegate "who had been silent shall have been heard if he choose to speak." Delegates were forbidden to read or to discourse with others or to pass in front of the chairman while a delegate was talking.

Everyone in the chamber felt in a mood for experimentation. To preserve that attitude, secrecy was necessary, and so we find a resolution passed against "licentious" publication of the proceedings. If any delegate's early guess were made public it would become increasingly difficult for him to change his mind or his vote.

With New Hampshire not sending delegates until July and with Rhode Island never represented, the eleven colonies proceeded to the business of amending the Articles of Confederation. A letter from the merchants and tradesmen of Rhode Island addressed to George Washington was read to the delegates as the first order of business. The sole purpose of the epistle was to let the convention know that:

It is the general opinion here—that full power for the Regulation of the Commerce of the United States, both Foreign and Domestick, ought to be vested in the National Council.

Thus did Rhode Island citizens pursue the Annapolis convention's objectives. This was the first and practically the only communication from outsiders. It pointed to the greatest problem of the day—interstate commerce.

The first close division was on the question of appointing a committee to "superintend" the minutes of the convention. The vote—five to four—showed confidence in the secretary, Colonel Hamilton's candidate, Major Jackson. No superintendence of the minutes was authorized, but Madison, by general consent, was permitted to take notes from his seat directly beneath the chairman's dais.

During the two weeks which had expired in waiting for eleven of the thirteen states to send representatives, groups of delegates listed up objections to the Articles of Confederation and prepared outlines of a new type of government. In these early discussions Pennsylvania went so far as to urge that the small states be reduced in voting power in the convention itself. Madison shrewdly suggested that the small-states problem be avoided until later in the convention.

The Four Proposed Plans

Randolph, the thirty-two-year-old governor of Virginia, arose to offer the Virginia plan. This was directed to "procure to the several states various blessings of which an isolated situation was incapable." In essence he proposed:

1. That there be two legislative houses—both elected on the basis either of wealth or of free inhabitants, "as the one or the other rule may seem best in different cases."

   Representation by wealth was considered democratic. If applied in 1937 Congress would be dominated by New York.

2. That Congress elect the executive, who should be either a single person or a group of people. In very few states were the governors elected by the people.

> *Many delegates urged three or five presidents, all chosen at the same time and for the same term of office. There was great distrust of a single president. It seemed a step toward monarchy.*

3. That the national legislature should have power to annul all state laws.

> *Generally accepted, but, the mails being slow, many feared too much time would elapse between the time a state enacted a law and Congress became aware of it.*

4. That the Supreme Court, consisting of *one or more* supreme tribunals, was to have limited jurisdiction.

> *The idea of several Supreme Courts was not disturbing, for many delegates thought of the Supreme Court as an agency designed mainly for deciding disputes between states on boundaries and for determining the legal owners of captured pirate boats.*

5. That the Congress shall have no part in amending the Constitution.

> *The sovereignty was to be in the people.*

6. That the executive and part of the Supreme Court be given the veto power—he called it a revision power—over acts of Congress.

> *The judges, not very busy, were to be outwardly and admittedly acting directly on legislative proposals.*

7. That the congressmen were to be elected by the people of the states, and the senators to be elected by the congressmen.

> *By removing the election of senators one more step from the people a higher class of senators would be*

procurable. A check on democracy was essential to protect the propertied classes.

Of course he listed many other features, such as the admission of new states and the ineligibility of congressmen, senators and executives for re-election. He was so honestly uncertain about his entire program that we find he left blank spaces in his report wherever numbers or dates were needed. Should a congressman serve for two or for ten years?

This plan, so radically different from the Articles of Confederation, was promptly attacked by several delegates who brought out in good lawyer fashion that the call from Annapolis and the act of Congress forwarding that call in no way permitted any discussion of a scheme of government basically different from the old Articles of Confederation. Was not our power limited to preparing amendments? By what right could we presume to forget the Articles of Confederation, and the present existing Congress thereunder? Did not the very call for this convention limit us and tie our hands?

And then we find in the record the second proposal—the Charles Pinckney plan for a new constitution. It was extensive and in great detail. It resembles closely the Constitution as finally adopted. But research shows that the Pinckney plan as incorporated in the minutes bears slight resemblance to the plan which he actually proposed on that Thursday, the 29th day of May 1787. For Mr Pinckney, it appears, in 1818, when Madison was getting his minutes in shape for publication, rewrote his original plan, making it conform to the Constitution as finally adopted so that he could boast to a gullible world that he was the author of the document. Thus was committed one of the slyest and most ineffective forgeries of our history.

In the ensuing discussion on the Randolph plan which covered many days after May 28, the issues were being clarified.

We find Hamilton bringing forth a third plan. He urged

that "we copy the House of Lords in all its aspects," particularly life tenure of office. Little did he foresee that the House of Lords was to dwindle in power and prestige after the Reform Act of 1832, while our elected Senate was to grow in power.

Jefferson wrote to Madison on June 20, 1787, from Paris. Madison received the letter in Philadelphia seventy-eight days later—September 6, 1787.

After the delegates had argued with great fervor either for or against the use of the words "national" or "supreme" as applied to the new government and whether the new powers were to be enforced against the people or only against the states, delegate Hamilton, on the 19th of June, made his only lengthy address to the convention. He outlined his plan which, at the close of the convention in September, he elaborated and submitted to Madison: a proposed constitution for the United States "which he said delineated the Constitution which he would have wished to be proposed by the Convention." Whether he had been subdued by Yates and Lansing, the two mediocre other New York delegates (neither of whom signed the final document), or whether, as he wrote Washington, he thought nothing of value could be accomplished, it is difficult now to appraise why this vital advocate of monarchies should have been so feeble in pressing his point of view on the floor of the convention.

He did, however, offer some striking suggestions all in the direction of monarchy and concentration. His later fiscal program, with tariffs and subsidies to merchants, was conceivable only through a centralized government:

1. Congress shall appoint the governor of each state, who shall have power to veto all state laws.

1936—Roosevelt's Congress would have appointed the governor of Kansas.

2. Indefinite powers shall be given to Congress, because if the federal government be limited, the states will gradually subvert it. "As states they ought to be abolished."

> *1936—the Supreme Court would not have been called on to consider the Wagner Labor Act, NRA or the balance of the New Deal program. Nor in fact could it have declared the income-tax law of 1893 unconstitutional.*

3. The president shall have absolute power to veto all laws of Congress.

> *1936—the Bonus Bill dies on the President's desk.*

4. The president shall serve for life.

> *1936—we elect our fifth or sixth life president.*

Hamilton saw government in terms of economics. The small states' fear of larger states did not disturb him. He did not believe that the three large states, Virginia, Massachusetts and Pennsylvania, would ever combine against all the others. The vast distance between them of itself would prevent any effective joint action. Did it not require more than a month for a letter to go from Boston to Richmond and back to Boston?

What he truly feared was the continued violation of the federal authority. Had not New Jersey expressly refused to comply with her constitutional requisition of money to Congress? Did not the files of Congress show complaints from many foreign nations, indicating specific violations by separate states of treaty provisions?

Must we not stop in the future those ill-conceived interstate commercial treaties? Had not Pennsylvania and New Jersey entered into such compacts without any "application or apoligy"? Had not Massachusetts raised a separate army? Surely we must keep in mind the experience of the kings of Persia, Philip of Macedonia, and the Amphictyonic Confederacy!

The Randolph plan, in the light of Hamilton's observations, was then discussed in detail but mainly on the question of whether this new federal power would be supreme. What if a state refused to obey? Were we to rely on good faith? What evidence was there to believe that the states would play any more fairly with each other in the future than they had done in the past? This line of debate forced the proponents of the Virginia plan into the open. The new government was to be more than a league of eleven nations. It must exercise its control over the inhabitants directly, not only over the states.

On the decision in favor of that philosophy the convention threw into the discard the old Articles of Confederation. By taking this step the delegates scrapped irretrievably the call for the convention. To carry through this expression it would become necessary to gain approval, not from the states as such, but from the people of the states. This basic departure in political thought created the need for an illegal method of circumventing all the state officials who, if permitted a vote on ratification, would kill the Constitution. Thus will we see the document detoured past the legislatures, the bodies required for ratification both by existing law and by the convention call.

Early at one troubled session Randolph, noting the general despair of the delegates, suggested that the convention adjourn and that the secrecy rule be abolished. "Let's adjourn for a time and let the citizens know what we have discussed and that we cannot agree on any program." A delegate from South Carolina, unmindful of any reflection on Philadelphian hospitality, declared: "I could not think of going all the way back to South Carolina and then returning to this place!"

On July 5, Yates and Lansing, two of the three New York delegates, went home quite sure that "the results of the Convention would be unsatisfactory."

Morris prophesied that "there is every reason why the gallows and halter will finish the work of the sword."

Early Americanisms of this period which struck European fancy were "I reckon" and "go the whole hog."

The president of Yale deplored pronunciations like vess'l, Brit'n, gard'n, warf, and weat. Americans also said virchue, natchure, fortchune, quietchude and distchurbed. And vulgar new phrases were coming in rapidly, such as "made up my mind," "hurt my feelings," "had committed himself."

The small states became alarmed. They must move quickly and definitely or be forever submerged. Paterson of New Jersey brought out a plan for organizing the eleven states. The Paterson, or New Jersey, plan proposed to strengthen the Confederation. It urged plural presidents, being also fearful of a single executive. Paterson was less courageous than Randolph on the tax features. The old Congress had no power to gather money from the states. It was a mere central beggar. Paterson suggested a plan under which Congress could levy duties and imposts and in case of non-payment might "direct the collection." He saw no need for financial teeth. The small states, so fearful of the large ones, appreciated the need of more central power but suggested something between voluntary paying of taxes and a definite central power to collect taxes.

But the essence of the plan was the continuation of the then existing method of representation in the Congress. Each state shall equal in voting power each other state. Size, wealth, income, population—all were to be immaterial. It was as if today we had a Senate only and no House of Representatives. Democracy was to be based on numbers of states instead of on numbers of human beings.

The balance of the plan dealt with admission of new states, regulation of trade, uniform naturalization and a judiciary in addition to the Congress. Essentially the plan was for a federal government, not a national government. Lansing, promptly speaking for the New Jersey plan, said, "It sustains the sovereignty of the respective states, while that of Randolph destroys it."

But Wilson did not believe that a citizen of Delaware would be "degraded" by becoming a citizen of the United States. Pinckney minced no words; he knew that if we gave

"New Jersey an equal vote in Congress with all other states she will dismiss her scruples and concur in a national system."

Randolph pointed out with great wisdom that a government relying on coercion was a weak government and that unless this assembly agreed on a plan "the people will yield to despair." Hamilton sneered at all the plans, for popular government to him was no government—all the plans were "but porc with a little change of sauce." Madison's clear analysis in favor of the Randolph plan was followed by a vote of seven states to three states preferring Randolph's plan to Paterson's. But Paterson's essential point of advantage for small states was still to win out.

The convention was far from peace and agreement. The controversy grew so acute that Paterson himself suggested: "If the Confederacy is radically wrong [allowing each state to have one vote irrespective of size] let us return to our respective states and obtain larger powers, not assume them ourselves."

There was little apparent logic or consistency back of the votes on any plan or proposal. The combinations between states were often inexplicable.

On the presidential term there were eight votes—Pennsylvania alone consistently for the longest term.

On the method of electing representatives three votes were taken, with the small states usually against popular elections.

Eleven votes were taken on the method of electing a president.

Five votes were taken on the resolution that money bills must originate in the House.

Pennsylvania alone was consistently against assuming the debts of the Confederation.

The delegates from Maryland divided twenty-seven times on different issues, and there were twenty-three occasions when, had there been no divided vote, the result of the vote at the convention would have been altered.

Maryland, Delaware and Virginia once joined together in favor of sumptuary tax laws, and later formed a similar alliance to fight against the power being given to Congress to subdue a rebellion even upon a request of an imperiled state. Martin of Maryland blandly suggested "leaving the states to suppress rebellions for themselves."

On the slave-vote question Delaware joined with South Carolina and Georgia for representation based on full slave population.

In 1936 Negroes in most courts in Southern states may not sit with white folk—except Negro lawyers, for lawyers are always preferred people.

Whenever it was suggested that new states might apply for admission, New Jersey joined with the Southern states opposed to giving them equal treatment.

The delegates became alarmed at current outside events. Although the crops of 1787 were better than most people had expected, the threats of thirteen types of separate inflations were ever present. Many other influences were working for cohesion. Georgia, threatened by the Creek Indians, had declared martial law. Savannah was fortified; Spain was suspected of backing the Indians; and Georgia needed national support from the other colonies. The convention also heard that it was "pretty certain that the seditious group had become formidable in Congress sitting in New York City, and that the seditious party had opened communication with the Viceroy of Canada."

Compromises had to be effected. In the process of give-and-take, votes were traded, principles were abandoned. An agreement had to be reached. On no single issue was there anything approaching unanimity. But throughout these sessions much more attention and time were devoted to the salaries of members of Congress than to the powers Congress was to exercise. A proper system of voting strength in the Congress seemed to make needless in the minds of many any attempt to define with precision the frontiers of congressional power. A few of those present agreed with Alexander Hamilton: "I never had any faith in the Constitution from the beginning because it was a frail and worthless fabric."

The delegates first had to fix the voting power of each state in the Congress. If this were once done to the satisfaction of both small and large states, no one would worry much about the power to tax or regulate commerce. So we find the great battle over the make-up of the Congress. But this problem was inextricably interwoven with the definition of boundaries, numbers of states and threatened subdivision of the larger states.

CHAPTER XII

The Four Great Powers

Throughout the debates on the four plans for a new type of union, the delegates never wandered far from the consideration of four main problems.

1. *The Boundary Question.* This involved far more than stretching surveyors' tapes along the lines of ancient British grants. It affected the number of states, the size of states, the control of Western lands and, in its most significant form, the balance of voting power between the states in the new government. This last dilemma of the convention which faced the Founding Fathers underlay every other problem. On its solution depended the amount of authority the states would vest in the state representatives sitting in a national congress.

2. *Guarantees of a Republican Form of Government.* Although discussed in metaphysical terms, this issue impinged on the threat of any of the states shifting to monarchies. Query: Should arms be used to perpetuate the republican form of government? This issue has not yet been put at rest either in the nation or in the states. The work of Huey Long and the activities of the Liberty League have now for the first time since about 1812 directed attention to this portion of the Founding Fathers' deliberations.

3. *Taxation.* Here was a practical test of how far the new government would become potent. Had the Articles of Confederation included the power to raise adequate revenues for war and peace, the convention of 1787 would have taken on a different form and complexion.

4. *Commerce.* This power and its use were discussed in words and terms not unlike those employed today by those who want a national economy instead of forty-eight com-

petitive ones. To the delegates the problem included: Should the slave business be continued either by importation or by domestic sale? What power should the states turn over to the new government to deal with foreign nations? Did we not need a stabilized currency? Should inventors be protected by monopolies? Should bankruptcy relief be available to debtors? How could the devastating interstate commercial warfare be abolished on fair terms to all states?

Boundaries and Voting Power

Twelve states were represented when the Constitution was finally adopted by the delegates. If any twelve human beings get together to form any kind of club or organization, the first questions invariably asked are: Who is going to own this club? Will new members be elected? Will new members have the same vote as charter members?

The thirteen colonies were vague geographical entities. Original grants of land had been set forth in loose language, for the kings of England had no idea whether oceans or deserts lay three hundred miles west of the Atlantic seaboard. In many cases the grants overlapped each other. It took us more than an entire century to settle all these disputes. As late as 1925 the Connecticut–New York boundary line was still in doubt, to be cured only by an interstate treaty and congressional approval in that year.

The Articles of Confederation under which we operated during five of the seven years of the Revolution were found unworkable, in part because of boundary disputes. Thousands of farmers and realty operators were in doubt whether they were in this state or that. Hence they paid taxes to neither. Maryland had insisted that all states should give up their Western lands, wherever they were claimed to be, to the national government; and this was tentatively agreed upon in 1781, four years after the Articles of Confederation had first been submitted for ratification.

The delegates at the Philadelphia convention could not see as far west as the Mississippi. None dreamed of as many

as twenty-six states, the number now lying east of the
Mississippi. It is hardly conceivable that the Constitution
would have been adopted in its present form had anyone
present imagined that as many as twenty-two states would
eventually be created west of the Mississippi. The main
concern of all related to the danger of the overwhelming
political power of the then large states. Ellsworth, with
courage, pointed to this peril. He and many others were
convinced that Massachusetts and Virginia were already so
vast that they could never govern the people within their
limits. Virginia was having great difficulty in controlling
what is now Kentucky. West Virginia finally became a
separate state during the Civil War period. Everyone knew
that Massachusetts was unable to keep peace one hundred
miles from her own seaboard capital. No one was dismayed
at the obvious break-up of the big colonies. Had not Massachusetts originally been three colonies? Did not Connecticut
and New Hampshire at one time comprise one entity? Was
not small New Jersey a union of two colonies, fused because
Pennsylvania and New York had threatened, through
interstate-commerce controls, to destroy their people?

There were lengthy observations by many deputies indicating which, if any, of the colonies would grow any larger
than they were at that time. Many agreed that "Pennsylvania will not increase, considering the present vast state of
her population."

*The number of Americans now living abroad is twice
the population of Pennsylvania in 1787.*

Bedford of Delaware anticipated that Georgia would
grow very big. It has today a population equivalent to that
of all thirteen colonies in 1787. Several delegates pointed to
the fact "that Berne and Zurich, two of Switzerland's can-
tons, were quite large and yet their governments are not
complained of by the inhabitants."

Gorham of Massachusetts felt that it was not unlikely
that Kentucky, Vermont and the "Province of Mayne"
might some day be added to the present number of states.

This was the nearest to a definite guess of a possible sixteen states.

Madison, with more vision than most of the delegates, shifted the consideration of the convention to the fundamental problem of future immigration. He foresaw that:

If we are to have a stable government, many "respectable" Europeans who love liberty and wish to partake of its blessings will transfer their fortunes here. If they do so it is proof of their attachments which ought to excite our confidence and affection.

Gouverneur Morris, conceding that the Western lands might be settled at a future date, was unwilling to admit these Western territories, stuffed with foreigners, into the United States. He would admit "foreigners" to his house, invite them to his table, but would not "carry complaisance so far as to bed them" with his wife.

Wilson, with a little bitterness, noted that almost all the general officers of the Pennsylvania line of the late army had been "foreigners" and that three of her deputies at the convention were not "natives."

The ignorance of the delegates as to what history would do with our Western lands is nowhere more clearly indicated than in the letter written by James Monroe, later to be a president, after a trip out West:

A great part of the territory is unspeakably poor, especially that near Lakes Michigan and Erie and that upon the Mississippi and the Illinois consists of extensive plains which had not had from appearance, and will not have, a single bush on them for ages.

Such prophecies, now proven so grossly inadequate, were to affect not only the adjustment of representation in the legislative chambers but also the decision as to the method of amending the Constitution. What, asked one deputy, would happen if there were ever to be as many as fourteen states? If we agree now that nine are to bind thirteen, should ten bind fourteen? The delegates, thinking only in modest numbers of states, failed to appreciate that to amend the Constitution by a vote of three fourths of the states would be vastly more cumbersome and difficult if the votes of thirty-six states were required rather than the votes of only nine.

New Jersey and the Southern states were quite generally agreed that, even if new states were to be added, they should not get equal treatment with the original thirteen. For hours the delegates argued, in effect: Surely everyone must admit that the original joiners should have some special advantages over all newcomers. Clymer of Pennsylvania went so far as to urge that the encouragement of the Western country was suicide to the old states.

The entire problem of the admission of new states was discussed more in terms of political than of economic power.

Not a single candidate foresaw that with the introduction of machinery these disdained foreigners would soon be cajoled, invited and even smuggled into our nation. Aside from ownership of Negro slaves, employers had not yet conceded that the profit of the owner of an industry equals that amount of wealth created by the workers which he is able to retain for himself. Little could they foresee that the United States Steel Corporation under Andrew Carnegie a century later would spend thousands of dollars scouting around eastern Europe to import cheap, profitable laborers.

The economic tangent of the state-boundary debate touched solely, and then only gently, on the latent values of these vast landholdings to the west. But had a single state clearly foreseen the coming Western real-estate boom of the next decades, the gift of its lands to the national government would never have been agreed to. Only Hamilton and a few of the moneywise delegates had even an inkling of the possible sales prices of these Western lands, later used to feed a starving national treasury.

The political implication of boundaries, as determining the number of states, was clear to all. In its simplest terms it resolved itself into: Should the power of the new government be vested in states or in men? Those states which were small or feared they might not grow in the future were naturally against a democratic control. Connecticut, New Jersey, Maryland, Delaware and New York were for the old system of the Confederation—voting to be solely on the basis of states, with each state having an equal voice in the government. To these should be added New Hampshire, never truly vocal on this issue. New York, fearful that it would remain a small state, was certainly ill advised by its delegates.

But the compromise ultimately effected could not be reached until the delegates were ready to decide whether Negroes were to be counted as part of the population. Even though slaves (more than 500,000 in all) had no votes, the slave-owning states urged that in apportioning representatives in Congress the South should have voting power based on total population—white or black, free or slave. The old Congress of the Confederation had passed two resolutions affecting slaves, one which proposed to abolish slavery for all time north of the Ohio River, and another in 1783, assessing the thirteen states for the expenses of the government on the basis of counting each Negro slave as equal to three fifths of a person. For many days Negroes were debated in terms of fractions of humanity. Why not count seven Negroes as equal to three whites? After such higher mathematics had been explored at length, the old five-to-three ratio was continued. Had representation in the legislatures been based on full population figures, including slaves as the equals of free whites, then certainly the Southern states would have greatly outnumbered the Northern states in the proposed Congress. On such a basis the small states would have wanted only one chamber—a senate—where states had equal voting power. If, on the other hand, the Negroes had not been included for apportioning representations, the small states might readily have agreed to only one chamber—a house based on population.

The compromise finally agreed upon established our two chambers—one democratic, the other territorial and artificially based on state boundaries. During the convention there was little of the silly twaddle about checks and balances which now fills our textbooks and American histories. No one conceived of bicameral legislative chambers as a double check on legislation. The only balance sought was between the then populous and the then unpopulated states. The

great compromise, of a senate in which each state should
have two votes, and a house in which congressmen were to
be apportioned to population, was the only way to reach any
agreement at all for a new government.

Bedford of Delaware arose to shout:

I do not trust you men from the large states. If you possess the power,
the abuse of it cannot be checked, and what then would prevent you
from exercising it to our destruction? Sooner than be ruined, there
are foreign powers who would take us by the hand.

From the debates it is entirely clear that not a single candidate had any idea that little Rhode Island in 1936 would
exceed in population the then largest state, Virginia.

After eleven days of debate the deal was effected. The
majority rule under which the convention was acting was
invoked, and by the slimmest of possible margins—six votes
to five—our Constitution included a house and a senate.

Into this compromise there was injected a real check on
the power of the people. The Senate was to be chosen by the
state legislatures—once removed from the electorate. Not
until 1913, by means of the Seventeenth Amendment, was
that device for the thwarting of popular will to be over-
thrown. Then did we reverse the Founding Fathers. Then
for the first time did we, the people, directly elect our own
senators.

But the salient implication of the Great Compromise lies
in the fact that with the two-house situation, with small-
state protection, with a stiff three-fourths rule for amending
the Constitution, even the small states were ready to grant
Congress and the president wide powers over taxation, commerce and public welfare. Had the small states been defeated, had they been forced to accept a governmental structure capable of outvoting them by the counting of heads
instead of states, the powers of Congress would have been
strictly circumscribed. No generous power over commerce
would have been granted to Congress under any other arrangement. But with the small states in a position to block
action in the Senate, and the large states controlling the
House, the convention was anxious and willing to put into

the Congress all the power needed to cope with all possible threats of disunion. Let such a Congress make treaties, coin money, lay taxes, admit new states and regulate commerce.

Thus was the boundary-large-state-small-state problem resolved. Thus do we find that Nevada, with 100,000 population, has an equal voice in the Senate of the United States with New York, with 12,500,000 inhabitants; and 250,000 citizens of Delaware have the same senatorial voting strength as 9,500,000 people living in Pennsylvania.

After a decision had been reached on the question of power between the states, some thought had to be given to the general type of government which was to exist in the states. Even the best-knit union could be broken up in a year or so unless the states followed a basically uniform pattern of local government.

Republican Form of Government

The delegates were concerned with procuring a degree of uniformity of political procedure in each of the separate states. No delegate was quite sure what the word *republicanism* meant. But by and large the delegates were in opposition to the extreme Hamiltonian philosophy. So the problem presented to the delegates was simply this: How far should the states, banded together, guarantee a republican form of government to each state? What if a state wanted to change its form of control? Should it be permitted to go outside of some form of republican government? What if the state wished to appoint a governor for life with hereditary power vested in his eldest son? What if a state desired to abolish entirely its legislative chambers; or, instead of electing a single governor, elect a commission of governors? How far should the other states, through the new nation, endeavor to prevent such experimentation in the forms of government? Gorham feared that

an enterprising citizen might erect the standard of monarchy in a particular state and extend his views eventually to other states while the United States would be an inactive witness to its destruction.

At the start of the debate many were unwilling to sacrifice the lives of the citizens of some states to protect the laws of other states. Several delegates arose to suggest that the new national government should never sacrifice human lives to perpetuate such "outrageous laws as existed in Rhode Island."

> *The college of William and Mary was required by its charter to pay to the governor on each November 5th two copies of Latin verse as quit rent for its lands. Rhode Island had a 2.5 per cent revenue tariff, and taxed in addition axes, shoes, hats, vehicles, soap, candles, paper, tinware, leather and apparel.*

Wilson stood for a compromise and suggested that it would be sufficient if the national government secured each state against "dangerous commotions, insurrections and rebellions." Houston declared "that the government of South Carolina" was "a very bad one," and he opposed any steps which would perpetuate such existing constitutions and forms of government.

Gouverneur Morris was disturbed. Dogmatically he shouted:

It has been a maxim in Political Science that Republican Government is not adapted to a large extent of country, because the energy of the Executive Magistracy cannot reach the extreme parts of it. Wealth tends to corrupt the mind, to nourish its love of power and to stimulate it to oppression.

The phrase "republican form of government" was bandied around in loose fashion like "Socialist" or "Communist" today. Some of the most intelligent delegates proposed a national government under which the president would hold office for life; others proposed that his selection be thrice removed from the power of the people by Congress selecting the senators and the senators selecting a committee by lot, and the committee selecting the president. Such devices apparently did not appear to run foul of the high-sounding slogans of republicanism of 1787.

They wanted to prevent dictators or kings. They knew that many delegates preferred a monarchy to a democracy. If a single state should decide to be governed by a king, the new national government might become impotent in his realm. To prevent such a happening the delegates gave to the Congress power to assure a republican form of government. Just what was meant by that phrase no one knew or will ever know. One thing is certain, it did not mean a democratic form of government, a government in which all adults have an equal voice. It referred to form, not essence.

Negro slaves, the women, the poor, the debtors were disenfranchised in 1787, and at no time on the convention floor did any delegate plead that republicanism meant universal suffrage. Nor did the phrase imply guarantees of personal liberty. If so, how could these delegates have omitted from the proposed constitution all such personal protections? Those demands set forth so fully and ably in the Declaration of Independence—the right of jury trial, the prevention of excessive bail, the rights to bear arms, to assemble peacefully, and freedom of the press—were nowhere referred to in the Constitution.

The final decision on uniformity of types of government became a single sentence in the Constitution:

The United States shall guarantee to every State in this Union a Republican form of government, and shall protect each of them against invasion, and, on application of the Legislature, or of the Executive (when the Legislature cannot be convened) against domestic violence.

Thus did we start with a national plan for national control of experimentations in state government.

This section of the Constitution may still be a battle ground for courts and lawyers during the coming decades. The Liberty League represents the monarchists of 1787. When the test comes, any judge or legislator can read into the section exactly what he pleases. There will be no right or wrong in the decisions, merely a question of which hands have the power to write the last words of the chapter.

Taxation

In the Congress, under the Articles of Confederation, each state paid the salaries of its own congressmen. Each state was allowed not less than two and not more than seven representatives. The number made slight difference, since each state had only one vote and the expenses of congressmen were borne by the states. The caliber of congressmen depreciated, possibly because of this imperfect machinery. To such nondescript congressmen there was not granted the power to tax but only the right to beseech money from the states.

We have seen that the need for an immediate national taxation power was essential to carry on the national government and the establishment of foreign credit. The delegates knew that France had been treated in a shabby fashion. Holland, the friend of every delegate, had obviously saved the United States from bankruptcy in Europe. It was generally known that the Dutch loan was obtained in the belief "that a Constitution then pending would be certainly, speedily, quietly and finally established and by that means put America into a permanent capacity to discharge with honor and punctuality all her engagements."

As far back as March 7, 1783, proposals were offered to amend the Articles of Confederation to establish a potent national treasury. The foreign creditors must be paid. No longer was reliance on state voluntary contributions sufficient.

In 1936 the Treasury Department estimated that, by a change in the tax law, the number of persons with incomes of over a million dollars a year would climb from 86 to 298. These 298 would have a total real income of 792 million dollars for the year 1936.

Although general agreement was easily obtained for a national tax economy the delegates were much more concerned with where the power for originating such legislation should reside. On what to us seems an unimportant issue—should revenue legislation originate in the lower or upper house—no less than five ballots were necessary before reaching a compromise. If the House alone could originate tax bills, then the congressmen, closer to the people because they were to be elected by the people and not by the legislatures, as was the case with senators, would control. But no matter where the origination of tax bills should reside, the delegates were also concerned with the extent to which the federal tax power might intrude on the states. The decision finally reached was predicated on facts and information which to us today must seem little less than ludicrous. A very circumspect delegate like Rufus King was sure that there could never be any temptation of the federal government to intrude on the states, particularly if the state debts were thrown into federal budgets, making a total of seventy millions. In the first place, his guess as to seventy millions was grossly inaccurate, but, beyond that, little did he dream that state and city debts would eventually rise to twenty billions of dollars.

Mercer of Maryland was frankly bewildered by the problem of national taxation and, although opposed to a national government having any general revenue powers, openly admitted that, because he had no other plan to propose, he would fall in line in favor of the federal government having power to place taxes directly on individuals. None of the delegates was prepared to discuss taxation in relation to the amounts of revenue needed, the methods of expenditure or the forms of collection. Many delegates felt that it would be a long while before substantial taxes would have to be levied. The great concern of all was over the threats and protests of state tax collectors who would lose their state jobs if the Constitution were to be adopted with such taxing powers. They were afraid that the state tax collectors would oppose ratification of the new national government unless provision were made that the federal employees could also hold state jobs. This overlapping of jobs, state and federal, was the impelling reason for requiring an oath of office for federal officeholders. Although Wilson declared even as to presidential oaths of office, "a good government" did not need them and a "bad one" could not or ought not be supported.

Grayson wrote to Monroe on May 29, 1787:

> N. Hampshire has not paid a shilling since peace and does not ever mean to pay on to all eternity; if it was attempted to tax the people for ye domestic debt 500 Shays would arise in a fortnight. In New York they pay well because they can do it by plundering New Jersey and Connecticut. Jersey will go great lengths from motives of revenge and interest.

To be sure, the foreign debt would have to be paid off, but obviously the delegates realized that this was no great problem, provided even a modest national tax program were inaugurated. In fact, by 1795 practically all of the foreign debt was paid off. The reason why the immediate tax program was to be worked out with such ease lay in the fact that in 1787 the nation possessed a vast national asset known as the National Lands. Without effort this wealth increased as the population grew and went to the West. In the very year of the convention five million acres of national lands, not even surveyed, had been sold at sixty cents an acre, payment to be made in national or state securities. At the very time that the convention was in session, realty speculation was rife. Free trips were being offered with great ballyhoo by land companies selling lots and acres to new settlers. They gave, as a bonus, free church and clergy services. Within a month after the convention closed, the existing Congress of the United States was deep in the land business. One hundred thousand acres of land were sold in the open market. Here was a treasure to be tapped for decades.

No modern methods of taxation entered the mind of any delegate. The delegates thought of taxes in terms of a levy on the number of windows in a home, a tax on carriages, a tax on lawyers or a tax on local auctions. Tariff and land sales would balance any possible budget. Little did they think that stamp taxes, so objectionable to the colonies, were soon to be adopted under the new constitution. The tariffs which the colonies had grumbled against for decades were to become the mainstay of the national treasury. The tax power was soon to be used as a method of fashioning a new society, curbing industrial practices and encouraging new forms of commerce. Even Madison thought that with "a country so vast the tax would have to be directed at industry. They can only tax through the medium of exports, imports and excises."

In the very first Congress of the United States our first national planned economy was to be adopted when we accepted a tariff program which was urged, not only for the purpose of revenue, but to encourage, and in fact to subsidize, merchants and manufacturers in the establishment and extension of needed businesses.

On this issue of the power to tax, as on every other one, the delegates were intent on granting to the national government all the power it needed in order to carry on a national program. That they did not foresee, in 1787, the social advantages of an income tax or a national inheritance tax should not be charged up to the discredit of the delegates. A fair interpretation, however, of their debates would lead any layman to believe that if those forms of collecting revenue had been in general use they would have granted to the national government the power to levy just such taxes, provided only that there was to be no discrimination in favor of certain states as against others. With the resolution of the basic problem of the method of electing congressmen and senators, the fears of delegates as to the abuse of the taxation power by the national government promptly evaporated.

In 1781 the Confederation had asked for power to levy a 5 per cent import duty to pay off the moneys loaned to the government to win the war. It was refused by the states. Such a tax, it was claimed, would "be repugnant to the Liberty of the United States as a full treasury would leave Congress independent of the states." Again, in 1783, Congress wanted to levy duties for a limited period of time. Again the states refused. Robert Morris wrote: "Talking to the states is like preaching to the dead."

But before 1787 the pressure of business competition between the states had educated many. On no single point did the new constitution peg a greater advance over the Articles of Confederation than by this full grant of taxation powers. And so freely was the power used that by 1836 the surplus of $28,101,644.91 in the Treasury of the United States was voted distributed to the states in proportion to representation in the Senate and House.

One controversy arising out of the wording of the tax clause in the Constitution portrays the degradation of legalisms. In the printed draft which the members had before them the clause read:

To lay and collect taxes, duties, imposts, and excises; to pay the debts and provide for the common defense and general welfare of the United States.

In the engrossed final draft the semicolon between "excises" and "to pay" was changed by the copyist to a comma. If there were a semicolon, Congress had broad powers of general welfare. If a comma, then the phrase "general welfare" was tied to taxes and in fact a limitation on the tax power. On this grammarian dispute, tomes have been written. Maybe we are being dragged into misery by a semicolon.

A National Commerce Power

These forty-two men were not dreamers. They knew that government did not arise full-grown just because words were put on paper. They knew that wealth arose from industry and labor and that even the idle landowners lived through human toil of others. But toil was of no avail without consumption. The conflicts between producers in their marketings were not limited to state boundaries. Madison, writing to Monroe, said of the states:

They can no more exercise this power separately than they could separately carry on war, or separately form treaties of alliance or commerce.

And later wrote:

As to the objection against entrusting Congress with a power over trade, drawn from the diversity of interests in the states, it may be answered: 1. that if this objection had been listened to, no confederation could have ever taken place among the States, 2. that if it ought now to be listened to, the power held by Congress of forming commercial treaties, by which nine States may indirectly dispose of the commerce of the residue, ought to be immediately revoked, 3. that the fact is that a case can scarcely be imagined in which it would be the interest of any two-thirds of the States to oppress the remaining one-third, 4. that the true question is whether the commercial interests of the States do not meet in more points than they differ. To me it is clear that they do; and if they do there are so many more reasons for, than against, submitting the commercial interest of each State to the direction and care of the Majority.

Commerce must flow with ease and be nationwide. The medium of payment must be uniform and stable. Against the foreign nations there must be a united trade front. The states were incompetent to handle bankruptcies. Only one commodity required separate treatment in the Constitution —the importation of Negro slaves.

The control and stability of commerce and trade called for the exercise of many powers by the new government. The delegates provided in the Constitution for regulation of commerce, regulation of coinage and money, bankruptcy relief for distressed commerce, the right to make foreign commercial treaties, grant monopolies to inventors, build roads and invite or stem immigration. Coupled together, these seven powers, vested in Congress, were to make this land one industrial and agicultural unit.

1. *Interstate Business*

At the end of the Revolution business of all kinds was in a chaotic condition. Importing and exporting relations with Europe had been greatly throttled. After each state in turn broke away from British control, separate resolutions or constitutional provisions were enacted under which "the internal concern of the colony resided in the respective colonial legislature."

As far back as 1782, Madison, appreciating the relationship between intercolonial and foreign commerce, wrote:

On a review of the doctrine of the Ninth Article of Confederation,
I believe the right of the State to prohibit in the present case the ex-
portation of her produce cannot be controverted. The States seem to
have reserved at least a right to subject foreigners to the same imposts
and prohibitions as their own citizens.

Throughout the debates the words *commerce* and *trade*
and *navigation* were often used interchangeably. The attitude in the convention toward industry and trade is difficult
to visualize because the mechanical and artificial processes
of economic production had scarcely started their march
toward the present times. Shortly before the convention
Jefferson received a letter from one of the delegates stating:

. . . to allow trade to regulate itself is to renounce the boon with
which Nature has favored our country, and if one set of men are to
be importers & exporters, another set to be carryers between the
mouths and heads of the rivers & a third retailers, trade, as it must
pass through so many hands all taking a profit, must in the end come
dearer to the people than if the simple plan should be continued which
unites these several branches in the same heads.

Many of the delegates agreed with Hamilton on at least
this much of his program—economic collision between states
must be prevented. Hamilton saw the issue as one of labor
supply:

With regard to scarcity of hands, the fact itself must be applied with
no small qualification to certain parts of the United States. There are
large districts which may be considered as pretty fully peopled; and
which, notwithstanding a continual drain for distant settlement, are
thickly interspersed with flourishing and increasing towns. If these
districts have not already reached the point at which the complaint of
scarcity of hands ceases, they are not remote from it, and are approaching fast towards it.

At the time of the convention, commerce as now was divided
into two major brackets—commerce with foreign countries,
and domestic commerce.

Pinckney enumerated the main commercial interests of the country: (1) fisheries and West Indian trade, which belonged to the New England states; (2) the middleman business of New York, which he thought would always urge free trade; (3) wheat and flour, the staples of New Jersey and Pennsylvania; (4) tobacco, the staple of Maryland and Virginia, and particularly of North Carolina; (5) rice and indigo, the staples of South Carolina and Georgia.

Pinckney foresaw that these specific forms of interstate commerce if not nationally regulated would be a source of oppressive regulation. Dickinson was confident that the danger of being injured by the power of the national government over interstate commerce was less than the danger of the national government being injured by the states.

The delegates were fully informed of the long line of universal demands for central control of commerce, the New Jersey Representations of 1778; the Witherspoon Resolutions of 1781, the action of the Pennsylvania general assembly which sent instructions to its delegates in Congress as far back as December 1783, that . . .

. . . this house is clearly of the opinion that the individual as well as the general good will best be consulted by relinquishing to Congress all the separate and independent powers in respect to commerce, now resting in the states.

In 1785 the Philadelphia town meeting, the Monroe committee report, the Rhode Island instructions to delegates all supported the same position. The Connecticut plan, the New Jersey plan, the Randolph and Rutledge drafts—all urged that the federal government rule where states were commercially incompetent, or wherever the harmony of the nation might be interrupted by the exercise of individual state trade legislation.

The powers which states had to destroy adjacent territories were, of course, different from the powers that exist today. But the difference is not a difference in effect. When the industrial era developed and cloth was made in factories instead of in homes, entire industries, as we know, were shifted hundreds of miles because of competitive industrial practices between states. The South has ruined the textile industry of New England with exactly the same precision and misery by child labor, low wages and long hours as if it had employed the weapons of 1787—embargoes, tariffs and taxation. Pinckney was correct. Tobacco of Connecticut and tobacco of Virginia are today staples crying for national treatment.

The delegates were aware of the need of centralized power over trade and navigation in industry, but they also appreciated the great power which the states were handing over to Congress. In the terms of 1787, the delegates knew that if the states were to relinquish their powers to create separate embargoes and tariff restrictions against other states, and Congress were to assume such powers, the particular methods of commercial control such as tariffs and embargoes would not disappear into thin air and evaporate. Congress was to exercise such powers. With this in mind, the debates were rather full as to whether the power of Congress over commerce should not be a special power used only on the vote of two thirds of the members of each house. Many delegates believed that there should be some check on the use of this power by a bare majority. But, as Randolph sagely noted, if this power rested in a two-thirds vote instead of in a mere majority of Congress, foreign nations would have the capacity "of instituting obstructive and retaliatory measures" in case a two-thirds vote was requisite and was unattainable. The final decision to allow commercial control by a mere majority of Congress emphasized the desire of the delegates to have this power clear and unrestricted.

Even those who feared centralization of power in other fields were in agreement on interstate commerce. Many were frank in admitting that the Southern people were "prejudiced against the Eastern states," but nevertheless believed that the overriding necessity of central control over commerce reconciled them to the national program.

The delegates appreciated that Congress, with this great power in its hands, would act only through the representatives of states and that protests of any few states would have an ample hearing in the halls of Congress. The very powers that the states had possessed to destroy each other economically were intended not to be annihilated in the Constitution but merely to be shifted to the states acting jointly in the new government. For this reason, as Madison wrote, "the regulation of commerce was in its nature indivisible." So great was this power that Congress was permitted to establish monopolies. James Wilson, later a chief justice of the Supreme Court, wrote: "As to mercantile monopolies they are already included in the power to regulate trade."

Repeatedly it was argued that it was unfair for any state to expect other states to bind themselves in a joint military defence in its behalf and still leave the other states "at the mercy for commercial advantage." The feared oppression of the uncommercial states was guarded against by giving this wide power over commerce to Congress.

Madison, writing to Jefferson, said:

The line of distinction between the power of regulating trade and that of drawing revenue from it which was once considered the banner to our liberties was found on fair discussion [in the convention] to be absolutely undefinable.

At one time Randolph went so far as to suggest that if the power over commerce were too broad the commercial power might be limited to the "mere and sole purpose of raising revenue." The defeat of this suggestion points clearly to generous and full use of the commerce power of Congress.

Thirty years after the document was written, James Madison reaffirmed this interpretation when he favored the establishment of an Undertaking Company which was to finance businesses located within separate states, a company resembling in many ways the Reconstruction Finance Corporation inaugurated by President Hoover.

In 1787 coastwise trade among the thirteen colonies amounted to about 185,000 tons a year. The cotton industry was being mechanized. But not till 1836 was the first strike of labor. The Journeymen Tailors, "insti-

gated by a set of vile foreignors (principally English)"
published "a most diabolical and inflammatory hand-
bill yesterday, headed by a coffin":

THE RICH AGAINST THE POOR!

Judge Edwards, the tool of the aristocracy, against the people!
Mechanics and working men! A deadly blow has been struck
at your liberty! The prize for which your Fathers fought has
been robbed from you! The freemen of the North are now
on a level with the slaves of the South; with no other privilege than labouring, that drones may fatten on your life blood!
Twenty of your brethren have been found guilty for presum-
ing to resist a reduction of their wages! and Judge Edwards
has charged an American jury, and agreeably to that charge
they have established the precedent that working men have
no right to regulate the price of labour, or, in other words, the
rich are the only judges of the wants of the poor man. On
Monday, June 6, 1836, at ten o'clock, these freemen are to
receive their sentence, to gratify the hellish appetites of the
aristocrats!

On Monday, the liberty of the workingmen will be in-
terred! Go! Go! Go! every freeman, every workingman, and
hear the hollow and the melancholy sound of the earth on the
coffin of equality! Let the courtroom, the City Hall, yea! the
whole park, be filled with *mourners;* but remember, offer no
violence to Judge Edwards, bend meekly, and receive the chain
wherewith you are to be bound! Keep the peace! Above all
things, keep the peace.

On this generous power in Congress over commerce Randolph, Paterson, Hamilton and Pinckney were in basic
agreement. Paterson's small-states plan read: "provided
that Congress be given power to pass acts for the regulation
of trade and commerce as well with foreign nations as with
each other." Such a provision is found in the report of the
Committee on Detail of August 6, but in slightly changed
verbiage: "to regulate commerce with foreign nations and
among the several states." When Madison was afraid there
might some day be a conflict between the state and federal
powers over commerce, Roger Sherman said:

The power of the United States to regulate trade being supreme can control interferences of the State regulations when such interferences happen; so that there is no danger to be apprehended from a concurrent jurisdiction.

Not one delegate disagreed with Hamilton's philosophy that it was easy to conceive

that cases may occur in which it would be beneficial to *all* the states to inaugurate or suppress a particular branch of trade, while it would be detrimental to either state to attempt it without the concurrence of the rest, and where the experiment would probably be left untried for want of concurrence.

In so far as there was trade, commerce or navigation, every control known to any state affecting any article flowing to another state was turned over to Congress for use by the delegates of the states elected to the House and the Senate.

The Articles of Confederation were inadequate to provide such a national control. This defect had to be cured. Delegate Morris stated:

Congress ought to have complete sovereignty in all but the mere municipal law of each state so as to alter irrevocably the present futile and senseless confederation which is incapable of preventing commercial destruction of one state by the other.

On September 4 an additional phrase was added so as to make sure that the clause was broad enough to give Congress the power to control trade with the Indian tribes. In such form it was unanimously adopted and became the interstate-commerce clause of the Constitution.

2. *Coinage*

The Constitution provided that Congress shall have the power:

To borrow money on the credit of the United States . . .

To coin money, regulate the value thereof, and of foreign coin, and fix the standard of weights and measures.

This was the answer to Daniel Shays and the inflationists. It was in reality a commerce clause. With each state determining its own currency, the tobacco growers of the Carolinas found it futile to ship their produce to Connecticut buyers for undetermined prices in skyrocketing dollars. Buyers and sellers could never reach prompt meetings of the mind when price meant so little compared to value of the currency used. No man would sell a farm for one hundred pounds if, at the time he was to receive his pounds, that amount of money would scarcely buy a new quill pen.

Congress was to be supreme in this field. Madison was much worried "about disorders of our coin and the want of uniformity in the denominations of the States." He suggested that the

Standard of Measure should be fixed by the length of a pendulum vibrating seconds at the equator and that the Standard of Weight should be a cubicle piece of gold of dimensions fixed by the Standard of Measure.

But not once did he or others bow abjectly to the so-called "gold standard." When the delegates discussed inflation they were not talking about printing more money than the amount of gold and silver held on deposit for the redemption of that money. There was no gold or silver sufficient to use as a basis for money. No delegate present would have been able to understand the money situation of the United States under Coolidge or Hoover, when the bankers caused an inflation of over sixty billion dollars. In 1933 they would have seen the government holding four billion dollars in gold, with inflation to the extent of two billions, in bills alone, since our demand gold bills exceeded six billions. In addition, in 1933, the bank deposits totaled fifty billion dollars, with checks being used the same as money. Not one ounce of gold was produced in this land until 1792. Not until 1792 was a coinage act passed, and that provided for coins of gold, silver and copper. Not until 1900 did Congress go onto a gold standard.

All that the delegates meant was that Congress should do everything necessary to have our currency stabilized in any way Congress saw fit and that no state or citizen should be permitted to take any steps to interfere with such a program. No one at the convention declared that gold shall forever be worth $20.67 an ounce or that about twenty-three grains of gold shall be put into each dollar. The figure later accepted for our gold standard might well have been $150,-000 per ounce or fifty grains per dollar.

The Constitution—to its credit—doesn't even mention gold. It called for uniformity, without which commerce could not flourish. And today, under this broad coinage commerce power, if the judges thought it wise, Congress might delegate to the Federal Reserve Board the power to give preferential credits to those commercial borrowers who abide by decent living standards of hours and pay for their workers. Thus might the coinage power, which includes banking, be used to stabilize our industries.

3. *Bankruptcy*

A necessary commercial device in a capitalist society is some method of periodically washing up private debts. In a profit-motivated civilization most long-term debts are never repaid. They are just adjourned or, in polite banking language, refunded. Year in and year out individuals and companies need relief from obligations.

The delegates were not entirely happy about the debtors' prisons which dotted the landscape. In many towns Quakers, refusing to pay taxes to carry on Protestant churches, lived and died in jails. Although those particular debtors aroused no great sympathy in the convention, and although debtors' prisons were not to be, and are not yet, abolished, the convention did want some provision for financial absolution for commerce. Inflation and depressions were unavoidable. Mere capricious avoidance of debt was not to be permitted, but wisely they set up a federal bankruptcy provision which has probably been used to a greater degree than any other portion of the Constitution. In fact today the federal courts are the biggest business managers in the world. They have run during the past years a goodly portion of our railroads, a fair amount of the motion-picture industry, cosmetic fac-

tories, chain stores, coal mines; in fact, a part of every trade
and industry in the land. This federal bankruptcy provision
—a plan by which the courts would take over the assets of
an individual or industry, continue to run the enterprise if
it thought wise, and then distribute to the creditors their fair
share in payment of the indebtedness—is the backlog of the
regulation of interstate commerce.

4. *Foreign Commerce*

The foreign commerce which was foremost in the minds
of the delegates was that which flowed between the colonies
and the West Indies. Rutledge announced that the West
Indian trade was the great object, and a navigation act was
necessary for obtaining it.

Foreign commerce, in addition to being a navigation
problem, was also thought of in terms of foreign treaties
and import taxation. Treaties and tariffs were part and par-
cel of the same objective. It is interesting to note that the
words which give Congress the power over foreign commerce are identical with those used for interstate commerce.
It is the power to "regulate." The method of regulating
foreign commerce was simple—either a treaty, or a tax at
the port of entry, or a complete bar to importation. By the
latter two devices Congress was enabled to exclude, for all
practical purposes, gloves from France, cotton goods from
England or rice from China. The domestic interstate sugar
industry has been regulated with exactness by the shifting
tariff laws. By tariff acts the virtual exclusion of any commodity—a regulation—is often based on lower labor standards in foreign nations. The use of child labor and the continuance in a distant land of pay so low as to be virtual
peonage have always been factors in the regulation of foreign commerce. By foreign treaties commerce in this land
was to be regulated, controlled, encouraged or destroyed.

5. *Patents*

Congress was to issue patents and copyright monopolies.
In 1800 two hundred and sixty-eight patents were issued.

In 1935 fifty-six thousand were issued. The first copyright for a book was for the *Philadelphia Spelling Book,* June 9, 1790, by John Barry.

The theory of the patent is to encourage inventions by the grant of a monopoly. From pine knot to candle, to lamp, to gas, to electricity, the industrial and commercial genius of man is recorded in these monopolies. Although most states still have patent laws and issue state patents, this function was and still is essentially an interstate one. No one at the convention thought that new inventions might mean misery in a later, undreamed-of industrial era. But Congress was given the power to issue or not to issue patents and copyrights.

It might even use this power today as a mechanical governor to determine the degree to which science must be retarded because of our industrial and judicial stupidities. Possibly, if the judges thought well of it, Congress could regulate interstate commerce by providing that patents may only issue if the user agrees to a minimum wage and such hours and working conditions as Congress may provide from time to time. Most of the large industries are dependent on patent monopolies. Congress, a half-century ago, provided that copyrights shall issue only for writings which meet a standard thought by Congress not to be hurtful to the people of the land. Interstate commerce might be likewise regulated through the power to issue or withhold patents.

6.   Post Roads

The right to establish post offices and post roads cannot be said to be unrelated to the flow of interstate business. Congress was empowered to build roads. For what conceivable purpose did the delegates want Congress to lay a road which would be entirely within one single state, except for interstate commercial purposes? Commerce and social intercourse within a state would not reasonably call for funds collected from other states to build roads of communication, but the delegates were clear in their desire for a national road program.

7. *Immigration and Slavery*

This section of the Constitution was directed specifically at the slave question. Not until seventy-five years after the Constitution was drawn was this nation to be deeply concerned with the problem of freeing the Negroes. At the convention few were so audacious as to urge seriously that our new Constitution free the slaves either in 1787 or at any later date. To the delegates the problem was simple and easy of solution. Rutledge declared: "Religion and humanity have nothing to do with the slave question." There was little division in opinion. The lives of five hundred thousand black men were handled as an importation traffic problem.

> *Robert (called "King") Carter left an estate of 300,-*
> *000 acres, 10,000 pounds, and 1,000 Negroes. Wash-*
> *ington had 317 slaves. One newspaper advertisement*
> *read:*

> To be sold, a young healthy negro fellow who has been used to wait on a gentleman and plays extremely well on the French horn.

To be sure, the New Englanders were opposed to slavery in theory, and Ellsworth of Connecticut, the delegate who most nearly represented our modern labor point of view, realizing that the question of slavery was not before the convention, philosophized that "as the population increases, poor laborers will be as plentiful as slaves and the pressure of the unemployed would determine the ultimate solution." Jefferson around this time wrote:

The whole commerce between master and slave is a perpetual exercise of the most boisterous passions, the most unremitting despotism on the one part, and degrading submissions on the other. Our children see this and learn to imitate it. . . . Thus nursed, educated and daily exercised in tyranny . . . the man must be a prodigy who can retain his manners and morals undepraved.

Pinckney of South Carolina then threatened the assemblage. He pointed out that no constitution which prevented importation of slaves would ever receive the approval of the Southern states. He went further and defended the institution of slavery by declaring: "In all ages one half of mankind have been slaves." If importation had been stopped immediately, at least two states would have failed to join the Union.

It soon became apparent that no one seriously wanted to discuss the freeing of the slaves. How then could the increase be curbed? The question of slavery and navigation was referred to a special committee. At this very time the Western settlers were calling for more slaves and Virginia was prospering in the business of breeding and jobbing black men. In vain did George Mason point out that "the poor despise labor when performed by slaves," and even a Northern delegate openly deplored "the lust for gain of the northeastern merchants" which had "caused them to embark on the slave trade."

Randolph suggested that there would be a revolt of the Quakers if slavery were not somewhat restrained. Luther Martin saw a national weakening if importation was permitted, because "slaves weakened one part of the union which another part was bound to protect."

The committee's report was accepted with obvious good will. Congress was empowered to pass a navigation act under its general commerce powers, but Congress could not prohibit the importation of slaves until after 1808. Another whip was suggested—social control by taxation. The delegates thought that the taxing power should be used to throttle the importation of Negroes. Ten dollars a head on Negroes imported was the figure suggested.

There is no part of the constitutional debates which shows more clearly the inability of these wise men to foresee the course of history. No one delegate foresaw that within a few decades his grandchildren would be killing the grandchildren of some other delegate because of this very issue.

The delegates were handling a practical problem in the year 1787. Looking into the distant future, they thought they could see as far off as 1808. Having no possible human conception of a place now called Missouri, they could not dream that Congress would enact, in 1820, a statute limiting slavery in those Western lands. No one pictured a man named Scott, slave in Missouri, taken to free Illinois and then to the Western Territory and then back to Missouri, and a lawsuit involving this Negro—a lawsuit which helped propel us into a civil war.

The delegates, facing the facts of their time, believed that the slavery issue could be handled by the use of three powers granted to Congress: taxation, navigation and interstate commerce. That the delegates were ready and willing to give to the senators and congressmen the complete power to treat with slavery and immigration after 1808 is beyond dispute. On this power Congress has rested its immigration laws. By those laws trade and commerce were aided or discouraged. Did business need more cheap foreign labor or not? Each immigration act, whether an open door or a quota exclusion act, was a medium for regulating, in its broader sense, interstate commerce. Once more we find the clearest intention to give vitality to the national instrument. A national program was conceived to control our national labor supply for commerce.

The four points that were mentioned at the beginning of this chapter were obviously not unrelated to each other. The delegates, in selecting these four major problems for peculiar attention, failed to sense the temper of the people. Sitting secure in Philadelphia, most of the forty-two framers of the Constitution were totally unaware of the insistent public demand for another basic relief: a guarantee of personal liberty. How far the convention was out of tune on this score with its own times did not become evident to the delegates until after the convention disbanded.

CHAPTER XIII

The Three Great Departments and the Right to Change

THE POWERS OF CONGRESS over our national life were set forth in wide spacious terms. Commerce in the dictionaries of 1787 was a synonym for trade, industry, business. Coinage implied banking and control of all currency and money. Each state, feeling that it would be fully protected in the halls of Congress, felt no concern over the extent of the use of the powers delegated by the states to Congress. Congress was given even the power to allow the states to have separate tariffs on imports or exports.

Much more time in the convention was granted to the discussion of the structure of the federal government than to powers of Congress. Three departments were agreed upon. But the conflict in the convention was not one of capacity of each department, the separate functions of the Court or the president or Congress, so much as the degree to which the common people were to participate in government. Were the mobs to elect the legislators, the president, the judges? How could the power be kept in the control of the wealthy, the successful, the aristocrats? The delegates—all of the same class of society, prosperous and literate and possessing the privilege of voting and holding office—were not in favor of a gradual spread of democracy. Most of them had nothing but disdain for the common people. Hamilton represented those who feared the power of the masses, and he never failed to preach: Let's copy England; that's the kind of government we want.

Madison, the leader of the opposition, foresaw the beginning of the class struggle and the futility of having a government remote from popular control. During the debates he enunciated a philosophy to which he adhered as late as 1829:

And it is a lot of humanity that of this surplus a large proportion is necessarily reduced by a competition for employment to wages which afford them the bare necessaries of life. What is to be done with this unfavored class of the community? If it be, on one hand, unsafe to admit them to a full share of political power, it must be recollected, on the other, that it cannot be expedient to rest a Republican Govt. on a portion of the society having a numerical and physical force excluded from, and liable to be turned against it; and which could lead to a standing military force, dangerous to all parties and to liberty itself.

The problem raised in the Hamilton–Madison clash of political philosophy was resolved by the conclusions reached on the methods of selecting executive, legislative and judicial branches of the government and on the ultimate decisions as to length of terms of office, eligibility to re-election and powers of each branch.

The Articles of Confederation had combined in the Congress alone all of the executive, judicial and legislative powers. Delegates were to be elected by the state legislatures annually. There was no president, and the Supreme Court was only an informal circuit-riding body of arbiters operating as a part of Congress. After 1778 it was difficult to get together a quorum of the Congress to transact business, and obviously still more difficult to set up the necessary officials to execute the decisions reached by Congress.

The English revolution of 1688 had established the principle that legislation could be enacted only by Parliament, and the Act of 1701 had removed judges from the king's exclusive control by providing Parliament with the power of removal in case of bad behavior. After 1748 the colleges in the colonies received outlines of the novel ideas of one Montesquieu, a French political theorist, who had urged the division of the state into three powers—executive, legislative and judicial.

Although the convention readily accepted the three-functional government idea, the duties and powers of each

were not discussed with any amount of clarity. They knew
that government does not operate itself; it is operated by
men.

The President

Many delegates expressed great fear that the president
of the United States would eventually become a dictator.
To prevent such occurrence, there was widespread support,
as we have seen, for plural presidents. But as the minds of
the delegates concentrated on the selection of a single president, the debates shifted to the length of office for which
such president should be chosen.

Martin moved for an eleven-year presidential term.
Gerry suggested fifteen years, and King raised it to twenty.
A delegate arose to suggest that twenty years was the
median life of princes. Davie thought it was too long and
suggested eight years. Mason referred to the fact that the
parliamentary term in England was seven, and the convention, by a vote of seven to two, adopted the seven-year term
of office. The seven-year term was again readopted by a
vote of seven to three, with Massachusetts not on the floor
and the Virginia delegates divided two to two, with Randolph not in attendance.

On July 19 the six-year term was adopted by a vote of
nine to one, and Ellsworth debated in slangwise fashion that
"there will always be outs as well as ins."

The length of term of the president's office was tied up
with the question of his eligibility for re-election. Re-
eligibility was finally permitted only because the term of
office was reduced by compromise to four years and because
many delegates believed that "if you shut the civil road to
glory, the president may be compelled to seek it by the
sword." But before the four-year term was adopted, life
tenure for the president received lengthy consideration. A
life term might well have been adopted had there not been
a general feeling that if a president were elected for life
from one of the three large states there might be a disturb-
ance to the balance of power between the various states. If
the delegates had had vision enough to foresee forty-eight

states and to appreciate that what was large in those days is small today, the term of the president's office might have been fixed either for life or at least for twenty years, even though Mason consistently argued that a life term for the president "would be an easy step to a hereditary monarchy."

But even after the delegates had voted repeatedly and inconsistently on the term of office for the president, they were still sorely troubled as to the method of electing him. The New Jersey plan as well as the Randolph plan suggested that Congress elect the president. The advantage of such procedure was that the president would be thrice removed from the people. In answer to this proposal it was argued that the executive should be independent of the legislature and, in fact, there appeared to the delegates to be more reason for the independence of the executive than for the independence of the judiciary. Eleven different roll calls were needed to decide the method of electing the president. At one time the popular election of the president was agreed to by a vote of nine states to one, Pennsylvania alone in the negative. On reconsideration of this vote the proposal was defeated by Wilson's prolonged argument when he proved to the satisfaction of the delegates that popular election had not worked successfully in Poland.

At one time in the convention the delegates had defeated every proposal submitted for the election of a president. The plans for the election of the president by the people directly or for the election of the president by electors chosen by the people had both been discarded. Wilson then urged that the president be elected in a fashion similar to the election of a Pope of the Roman Catholic Church. He outlined his plan in detail as follows:

The Executive is to be elected for six years by a small number, not more than fifteen of the National Legislature, to be drawn from it, not by ballot, but by lot and who shall retire immediately and make the selection without separating. By this mode intrigue would be avoided in the first instance, and the dependence would be diminished.

No matter how the president was to be chosen, no matter what length of term was to be granted to him, no matter how the question of eligibility of a second election was to be determined, many delegates supported the position of Franklin and Hamilton when they urged that the president should act without salary.

Madison favored the removal of the profit motive by stating that "in all cases of public service the less of profit the greater the honor."

> *Monroe left the White House insolvent, spent the balance of his life in absolute poverty; Madison's and Jefferson's estates were overburdened with debts.*

These were rich men, and few of them foresaw that the failure to give compensation to governmental officials would prevent poor people from holding office. As they viewed life, there were no poor people competent to hold office.

The final decision of the delegates indicated, in the first place, the necessity of preventing a monarchy by shortening the term of office of the president; in the second place, the need for the right of re-election to prevent an existing president from keeping power by the use of the sword; and in the third place, the avoidance of the question of compensation, by leaving the matter to Congress in the future.

During these very debates the suggestion was made that the value of the dollar would fluctuate in time and that dollars were myths if unrelated to the price of wheat, cloth and shoes. Morris suggested that "the state of society may alter as well as the value of money in which event wheat would not be a sound basis." The salary question was left open with the clear intimation that a fluctuating commodity dollar might in time be found advisable for general use. But beyond all these considerations the delegates wanted to make sure that the people of the land would have no direct control over the election of a president. Even though only a few people had the right to vote, and even though that vote was limited to the rich, the convention agreed that the selection of the president should be removed from the direct control of the people.

And thus we find the establishment in the Constitution of

a provision for the election of the president once removed from the people by the injection, between the people and the president, of a group of persons to be known as the "Electoral College." It did not take long to prove that this provision was a device unwise and unworkable. As provided in the Constitution, the person receiving the highest number of votes was to be elected president, and the candidate with the second highest number of votes would be vice-president. Of course there were no political parties in those days; political thinking was based on geographical locations and economic interests, not yet made articulate through party organizations. If we had continued the system laid down by our Founding Fathers, Alfred M. Landon would have been vice-president in 1937.

By 1804 an amendment to the Constitution was passed to correct this now obvious stupidity. But even this amendment was squeezed through by the narrowest possible vote. This amendment to the Constitution, requiring a two-thirds vote in the House and the Senate and a three-fourths vote of the states, passed the Senate by a vote of only twenty-two to ten, and the House by a bare vote of eighty-three to forty-two, thus requiring the vote of the Speaker of the House to give the required two thirds. When the amendment was put up to the states, Connecticut, Delaware, New Hampshire and Massachusetts rejected it.

Thus we see that by chance and compromise the four-year term with re-eligibility for election was established; by the slimmest shift of votes the president of the United States might today be elected for a six-, seven- or ten-year term. Thus we see that the present simple system of having a president and vice-president in agreement as to political issues never occurred to the Founding Fathers as a wise precaution. Today, if anyone proposed that the president of the United States should not be selected by the people but by a system of checks on the people through a legitimate and real electoral college, the proposal would gain little support. We have in fact nullified the significance of the electoral college.

Nevertheless the system of our day is still quite far from

pure democracy. We can repeat the pattern of Andrew Jackson getting more electoral votes than Adams in 1824 and still not being elected president. In 1932, 28,756 votes in Nevada counted as three electoral votes for Roosevelt, while 1,937,963 votes in New York for Hoover counted not at all for Hoover in the electoral college.

Twice already the result would have been different if we had counted votes rather than pluralities in each state. Tilden in 1876 would have been seated instead of Hayes, and in 1888 Cleveland would have taken the place of Harrison. Wilson, in 1912, received only 42 per cent of the popular vote but practically all—82 per cent—of the electoral vote.

John Adams, to be the first vice-president and later a president, arranged by intermarriage to unite his family with the royal house of Great Britain, the bridegroom to be king of America. Washington, in white clothing as a sign of conciliation, a sort of flag of truce, called on Adams and objected. Adams rebuffed him.

The Constitution says little about the president's powers. He was to be the commander of the army and navy, to grant pardons, and beyond that the Constitution gives him specifically no powers, only a duty to consult his cabinet and keep the Congress informed as to the state of the nation. He was to nominate, but not appoint, certain judges and ambassadors, but even that power under the Constitution may be taken from the president by Congress and vested in the heads of departments (nowhere enumerated in the Constitution) or even in the courts of law. In other words, Congress could tomorrow empower the Supreme Court or some other court of law to nominate the local postmasters in Uniontown, Alabama; Los Angeles, California; or Williamstown, Massachusetts.

The Congress

Although the method of selection of a president and his term of office were matters of great concern to the dele-

gates, they all realized that the seat of power lay in the legislature. In the main, just as the delegates wanted to keep
the people from having power in the selection of the president, so also they wanted the legislators removed from the
will of the people. There was a very strong drive in favor
of having the United States senators elected by the congressmen. Many delegates felt that an economic filter would
be established by such a device. In certain quarters it was
urged that the congressmen should be elected by the state
legislators. Some delegates went so far as to urge that the
state legislature should not select the congressmen but that
the congressmen should be selected by the members of the
higher house in each state. It must be recalled that in most
states, to be elected to the senate—the higher house—required the possession of very substantial acreage or wealth.

The system now known as checks and balances was not
really one which related to checks and balances between the
president and the Congress, but was rather a system of
checks against the wishes of the population.

If the congressmen or senators were to be elected by the
people, what formula was to be adopted to define "the people"? Should they count heads, or area, or wealth?

All of the territorial jealousies reappeared during this
discussion. Wilson and others did not want the states swal-
lowed up. Hamilton wanted to destroy the states. King injected the idea that the states had never really been
sovereign in respect to making war or peace. At one time
during these discussions the word *national* was stricken out
of the Randolph plan, clearly implying that all hope had
been lost for a national government. But even Randolph
was in doubt as to how congressmen and senators should be
selected. One delegate saw a distinction between Senate and
House:

The Senate will be detained longer from home, will be obliged to
move their families, and in time of war perhaps to sit constantly.
Their allowance should certainly be higher.

It must be remembered that as far back as September 6,
1774, when under the Confederation a provision was made

that each colony was to have one vote, the resolution providing for state per-capita representation contained the following rider:

. . . The Congress not being possessed of or at present being able to
procure material for ascertaining the importance of each colony.

When Randolph and others at the Philadelphia convention urged that both houses should be elected on the basis
either of wealth or of free inhabitants, they were quite convinced that wealth and population traveled together. But if
we shifted our election system from population to wealth
today the actual representation at present in the House of
Representatives would be changed as follows: Virginia
would lose two congressmen; Georgia, seven; North Carolina and South Carolina, five each; while New York would
grow from forty-three to seventy-seven; Pennsylvania, from
thirty-six to forty-four; Massachusetts, from sixteen to
twenty-five, and of the thirteen original states Delaware
alone would remain with its one congressman unvaried.

The large-state-small-state compromise resulting in two
houses had not answered the problem of how each state
should elect its senators or representatives. Again great heat
developed. The delegates from Delaware held credentials
forbidding them to vote for any amendment to the Articles
of Confederation which would create representation on the
basis of wealth or population. Each state must forever have
the same voting power in Congress granted to each other
state.

Assuming that the legislature of each state would pick its
own two senators, the aristocrats at the convention were
confident that the senators of each state rather than the
assemblies would dictate such selections. Then true bewilderment was evident. Higher mathematics were involved in
the debates on the question of electing the members of the
House of Representatives. How big a House did we want?
Should it not be small enough to transact business?

*At the time of the convention six states contained four
fifths of the population. Many delegates were sure*

Congress would not meet every year, for the only acts of national importance would be "commerce and revenue" and "when these were once settled alterations would be rarely necessary and easily made."

The delegates took out their quill pens and started to figure. After guessing and logrolling had continued for many sessions, a schedule was adopted: one congressman for no less than 30,000 population, counting slaves at five to three, with Congress instructed to organize a census every ten years.

In the meantime the votes in the House were set forth in the Constitution by guessing at population figures. The number of congressmen was apportioned none too well, for by 1793 the total in Congress grew from sixty-five to a hundred and five.

As Fixed in Constitution		*As Determined by First Census*
New Hampshire	3	4
Massachusetts	8	14
Rhode Island and Provdence Plantations	1	2
Connecticut	5	7
New York	6	10
New Jersey	4	5
Pennsylvania	8	13
Delaware	1	1
Maryland	6	8
Virginia	10	19
North Carolina	5	10
South Carolina	5	6
Georgia	3	2
Vermont	—	2
Kentucky	—	2
Total	65	105

After these adjustments were once adopted, many of the delegates lost interest in the convention. No more speeches were heard from Bedford. Brearley was silent for weeks, and Paterson disappeared from the scene. But even after it was decided that the Senate should be representative of the states as such, the delegates still quarreled over whether the senators from a particular state should vote as members or as a state, and Martin continued to debate whether the two senators from a single state should not be compelled to vote in unison or not vote at all.

The net result of the convention was to prevent the popular will of the people controlling national legislation. Even today, if an overwhelming proportion of the people of the land want Congress to fix the hours of labor or the minimum of wages to be paid, a few senators from sparsely populated states can block the move. Legislation supported by 80 million of the 120 million people in this land can be defeated by the senators in Congress representing the other 40 million people. This was the check the Founding Fathers sought and obtained. But after this check was agreed upon, few if any of the delegates were worried about the extent of the congressional power. If Congress did go too far to override the wishes even of a small minority, the president could always exercise his veto. Then two thirds of the senators would have to vote against the president.

The Court

In the index to the debates at the Constitutional Convention less than half a column out of forty-four pages of references directs a reader to the subject of the Supreme Court. Its power was scarcely mentioned.

Madison wrote, shortly after the Convention closed:

As the Courts are generally the last in making ye decision it results to them by refusing or not refusing to execute a law to stamp it with its final character. This makes the Judiciary Department paramount in fact to the Legislature, which was never intended and never can be proper.

The delegates were fully aware of a judicial decree in 1780 in New Jersey, where the court endeavored to invalidate a legislative enactment. Just as the delegates were gathering, North Carolina's highest court declared that the elected legislators could not pass an act which would repeal or alter the constitution of the state because if they do this, they would at the same time destroy their own existence as a legislature and dissolve the government thereby established. In Rhode Island the people had made short shrift of judges who tried to step on legislative powers.

That the new constitution was to be supreme over state legislators and courts within certain fields was definitely in the minds of all. To this end suggestions were made that Congress itself should be allowed to veto all state legislation. Congress was to be the judiciary as to state legislation. Twice it was unanimously voted that Congress could nullify state legislation. In fact the main objection to such a plan was made clear when it was pointed out that the delays of mail would create a void of many weeks before an act passed in far-off Georgia would be reviewed in Philadelphia and then returned, approved or vetoed, to Georgia.

Air-mail round trip to Georgia from Washington, 1936, in less than one day.

Madison consistently urged that the executive and the Supreme Court should jointly have the veto or revision power over all legislation, with two provisos: (1) that if either the president or the Supreme Court should disagree with Congress such veto could be wiped out by a two-thirds vote of Congress; (2) if the president and the Supreme Court should both veto an act of Congress, then three fourths of Congress would be required to override these two other arms of the government.

On the motion to give the judges this great power the vote was three states for, three states against, two states divided and one state not voting. New Hampshire delegates had not yet appeared at the convention. The convention rejected this proposal in part because many delegates felt that the judiciary should not enter into legislative matters so early in the stages of enactment. Madison's plan was in effect a form of modified advisory judicial opinion such as some states have in use today.

The following seems to be the nub: No delegate believed that Congress was to act untrammeled as it wished. For example, it was not to have the power to pass an act lengthening the term of the president's office beyond that contained in the instrument, or extending terms of office of congressmen, even though the delegates knew that in England the Parliament, in 1716, had extended its own life for an additional four years. But no delegate conceived of the Court having the power to override an act of Congress regulating the economic welfare of the nation.

No one objected to the Court having the final power on disputes between states, but "as to its cognizance of disputes between citizens of different states many delegates suggested that it was a matter of slight importance which might be left to the State Courts." But to make the Supreme Court anything but a "department" of the government was not proposed by a single delegate. Jefferson was to write:

No, no, my countrymen. The opinion which gives to the judge the right to decide what laws are constitutional and what are not . . . makes the judiciary a despotic branch. The Constitution has erected no such single tribunal, that to whatever hands confided . . . its members would become despots.

The problems of interstate commerce, taxation, addition of new states, fixing up boundaries, making treaties and standardizing currency were the objectives of the government. No legal disputes were in sight on these subjects except on boundaries.

The powers of the Supreme Court were quite undefined. After much debate it was agreed that there should be only one supreme court. Many delegates urged several supreme courts because of the distances the judges would have to travel if there were only one court. The number of judges was left to Congress. Congress was empowered to create inferior courts and to decide just what cases might go on appeal to the Supreme Court. Thus tomorrow Congress could abolish all lower federal courts and take away from the Supreme Court all rights to hear appeals, with but one exception—the Supreme Court under the Constitution was to possess the right to hear cases involving either foreign ministers or any state of the Union. But even this jumbled machinery was found quite objectionable within six years of the adoption of the Constitution, and by an amendment, the Eleventh, the Supreme Court was deprived of hearing cases when either a citizen or an alien sued any state of the Union. For a full hundred years there was no right of appeal to the Supreme Court in criminal cases. Until 1889 even cases of life or death could only be argued in that court upon a certificate of division of opinion.

A century and a half after the convention, congressmen representing more than three quarters of the American people enacted legislation for the general welfare; and the Supreme Court, by a vote of five to four, announced to the American people that the legislation was void. The true irony of such a procedure lies in the fact that the deciding jurist, the ninth man, holding the final power in many such decisions, only a short time before was just one more senator with one vote among ninety-eight. On the bench he becomes an economic god.

For nearly a century the Supreme Court behaved like a department of the government. It acted as if there were intended to be three equal departments. Twice and only twice during that period the judges broke through the traces. On two occasions when litigants were before the Court the judges wrote long political tracts in favor of the judicial power to veto acts of Congress. But in those two cases the remarks of the judges were off the record and the actual decisions in those cases did not invalidate any act of Congress. Not until after the Civil War did the Supreme Court take on its supremacy over all other governmental officials, elected or appointed. In mounting numbers of cases since the turn of the century the judges of this highest court have voided acts of Congress.

Franklin, Bedford, Mercer, Dickinson, Charles Pinckney and other delegates resented any suggestion that the Court should ever have such a power. Gerry, King, James

Wilson and Luther Martin were quite cynical, foreseeing that the Court would assume the power whether it was intended or not.

Madison, appreciating the dilemma, proposed the only practical answer to a Congress with power to discard the provisions of the Constitution or a court overriding the Congress. His plan still makes real sense.

The Amending Process

The Articles of Confederation could be amended only by a unanimous vote. The constitution of New York had, as the delegates knew, a provision for a "council of revision" to prevent fluctuating and undigested laws, a kind of veto mechanism. The Massachusetts constitution provided that it could not be altered until 1790, but it was noted that the sending of delegates to the convention by Massachusetts was in itself a negation of that adamant clause. Other colonies had tried provisions for periodic reconsideration of their constitutions.

The amending clause selected by the convention was dictated in part by the failure to procure unanimity at the convention on any single subject. Randolph arose to declare:

If the last Article of the Confederation is to be pursued the unanimous concurrence of the States will be necessary. But will anyone say, that all the States are to suffer themselves to be ruined, if Rhode Island should persist in her opposition to general measures?

The delegates thought that twelve states might eventually join the new nation. If twelve signed up, the game would begin. They decided that, to amend the document, eight of the twelve states would have to agree, and in the usual method Congress would have to agree also, by a two-thirds vote. There were some delegates who queried: What would happen if there should be as many as fifteen states? But on the method of amending there was no wide dispute or lengthy argument. With only a dozen states the scheme they devised for procuring amendments seemed workable and fair. With forty-eight states it has become cumbersome and unresponsive.

> *In France constitutional laws are amended by the absolute majority of the houses. The Constitution of Canada can be amended by Parliament at Westminster; the Constitution of Australia is amended only after referendum in which a majority of electors in a majority of states have approved of the amendment. The Irish Free State constitution after a preliminary period of sixteen years is amendable by a majority of the electors at referendum. The British Parliament can do as De Lolme once said: "anything except make a man unto a woman and a woman unto a man."*

CHAPTER XIV

A Close Shave

WHEN THE CONSTITUTIONAL CONVENTION adjourned, the report, with a letter from George Washington, was sent over to the Congress of the Confederation then sitting in New York City. The General's letter made clear that the document was far from perfect. It did not express the full desire of any single delegate. There were compromises and concessions in every phrase.

When the delegates broke the seal of secrecy on September 17, 1787, the members of Congress sitting a hundred miles away in New York City had no idea what to expect. There was a general feeling that the existing Congress would be wiped out. But everyone who believed in law and order had a right to expect that the new document would suggest only a few amendments, which in turn would be acted on by Congress and then in turn be submitted to the legislatures of the thirteen states. There had been no public intimation that the Constitutional Convention was going to be so radical as to suggest an entire new form of government.

When the new instrument was read, the main bewilderment arose not because of its contents but because the convention had the gall to suggest that neither the old Congress nor the state legislatures were important. The instrument must be submitted to the people. The deputies in Philadelphia had been acute enough to realize that submission to the legislators would be futile. "Whose opposition," asked Randolph, "will be most likely executed against the system?" Had several thousand burgesses, senators, councilmen or assemblymen been allowed to ratify or reject the new Constitution, they would naturally have voted against this new machinery which would spell loss of salaries, loss of jobs and loss of powers. And so, in clear violation of the law the existing Congress allowed the convention in Philadelphia to run away with the show. What was to be said for this anarchistic provision in the proposed new constitution—acceptance to be effective when any nine of the thirteen states had ratified?

A few mossbacked lawyers sitting at the New York City Bar Association shook their wigs and wept, "It's unconstitutional." No doubt some local wag interjected: "Don't go back on the Founding Fathers of 1776." But the practical men of the day were concerned only with their hopes of getting even nine states to accept the instrument. If nine came in, pressure would bring the others. The dire need for union, the prevention of destructive interstate competitive business practices, were to be used to drive the others into line. Everyone knew that this would not be a union by volition. The states had to be cajoled or coerced.

The daring of the convention in its proposals for ratification can only be appraised by a supposititious analogy in our day.

Let us assume that a convention of tax commissioners, meeting annually and sent by state legislatures at state expense to discuss amending the taxing powers of the federal government, were to work out in 1936 a new federal constitution. Suppose then that this convention proposed, not an additional amendment or two to the present constitution, but an entire new document. Suppose, then, it forwarded this document to the states and, in total disregard of the present provisions for amending the federal constitution, suggested that the new constitution be adopted, not by a vote of Congress and of three fourths of the states, but by a majority vote of all the people of all the states.

Suppose that the new constitution were so ratified. We would have a comparative analogy to the scrapping of the first constitution of the United States, called the Articles of Confederation. The Constitutional Convention of 1787 did not even decently bury the old corpse. Nowhere was there a polite reference to the old instrument being superseded. It was just completely disregarded. And so to the people, instead of to the legislatures, the Constitution was submitted in 1787.

We have seen how the franchise for electing legislatures was severely limited in practically every state in 1787. If these restrictions were all that acted contra-democracy in the voting on ratification of the new constitution, we might rest with the declaration that a few rich people voted to send delegates to the state conventions on ratification and that in time these delegates approved the document. But, beyond that, it is now evident that the population as a whole was quite ignorant of what was being considered. Few copies of the proposed constitution were printed in any state, and the discussions carried on in the ninety-three newspapers seldom set forth the specific words of any of the now debatable clauses.

The agrarian people of the countryside were completely in the dark. Only four hundred copies of the Constitution were ordered printed in New Hampshire. "There was not a grammar, geography or history of any kind at the time when the Constitution had been adopted," writes a leading citizen of Ridgefield, Connecticut. In many towns no meetings were held prior to election of delegates to state ratification conventions. Not on any uniform date were the elections held, even in any one state. New York was the only state which permitted manhood suffrage for the election to its Poughkeepsie convention on ratification, and this false generosity in New York was due to the feeling that the large patroons controlled the votes of all their servants and tenants. Elsewhere the property tests necessary for the election of legislators were applied. At least two thirds of all adult males were thus excluded from voting by these property tests.

But voting had never been a popular pastime. It was really not a cherished privilege. In Connecticut, with a population of 200,000, fewer than 3,500 men bothered to vote. In Massachusetts, 17 per cent of the population was entitled to vote, but only 3 per cent of the population exercised this high privilege, even in contests where the community was greatly aroused.

In New York all analyses show that the popular vote in that state was clearly against ratification. In what is now Greater New York plus Westchester, 85,000 people elected 23 delegates to the convention, while the rest of the state, with 260,000 population, had only 40 votes instead of about 70 which a true democracy would have provided.

> *In 1785 New York City boasted a new Tammany Hall, one theater, but had no system of numbers on buildings until 1790. To row to New York from Brooklyn one had to take*

>> clumsy row-boats, flat bottomed square ended scows with spirit-sails, and two-masted boats called periaguas. In one of these, if the day were fine, if the tide were slack, if the water-man sober, and if the boat did not put back several times to take in belated passengers who were seen running down the hill, the crossing might be made with some degree of speed and comfort.

> *Under less favorable conditions, people*

>> counted themselves happy if, at the end of the hour's hard pulling the passengers were put ashore opposite Governor's wharf or on the marshes around Wallabout Bay.

In Maryland "the common class of people" knew little of the Constitution. Only 2,000 copies were printed by order of the assembly. Of the 25,000 voters in the state, only 6,000 voted, and 4,000 of these were in the densely populated portions of the state.

In many towns the voting on delegates was on a *viva-voce* ballot, names being suggested at the general town meetings. In many districts no meetings were held until too late to send delegates. Some delegates elected were unable to attend. In some states the high snows and the conditions of the roads made attendance of all the delegates elected impossible. In other states, like Massachusetts, towns which were in arrears in contributing to the state treasury were not allowed to send delegates. Sober commentators allege that the Massachusetts vote for ratification was purchased by money sent from the merchants of New York State.

The election returns in Philadelphia, with 42,000 population, show that George Latimer, the successful candidate for delegate, received 1,215 votes against 235 votes for his adversary—a total for the two candidates of about 3 per cent of the population.

Many kept away from the polls out of ignorance of what was going on. Some opposed the entire new machinery. In Pennsylvania only 13,000 came to the polls. The voters of the countryside were unable to be articulate on the issue. In the towns, the poor, the debtors had no money to carry on an effective campaign. The opposition uniformly lay in areas where debtors wanted relief by paper-money issues or where farmers working the soil for themselves and living off their own labor felt that the new instrument was a rich man's tool.

Slowly the news of the document seeped through the land by word of mouth. The mass of citizens looked to the old leaders. Where did Samuel Adams, Patrick Henry, Thomas Jefferson, John Hancock and the other old fighters stand? Were they for or against ratification?

> *Jefferson and Madison were also excited about other matters of great importance. Jefferson sent to Madison a pamphlet on animal magnetism and the last aeronautic expedition, together with facts about phosphoretic matches. Madison bought the original works of Buffon of thirty-one volumes, ten volumes Supplementary, and sixteen volumes on birds. He was much excited about a pocket compass the size of a watch. He suggested inventing a pocket telescope with "inches engraved" on the outside.*

Without Samuel Adams and John Hancock, Massachusetts could not be won over. Hancock was always an anomaly. The richest man in New England, he usually stood out against the bankers. He found his political support among the paper-money groups which feared the new na-

tional government, and he had wisely taken temporary leave
of office during Shays' Rebellion—avoiding the onus of fir-
ing on his voters. General Knox had explained the Massachusetts position when he wrote to Washington that the
Constitution is being supported "by the commercial interest,
all men of considerable property, the clergy, the lawyers,
the judges, the courts and the army officers." Hancock was
smoothly converted. Two alternative bribes were dangled
before his reach. If Virginia did not come into the Union—
and her joining was very doubtful with Pat Henry and Richard Henry Lee fighting against it—Hancock would be given
the nomination for first president of the United States.
Even if Virginia ratified and joined the new union, Hancock would receive the nomination for vice-president. Hancock came out for ratification, but received neither nomination. This was our first important political double-cross.

Old Sam Adams could not be reached in any such crude
manner. Samuel Adams, the great old man of the Revolution, was more than cool to the new constitution. This bat-
tler for individual liberty and freedom had never been excited about the need for developing a technique of government. He did not appreciate that the United States had no
working machinery to take over from Great Britain. He
never understood that we were unlike France at the termi-
nation of its revolution. We had no government available
for conversion to our purposes as had Oliver Cromwell in
England. Adams finally favored ratification, but coupled his
acceptance with proposals for amendments. A bill of rights
must be added promptly to satisfy the great personal radical.

With all the local leaders in Massachusetts finally in favor of ratification, the vote was nevertheless too close for
the comfort of the proponents: 187 for, 168 against. A shift
of ten votes would have defeated the Constitution, and with
Massachusetts rejecting the instrument it would never have
been revived.

*Massachusetts shippers were keeping the Southern
states well supplied with slaves from the African coast.*

*There was one college student to every 3,300 persons
in 1790—today, one to every 130 persons.*

The Pennsylvania convention was called for November 21, 1787. Here also the main attack was leveled at the
absence of a bill of rights. What of these charters of liberty
which England had denied us and for which our boys had
died? Reading through the Constitution of the United
States, no mention of right to a jury trial, to freedom of
speech, press or religion was to be found.

For five weeks the debates continued. Amendments were
offered, in fact many of them in the form later to be submitted to the states as the first ten amendments to the Constitution. By December 12 the Federalists thought they
could carry the vote, and the Anti-Federalists, appreciating
this fact, refused to attend any meetings. No quorum was
possible. The police were called, supported by large mobs
of citizens. Opposition delegates were dragged into the hall
and held there until, by a vote of 46 to 23, Pennsylvania
ratified our constitution.

By February 7 Massachusetts, Pennsylvania, Delaware,
New Jersey and Georgia had voted for ratification, the latter three with unseemly haste and scant deliberation.

Meanwhile a sharp struggle was going on in New Hampshire. In that state the convention at its first meeting, in
February 1788, was opposed to ratification. Here no Federalist mob, as in Philadelphia, was employed to push
through the Constitution. An adjournment was engineered
until June. The postponed gathering had a somewhat different personnel. The pro-Constitution machine had been at
work. Washington had written a letter published throughout the land. He scared many into favoring the Constitution
by declaring "And clear I am if another Federal Convention
is attempted [he doesn't say called or convened] that the
sentiments of the members will be more discordant." After
days of discussion a vote was taken. By 57 to 47 the Constitution passed. A change of 5 per cent of the convention
would have left New Hampshire out of the Union.

In South Carolina the attack opened up right in the legis-

lature in January 1788. When the legislature finally and
reluctantly decided to call a convention for ratification or
rejection, the views of adoption elsewhere, particularly in
Georgia, brought a prompt vote and ratification by a vote
of about two to one.

> *To the thriving village of Augusta, Indians came to
> barter skins for powder and rum. Savannah was a
> pretty village with no street paving. Georgetown had
> one hundred houses. Elections were the occasions of
> fights between rival mobs, because personal votes at
> the courthouses were required. Small change was so
> scarce that silver dollars were cut into halves. Quarters
> were called "sharp-skins."*

And still, if Virginia or New York refused to join, the jig
was up.

In Virginia, the home of political genius, the state of the
outstanding delegates, the fight was keenest. The Lee group
had long been bitter enemies of Washington. Here was a
rare chance to get even. But the opposition was more than a
personal grudge. Mason, who had been at the convention,
was genuinely of the opinion that the Constitution should
be rejected because it clearly gave to Congress the authority
to regulate interstate commerce. This argument, surprisingly enough, was popular in Virginia, the very state that
had incited the convention at Annapolis—a kind of preliminary bout for Philadelphia—in order to stabilize interstate
commerce. Even Monroe lined up in opposition to the Constitution. Patrick Henry again and again queried what right
those delegates had to say "We, the people." The old liber-
tarian wanted the clause to read "We, the states." He was
still seeking a league of states instead of a nation.

Jefferson, viewing the scene from abroad, supported
Washington and Madison, with many reservations. Jefferson wrote:

There are indeed some faults which *revolted* me a good deal in the
first moment; but we must be contented to travel on toward perfec-

tion step by step. . . . We must be contented with the ground which this Constitution will gain for us and hope that a favorable moment will come for correcting what is amiss in it.

Throughout the arguments Madison gained support by persistently pointing to the ease of amendment by any nine states of the possible thirteen.

But in Virginia as elsewhere the ratification was procured only by virtual promises of many immediate amendments. That these pledges were kept is evident from the fact that during the next decade more amendments were passed than during the next 140 years. When the vote on ratification was counted it showed 89 for and 79 opposed. A change of six votes would have caused the breakdown of the entire plan.

If Massachusetts and Virginia were tight squeezes for the Federalists, the outcome of the struggle in New York was even more in doubt. In New York the main issue was outspokenly that of interstate commerce. It was estimated that nearly half the goods consumed in Connecticut, New Jersey and western Massachusetts were brought from New York. Thus New York, by a state control of commerce, enacted a tax on all the consumers in these adjacent territories. Three economic groups—the strangest of bedfellows—joined forces to oppose the surrender of interstate commerce to this new united government. The conservative large landowners feared loss of revenue on their produce if the state imposts on exports were removed. New York would lose those economic advantages derived from competitive commerce which overwhelmed New Jersey. The poor downtrodden debtors saw in the Constitution the surrender of all hopes for mortgage moratoria and cheap paper money. And, finally, all the officeholders feared loss of power and even reduction of salaries if the state revenues should be cut in half by loss of these interstate tariffs.

In this notoriously dirty country, New York City was as dirty as the Southern villages. Water was taboo for

*drinking purposes. The yellow fever of the 90s did
great damage in Philadelphia, and the cholera of the
early nineteenth century found it ready prey.*

Within the state there was a clear division. New York
City and Long Island were strongly Federalist. The upstate
representatives came down to the convention at Poughkeepsie so bitterly opposed that many talked of lower New
York adopting the Constitution and forming a separate
state. On Hamilton's suggestion the "Federalist Papers"
were written for the *Independent Journal,* the *Daily Advertiser* and the *Packet.* Most of these anonymous articles were
from the pen of Hamilton. Of the 85, Hamilton contributed
51, Madison 29, and Jay 5. Hamilton's strategy was astute.
His approach was to attack the ineffective machinery of our
confederated government and to show up the danger of
establishing separate little governments.

At Poughkeepsie, in June 1788, two thirds of the delegates were opposed to the ratification. Hamilton, Robert
Livingston and Jay led the battle against Clinton, Lansing
and Melancthon Smith. Had a vote been taken during the
first few days, the Constitution would surely have been rejected. But within a week news came from New Hampshire
that ratification had been voted. On the heels of this was the
news of the earlier action in Virginia.

The delegates then saw New York isolated. What could
Rhode Island, North Carolina and New York do if all
others combined, with joint power of taxation and federal
control over interstate commerce? Could not the new nation
starve out New York? What if the ten-colony union imposed an embargo on shipments to New York and boycotted
her products by nonimportation legislation? Surely New
York had to join, whether the instrument was to her liking
or not.

Innumerable amendments to the Constitution were proposed by the New York delegates. Hamilton was ready to
make deep concessions to the opposition. A resolution was
passed unanimously favoring a second constitutional convention to correct this frightful instrument which New Yorkers

accepted only under duress. On the strength of such a resolution, letters were sent to all the states; and although Madison termed these epistles the "most pestilent tendency," New York ratified, in the hope of a new convention, by the slim margin of three votes—a vote of 30 to 27.

The newspapers of the period, when the states were voting on the Constitution, lead a reader today to believe that most people were plumb weary of planning a union and discussing a constitution. Although few of the citizens could read (and probably, outside of the delegates to legislatures and conventions, not one per cent of the public read the Constitution prior to its adoption), nevertheless New York's suggestion for a new convention caused quite a stir.

Patrick Henry took it up. In Pennsylvania the brilliant young Albert Gallatin followed with demands for revision. In North Carolina the New York letter, plus the close votes in other states, was interpreted to the sparsely settled frontier in such fashion as to delay ratification still further. Meanwhile, in Rhode Island, town meetings were called, and local plebiscites showed a vote of about ten to one against adoption.

With North Carolina and Rhode Island still not joining up, with eleven states ratifying, the old Congress scrapped the old constitution, while all the legal luminaries chuckled at the most important clause of the Articles of Confederation: No changes to be allowed except by unanimous consent!

The old Congress was ready to retire. The most graceful and important *coup d'état* had been accomplished. All that was now needed was the setting of dates for the election of new officials under the new constitution of the eleven colonies—joined into the United States of America.

From Maine to Georgia the staples of diet were brown bread, corn pone, or hoe cake, and rum, cider or whisky; and throughout the South the traveler was fed monotonously on bacon, eggs, hominy, coarse bread and rum. Lodging cost 50¢, breakfast 6 shillings, dinner $1.00. White bread was a luxury.

The adoption of the Constitution was celebrated by the Federal Procession on June 4, 1788, in New York City. It was an industrial parade—a commercial fair, a manufacturers' celebration.

On the right of the first carriage was a lace loom with a worker weaving a scarlet-and-white livery lace; on the left a worker using the new fly shuttle. Behind the loom was a printing table stamping elegant patterns on chintz for shawls. The Manufacturing Society dominated the affair. One float thirty feet long and thirteen feet wide, drawn by ten bay horses, carried cotton carding machines; a spinner was being worked, said the local gazette, by natives of New York City. The calico printers' flag waved on the rear end. The flag bore the motto of the industrialists: "May the Union Government Protect the Manufacturers of America."

CHAPTER XV

The End of the First Revolution

THE FIRST REVOLUTION in our history officially ended on April 30, 1789, when George Washington left the home of Governor Clinton on Cherry Street in New York City to be inaugurated president of the United States.

He had been elected president in a field of twelve candidates, receiving sixty-nine electoral votes; Adams, thirty-four; John Jay, nine. The rest of the votes were scattered. Only ten states had voted. Rhode Island had not been admitted to the Union, and North Carolina and New York failed to vote. The election had been held on January 7, with the electors meeting a month later. The time for the inaugural had been fixed to coincide with "a prospect of spring importations."

Washington had left his beautiful, peaceful estate at Mount Vernon to journey for two weeks by coach and boat to New York City. Crowds gathered all along his route to shout words of enthusiastic welcome. At Elizabeth Point, New Jersey, he was escorted to a special barge, manned by thirteen masters of vessels. When the boat carrying the newly elected President was reported as off Murray's Wharf, Manhattan, Governor Clinton of New York drove down to the dock in his handsome coach to take the future President to the Governor's home.

Major L'Enfant, the great architect and city planner, had organized, the previous year, a huge city parade "in honor of the Constitution of the United States," a parade which was repeated on Washington's arrival in Manhattan.

For several days the First Senate of the United States had been in session debating a most disturbing question. What should they call the President when he entered the

room? Many suggestions were offered. Everyone wanted
something grander than "His Excellency." Lee suggested
"Highness." Washington had intimated he preferred "His
Highness, the President of the United States and Protector
of the Rights of the Same."

James Madison took another look at the Constitution
and quietly arose to suggest that the document had solved
the difficulty by granting the title of "President of the
United States."

*On March 4, 1789, the date set for the start of the
Union, only eight of the twenty-two senators and
thirteen of the members of the House were present.
Not until April was even a quorum obtained.*

The General was received in the Senate Chamber on Wall
Street and Broad. He was escorted to the balcony. The oath
of president was administered by Robert Livingston. The
heroes of the Revolution stood near by. Livingston shouted,
"Long live George Washington, President of the United
States!" Cannons boomed. The President withdrew to the
Senate Chamber. Trembling, he delivered the first message
of any president of the United States. He made no recom-
mendations.

He left the building on foot, walking through streets
without sidewalks. Dressed in deep brown, with metal
buttons, an eagle on each, with white stockings, a bag and a
sword, he went past the street-corner signs—mostly in
Dutch, which he couldn't read. With dignity he returned to
the beautiful house on Cherry Street which New York had
provided for him.

New York was a dull and dirty little town in 1789. It was
a city without a bathroom, without a furnace, with bed-
rooms which in winter lay within the Arctic Zone, with no
ice during the torrid summers, without an omnibus, without
a mustache, without a match. Pigs ran wild in the streets,
scavenging. At what is now 77th Street and Broadway was
that favourite of all rendezvous—the Kissing Bridge. A
state law required people going north on Pearl Street always

to make way for people coming south, thus disposing of the traffic problem. New Yorkers excused themselves for the frequent robberies by claiming that footpads came from Philadelphia. They did little, however, "to drive the punks out."

Promptly after the inauguration President Washington ordered a new coach to be delivered to him from England— a coach of state, globular in shape, canary in color, decorated with cupids, nymphs and the Washington coat of arms.

Although the records are obscure, a house still stands on Cherry Street where the First President probably lived during the first year until he moved to his new residence at 39 Broadway.

The house on Cherry Street, once the hub of government and the court of our aristocracy, is now a dingy tenement with twelve windows on the street. On the lower floor is the sign of "Cocossa—Tobacco and Stationery"—destined to be the last tenant, for the building has been condemned as unfit for human habitation. Soon the sign on the window, "Skates—five cents an hour," will be removed. The old lodgers have been evicted. Cold water runs down from the tank on the roof into an iron sink in the hall behind the shop. No other plumbing exists in the building. As in the day of the President, a toilet stands in the yard; any other arrangement would be considered unusual by the inhabitants of Cherry Street, New York City, 1936. But plumbing is a modern contraption which takes second place in the concern of Cherry Street humans. The rats in the cellar become bolder every day. The wit of the street, leaning against the Washington mantelpiece, says with the authentic air of one who lives near to our first White House, "If you saddled them you could ride 'em."

PART IV

The Second Revolution

SOME *time after the Constitution was adopted by twelve states Rhode Island reluctantly joined the other states.*

The thirteen states in a new nation took a grand commercial spurt. The diminishing state economic conflicts were a relief to manufacturers and merchants. Territorial expansion, immigration, the working of a yet rich soil, the discovery of new wealth, led to a favorable financial future.

Was there easy sailing for long, or did the reluctance to accept the new rules indicate immediate trouble? The fight for the Bill of Rights, coupled with the Jefferson defeat of Hamilton, was a second revolution of great significance. From it the suffrage was enlarged and the monarchists put to rout.

The fourth part of this book is directed at the first great changes in the Constitution. The Bill of Rights was inserted in the document by ten separate amendments. All ten of these amendments were to be promptly nullified. The Court did not preserve the rights set forth in these amendments. But not until after the defeat of Hamilton did we start to establish for the first time a tradition of democracy. Had Jefferson been defeated we might today be governed by a monarch.

CHAPTER XVI

The Bill of Rights

The First Slap at the Founding Fathers

IN THE CONVENTION Mason proposed the inclusion of a bill of rights in the Constitution. Had we not objected to Great Britain's disregard of our fundamental private liberties? What else was the Declaration of Independence but a plea for freedom of press, of speech and of religion, freedom to bear arms, the right to a fair jury trial and freedom from excessive bail! We wanted decent due process in the courts. Now, in this new government which would act directly on the people, the government might or might not respect these basic rights, and surely the new constitution ought not be silent on such matters. "It will give great quiet to the people," Mason declared, "to provide these liberties in the Constitution."

It was no oversight that led the Founding Fathers to reject the Mason proposal, for when it was put to a vote not a single state voted in his support.

> *Jefferson had insisted, over the opposition of most of those signing the Declaration of Independence, that it refer to "life, liberty and the pursuit of happiness," instead of to life, liberty and property.*

At eight of the state ratification conventions the Constitution was adopted only because delegates were led to believe that a bill of rights would be added as amendments. And so it was. And still to this day few Americans appreciate that the Constitution was not originally that great document of personal liberty we suppose it to be. In a way, however, the omission is peculiarly important. Can it not be truthfully said that amendments to the instrument take on a higher validity than that of the original sections, since amendments imply separate, isolated, considered public opinion? Just so with the first ten amendments. They are clear and certain, and to anyone but a lawyer or a judge most of them mean what they say.

Within a few months of its first session the Congress received 100 resolutions setting forth amendments. On September 25, 1789, Congress submitted twelve to the states, and ten were ratified in December 1791. Connecticut, Massachusetts and Georgia failed to ratify any of them. Rhode Island was outside of the Union. The two amendments which failed related to salaries of congressmen and reapportioning the numbers in Congress.

In reviewing these new amendments it must always be remembered that they are not a truly national charter of liberties. For a long time the Court held that they limited the action of Congress only. The states were still to be free to cut down our basic civil liberties. The situation is further complicated because the due-process clause of the Fifth Amendment was repeated seventy-seven years later in the Fourteenth Amendment to the Constitution. Even lawyers fail at times to appreciate that the Fifth Amendment refers only to the federal government whilst the Fourteenth operates on the states. Although the Court decided no cases under the due-process clause of the Fifth Amendment until 1886, both amendments are now being construed as a double-barreled repeating gun, taking potshots against decent minimum wages on federal property such as the District of Columbia, and in the separate states.

At a later date the Supreme Court indicated that at least parts of the First, Sixth and Eighth Amendments bound the separate states through the Fourteenth Amendment. In a courageous opinion the Court recently vetoed an act of the Louisiana legislature because that state had violated the freedom of the press. On the other hand a candidate for president is denied the right of free speech in Terre Haute, Indiana, and no one dreams that the Supreme Court would interfere with such a violation of free speech. Then again no one knows just which of these ten amendments will be held by the Court as protecting us against both state and federal governments.

In the following notes on the amendments will be found references to deprivation of liberty by states as well as by the national government. To an individual it makes slight difference whether he is forbidden free speech, free press, the right to bear arms or any other freeman's privileges by one government or the other. You are equally throttled by a state or federal gag. It is important to view the complete scene because so many people are under the impression that the Supreme Court of the United States has been and is the protector of our liberties. Liberal groups throughout the land point to the new trials granted to the Scottsboro boys unmindful of the innumerable unpublicized counterparts of Tom Mooney and Eugene V. Debs.

Let us see what these amendments gave us in real liberty:

First Amendment

Congress shall make no law respecting an establishment of religion, or prohibiting the free exercise thereof; or abridging the freedom of speech, or of the press; or the right of the people peaceably to assemble, and to petition the Government for a redress of grievances.

These rights had been won by Englishmen long before 1791. Their importance in the Constitution lies in the fact that this national government was to protect the citizens of the land against itself. But Mercer was no doubt sound when he declared: "It's a great mistake to suppose that the paper we are to propose will govern the United States."

Despite the amendment and until 1828 religious qualifications for public officeholding existed in Maryland, and as recently as 1930 those who did not believe in a God and a Hereafter were denied the right of testifying in the New Jersey courts. All through the Coolidge–Hoover administrations newspapers of left-wing economics were denied the mails. In 1936, in Arkansas and California, as two outstanding examples, the right of peaceful assemblage has been denied, and in many states citizens have been convicted while peacefully petitioning the government to redress grievance.

How is this possible? Aren't the words of the First Amendment precise and certain? Could we rewrite the phrase with greater clarity?

The answer lies elsewhere. The judges of the Supreme Court have always construed the Constitution in accordance with their own human prejudices. This is no cruel criticism because, having once taken the position that they could declare laws unconstitutional, the reverse must inevitably follow: they declare certain laws constitutional. And so we find the courts saying that the freedom of the press doesn't mean freedom but only that amount of freedom which the judges deem wise. If a majority of the judges are opposed to the general public use of birth control, then a statute taking from the press the right to spread that gospel of family limitation becomes constitutional. During each war the judges naturally disregarded this First Amendment and in effect said freedom of speech must be used only if it does not hurt the common cause. But these limitations and exceptions inserted by congressional acts and approved by the Supreme Court are not in the words of the amendments. Nor did the Founding Fathers so mean. The judges carved a piece out of Liberty and called it License. License is the liberty they did not approve.

There is a story in American history which shows how the courts have permitted Congress to cut deep gashes into this First Amendment.

In 1835 the South was sorely troubled. Abolitionist literature mailed to the Southern states was stirring the Negroes toward rebellion. Southern senators urged at Washington that Abolitionist literature be excluded from the mailbags. The states were in peril. Three giants of that era arose to argue against the proposal. Clay, Calhoun and Webster declared that any such censorship of the mails would be clearly unconstitutional as well as socially unwise. Van Buren, as vice-president, sided with this point of view, and the mails remained uncensored at that time.

But thirty-five years later Congress passed legislation censoring the mails. The Supreme Court approved the right of Congress to limit the free flow of ideas in the mails. To us at this time the importance of such action by the judges lies in the fact that many people believe the power of judicial veto is needed to protect our civil liberties. But the judges have read the simple words of the First Amendment just as they have the other clauses of the Constitution and by legal turns and twists in opinions utterly unintelligible to laymen have taken out of or put into the words those concepts of life which to them at the time were comforting. Law is the expression of prejudices, and we might always remember that William Penn was acquitted only because he had some Quakers on the jury; and that in 1933, despite the First Amendment, the Secretary of Labor in President Roosevelt's cabinet was not permitted to address a gathering in the steel town of Homestead, Pennsylvania, except by going to the steps of the post office, which was federal-government property.

If the Court will agree that Congress may bar from the mails, from express and interstate shipment sexually exciting literature, surely we have no constitutional right to hope that the Court will not also ban writings which are economically or politically exciting. Surely the state as such is in more danger from political than from gonadic stimulation.

Matters relating to sex are properly excluded from the mail pouches, says the Court. Anything libidinous or lewd or indecent would corrupt the people of the land. To a non-lawyer a free press, as referred to in the amendment, implies the dissemination of such literature, but Congress limited the First Amendment, and the Supreme Court acceded to the limitation. Having permitted any exception to a free press, the extent and number of further exceptions depend on the mere whim of the Court.

Second Amendment

A well-regulated militia being necessary to the security of a free State, the right of the people to keep and bear arms shall not be infringed.

The answer to these words is, Try to get a gun. Again the right has been cut down. The amendment has been construed to read: "The right to bear arms shall not be infringed except if a state or the federal government sees fit and the judges approve." But if you had been the draftsman of this amendment and you wanted to say "no infringement —never—nohow—under no circumstances," how better could you have declared it than was done in the amendment itself?

I am not arguing that the amendment is any longer wise. It may be that the right to bear arms is valueless today. The use of air bombs and gas may well make this provision useless for the purpose intended—resistance to governmental dictatorship. That isn't the point of my attack. I merely call attention to the clause and ask if under it you find any loophole for the Supreme Court to say: You can't carry arms unless you know a local judge or a ward politician.

On the other hand the Supreme Court has rejected the Madison position that "no person religiously scrupulous of bearing arms shall be compelled to render military service in person."

Third Amendment

No soldier shall, in time of peace, be quartered in any house without the consent of the Owner, nor in time of war but in a manner to be prescribed by law.

This amendment is outworn. Barracks built by the government have made it unnecessary. But note that here the amendment gives Congress the power to make exceptions by the phrase "but in a manner to be prescribed by law." No such exception was added to Amendments I and II. Is it not fair to say that no exceptions were intended to those other amendments, even though the Supreme Court has permitted such exceptions?

Fourth Amendment

The right of the people to be secure in their persons, houses, papers and effects, against unreasonable searches and seizures, shall not be violated, and no warrants shall issue but upon probable cause, supported by oath or affirmation, and particularly describing the place to be searched, and the persons or things to be seized.

This amendment was to protect us against unlawful search of our persons, papers and effects. But the United States Supreme Court has held it to be lawful for the government to tap your telephone wire and hear what you are saying. On the basis of this decision a government X-ray radio might some day pierce the walls of your home without previous application to any court and without notice to you. A marshal can take away your privacy. The Supreme Court has not protected your privacy under the Fourth Amendment.

Fifth Amendment

No person shall be held to answer for a capital or other infamous crime unless on a presentment or indictment of a Grand Jury, except in cases arising in the land or naval forces, or in the militia, when in actual service, in time of war or public danger; nor shall any person be subject for the same offense to be twice put in jeopardy of life or limb; nor shall be compelled in any criminal case to be a witness against himself, nor be deprived of life, liberty, or property, without due process of law; nor shall private property be taken for public use without just compensation.

This is the amendment no layman will ever understand and on which lawyers seldom agree as to interpretation. Since the judges of the Supreme Court have divided by five-to-four votes on these words more than on any others in the Constitution, we might have to admit that the drafters of the amendment did as miserable a job as has ever been done with the use of words of law.

Read it carefully. Don't be bewildered by the fact that it is called law. What does it mean? It sets forth five ideas:

1. You are entitled to a grand jury hearing before being tried for certain crimes—those punishable by capital punishment and other infamous crimes.

But surely *infamous* is a word that changes with the years. It was infamous in 1791 to steal a horse or conceal a

Quaker. Comparatively few people sent to jail today are in-
dicted by a jury—even though the sentences they are serv-
ing run for long years.

2. You are not to be tried twice for the same crime.

Here a joker developed against you. If you were a boot-
legger you could be sent to jail twice for being in the same
business, since the federal government would convict you
under the federal law and the states would get you under
the state laws. The Supreme Court said that was in order.
It held that the amendment means only that the same government can't get you twice. I still have a suspicion that
those who fought for the Bill of Rights would have believed
that it made little difference whether the same or different
agencies of government got after you, and that the point
of their plea was, "Don't make any man pay twice for the
same essential sin."

3. You need not testify against yourself.

This was and still is essential to prevent the thumbscrew
and torture of trial by ordeal. Many court decisions, however, have approved confessions induced by the third degree.
Many persons have been jailed for failure to testify even
where they thought they would imperil themselves. But
maybe the framers meant this relief only to apply where
you were on trial in a criminal case and not to testimony
before legislative committees.

4. You are not to be deprived of life, liberty or property
    without due process of law.

Read with the rest of the section, would you not think
that this meant you were to be proceeded against in a fair
manner, with proper notice, a chance to be heard, a right
to appeal, and ample time to prepare your case? Don't be
silly; it means primarily that the United States may not fix
a railroad rate unless the Supreme Court thinks it is reason-

able and fair, because the stockholders of the railroad have a constitutional right to earn enough to pay them such dividends as the Supreme Court judges think capital should receive. These words *due process* have been stretched to mean that a state may not arrange to have ample ice to protect the milk of the babies and that no state may protect the health of children and women by fixing minimum rates of pay. For a long time the Court held we were not getting due process if a state said men shall not be worked more than ten hours a day in difficult, hazardous jobs.

5. If property is taken by the government it must be paid for.

Here is the udder of the co-operative cow. What is just compensation? Is it what you paid for something? Is it what you can sell it for today? Is it what you expect to make out of it?

When a city buys land for playgrounds and parks, due process demands, so the Courts say, that a much larger sum be paid than the amount the landowner claimed it was worth when the city assessed the same land for tax purposes. On such legal legerdemain the city slums remain intact and new housing, so sorely needed, is unobtainable.

Sixth Amendment

In all criminal prosecutions, the accused shall enjoy the right to a speedy and public trial, by an impartial jury of the State and district wherein the crime shall have been committed, which district shall have been previously ascertained by law, and to be informed of the nature and cause of the accusation; to be confronted with the witnesses against him; to have compulsory process for obtaining witnesses in his favor, and to have the assistance of counsel for his defense.

Seventh Amendment

In suits at common law, where the value in controversy shall exceed twenty dollars, the right of trial by jury shall be preserved, and no fact tried by a jury shall be otherwise re-examined in any court of the United States than according to the rules of the common law.

Eighth Amendment

Excessive bail shall not be required, nor excessive fines imposed, nor cruel and unusual punishments inflicted.

1. These sections were to assure a jury trial in all criminal cases.

More people are in jails of the land today, having been tried by judges without jurors, than by judges and jurors.

2. Excessive bail was to be forbidden.

> *Bail of $350,000 was recently held lawful in New York City in the case of a racketeer. Innocent people, merely perchance witnesses to a crime, have been held in jail, without the right to get bail, for periods of months.*

3. No cruel and inhuman punishment is to be inflicted.

Today, 1936, we have the longest and most inhuman punishments for even minor offences imposed in any civilized nation of the world, including even Germany and Italy before their fascist regimes. Whipping, bread-and-water diets, dungeon cells and chain gangs are customary.

4. Jury trials in civil cases are guaranteed where the amount is over twenty dollars and the suit is one "at common law."

This may have had some meaning to the lawyers of 1791. They wanted to assure a right of jury trial in certain lawsuits; but had they known, as we do, the difficulty of finding out what was the common law of 1791, they might well have adopted far different language than they did. In any event this provision indicated a faith in the jury system now fast evaporating in this nation, where many states are persistently ordering trials by judges without jurors.

Ninth Amendment

The enumeration in the Constitution of certain rights shall not be construed to deny or disparage others retained by the people.

Tenth Amendment

The powers not delegated to the United States by the Constitution, nor prohibited by it to the States, are reserved to the States respectively, or to the people.

These are catch-alls. The Ninth pegged definitely that the people had many rights in addition to those set forth in the first eight amendments, and the Tenth wanted to make it certain that the powers not turned over to the federal government by the states did not disappear but still remained in the states. This amendment was originally drafted in stricter terms. But the idea of giving to Congress only those powers *expressly* delegated was rejected. The people knew that no powers were delegated in tight-frozen terms.

CHAPTER XVII

Democracy Advances

In 1789 the crops were lush. To the twelve colonies the stars and the moon were kind, and the history of every new government is determined in part by the weather.

When Washington became president, twelve states had signified to the world and to each other a new relationship. The blood of the war had not been wasted. We had cut loose from the distant controls of the mother state, Great Britain. The twelve heterogeneous states had found a meeting of the minds in a few important spheres.

The Constitution, originally silent on the question of human rights and human liberties, was promptly corrected. It was still a close question whether we would remain an aristocracy with monarchical leanings or eventually turn toward democracy.

By the separation from England we had not veered very far toward democracy. But in our effort for a collective economy great strides had been made by the new constitution. No longer could any state by separate action destroy the economic welfare of any other state. Much sooner than anticipated, the whip of national economic pressure was to be used with effective precision. Congress threatened Rhode Island with economic destruction unless it joined our nation of twelve states. The national use of commercial control brought Rhode Island into the union.

The first Post Office Act, under the Constitution, was not signed by George Washington until February 20, 1792. This act set the rates at 6 cents for letters not exceeding a 30-mile distance, 8 cents from 30 to 60 miles, 10 cents from 60 to 100 miles, and 12½ cents from 100 to 150 miles.

The states had pooled their vast, unknown, unexplored landholdings. This co-operative generosity is probably the most unbelievable action of that era. In those distant lands lay the latent wealth of the separate states. Toward the West each state had had its chance for imperialism. In those far Western lands stretching to the Mississippi rested the possibilities of land sales so vast that the budget of the nation could be balanced for decades with scarcely any taxes. Although in 1790 only two hundred thousand people lived west of the Appalachian range, with over three million east of those mountains, by 1815 the additions to the population in the east and in the west were about equal, and by 1840 the population in the East and in the West was in fact equal. Few of the wise men of the Revolutionary era foresaw this, but the difficulties of each separate state protecting itself against Indians, the dangers of Spanish warfare on the Mississippi, the indefinite vagueness of the boundaries, and the many claims lodged by two or more states to the same lands led to a common donation of all these Western lands to the central government. With transportation limited and communication difficult and costly, states like Virginia and Massachusetts realized that their governments would break down because of mere vastness. It was a real relief to the larger states when the unburdening of these distant responsibilities took place. This donation was to ease the budget of the federal government, but also, in time, to complicate the entire numerical equilibrium of states in the House of Representatives as apportioned under the Constitution.

> *Township names for Western lands were chosen by the office boy of General Simeon de Witt. Being a lad of classical bent he selected Tully, Hannibal, Cincinnatus, Fabius, Manlius and Marathon.*

Under the Articles of Confederation the central government had to behave like a poor and unpopular distant rela-

tive. Funds were begged, not ordered. A failure to pay led
to nothing but obsequious further requests and secret concessions. Now the states had given to Congress the power
to tax. Not only did this mean a solvent, potent government; it meant that credit abroad could be re-established. It
was high time that we started to repay that gay opera writer
Beaumarchais, author of *The Barber of Seville* and *The
Marriage of Figaro,* for the substantial loans he had made
to the colonies during the war. Without his money we might
today be part of England. Even though we never did fully
repay him, at least the new government had the power to
refund and repay all debts abroad to Beaumarchais, the
Farmers General of France, and the valiant government of
Holland. For a very few years after 1787 the people of the
United States appreciated that without those foreign
financial credits we could never have accomplished our first
revolution. Within two decades our appreciation was to
turn into active animosity.

This power to tax meant by indirection the power to
direct society into definite social and economic channels.
Had not England determined the extent of the use of our
sugar or tea by the taxing power? Was not the Stamp Act in
principle to be carried over by us to control our predilections
for liquor? Would not the impost duties directly affect fishing, shipping and manufacturing businesses? We could have
employed the power to tax so as to force the President, Mr
Washington, to order his presidential coach from some local
wagonmaker instead of from London, England. Would not
the power to tax be capable of application so that backward
territories could be made more prosperous and less successful merchants could be aided with government funds?

Now that we were one nation, the power to make treaties
became important. Except for the radical worker group in
France the people of Europe, through their governments,
were looking at this new nation with suspicion, mingled with
high hopes that the joint venture would soon be disrupted.
Commercial treaties were important to our agriculture.
Although our foreign trade was most intimately wedded to

the Caribbean Islands, the wars between European states of necessity affected our imports and exports. Madison warned that if our new foreign treaties threatened war, we would get war. Rather should our treaties threaten embargoes and sanctions. Thereby we get peace, he said. But little did he appreciate that a system of sanctions in the world of 1776 would have made a United States of America impossible. Our opera-writing benefactor would have been forced to keep his money at home, and our treasurer Robert Morris would not have been able to overdraw, without permission, those vast amounts of French francs. Treaties were essential for the economic world trade of this new nation. By the new law of the land one treaty took the place of thirteen.

In 1795 Russia, Austria and Great Britain consum-mated the Triple Alliance. The massacre of hundreds of whites had occurred in a Negro rebellion in Santo Domingo. The recognition of France—the godless, bloodthirsty country of revolution—was an official act meeting with strong disapproval in Puritan quarters.

There was one other power created by these twelve states to gain peace at home. That was the creation of a forum for settling disputes between the separate states. During the war and for the years thereafter the Continental Congress had established a Supreme Court rotating in membership and modeled much like the present informal voluntary arbitration boards used by merchants. Arbitration between states was suspected because the decision in a case between New Jersey and Pennsylvania was influenced no doubt by the fact

that while one of the states had paid her quota of the impositions levied by Congress to pay the Continental debt and expenses, the other state had neglected to do so.

This court, composed in the main of members of Con-gress, had been principally occupied with maritime and boundary matters. Naturally, the new Supreme Court of the United States was to be engaged likewise with similar cases. To whom would the bounty ship belong—to the state whose ship brought in the prize or to the state whose port first welcomed the capture? To such problems the Supreme Court was to address itself, everyone realizing that the Constitution gave the judges no power to enforce their decrees. The judges might have a marshal or sheriff if Congress so voted, but the president had an army and a navy.

The coinage of currency and the carriage of the mails through the states were to be standardized. No longer would dozens of different coins circulate in each community. No longer would shillings have different values every hundred miles up and down the coast. No longer would the mails be a private privilege, costly and insecure. The conveniences which we now take most for granted were the confused uncertainties of that era.

The vested interests of private mail carriers clung on for five years. Not until 1794 did the government go into the business in earnest. The profitable enterprise of handling letters was not to be surrendered by the private interests without a battle. The postal companies argued that the mails were not clearly affected by a public interest. And although the Constitution provided that Congress shall fix the weight and value of coins, it wasn't until three years later that our legislators got around to this fundamental of efficient business. And not until about fifty years later were postage stamps used and rates fixed irrespective of the distance the mail was to be carried.

Through such measures a uniform pattern of daily living was being superimposed on the separate states—against, of course, a background of wide illiteracy, severe restrictions on the right to vote, and an educational system reposing in private profit-making hands. It took years before public education was generally established even for white folk. Not without a bitter struggle were the private schoolmasters to allow the competition of the government in this strictly private business of education.

But as soon as the First Congress assembled we were on

our way to the second revolution—the battle for the extension of the people's right to dominate their government.

In that first Senate chamber, with its canopy of crimson velvet over the chair of Vice-President Adams, inside that door guarded by the "Usher of the Black Rod," the forces were to line up behind Jefferson or Hamilton. A week after the date set for the opening of Congress in April 1789, only six senators had appeared. A circular letter was sent urging attendance of others. Two weeks more and neither house could muster a quorum.

Neither President Washington nor his court chamberlain, Colonel Humphreys, sensed the impending struggle. They lived a pleasant life. In New York the sewage was carried away at night by Negroes, six livery stables served the wealthy on jaunts all the way to Florida Tea Gardens on the North River and thence to Perry's at Union Square; 131 tavern licenses had been granted, and the Black Friars ran the only night club. A gallows stood where City Hall now stands, and in the slave market two thousand slaves were sold on Manhattan Island in that year. The wooded island, with its hills and many streams and rivers, was a delightful place.

Ice was shipped in that year from Boston for sale in India, and Mrs Knox, the wife of the General, wore her hair a foot high in the new butter-churn fashion.

But back of this scene the President presided at his dull and silent dinner parties to which guests were summoned by beautifully engraved stock form invitations. The General toyed in bored fashion with his heavy, large fork. Little time did he spend on playing his flute. Entertaining high society took his every evening. Jefferson was shocked by the "unrepublican tone" of the city.

Several early economic issues were to give the opposing forces opportunities to appraise the power of the leaders and the extent of their followings. The battle of the vested interests was directed by Alexander Hamilton. He wanted a government of strength, and money was strength. With

great wisdom he gathered together the data on all governmental debts outstanding. He found:

Foreign debts and interest	$12,000,000
Domestic Continental debts	
including army certificates	40,000,000
State debts (estimated)	25,000,000
	$77,000,000

This was the face amount of the debt. There were no
stock exchanges, no free market places. Hamilton's idea of
a planned economy required that all these separately in-
curred debts be funded and put down on uniform rates of
interest, set with fixed due dates, in one or more large national bond issues. Only thus could the debt be handled in
the annual budget. This genius, Hamilton, secretary of the
treasury under Washington, remembered that under the
Articles of Confederation our government had not paid
even the interest on the national debt. Our government
paper had depreciated until it was selling at one twentieth
of its par value. Thousand-dollar bonds were bought and
sold for as little as fifty dollars.

*The French consul took his cook along when he visited
the presidential homestead, the food being none too
good.*

As soon as news leaked out that Hamilton intended to
take in all the state and federal bonds and issue new federal
bonds at par to be met out of federal taxes, the congressmen, the senators, their relatives and their friends, consistent with the prevalent morality of the day (of almost
any day, for that matter), saw a chance to benefit personally
and become fabulously rich. Most of them lost no time.
Robert Morris, consulted by Hamilton on the program,
was deep in the speculation. One of his partners grabbed
options on $40,000 of the outstanding bonds from the un-
suspecting and uninformed public. *The New York Daily
Advertiser* of February 13, 1790, prophesied that Robert
Morris would benefit by eighteen million dollars, Jeremiah

Wadsworth nine million and Governor Clinton five million.

Twenty-nine of the sixty-five members of Congress speculated. Christopher Gore, the richest lawyer in Massachusetts, a district leader in the Hamilton machine, made an independent fortune buying bonds in the hinterland of the Berkshires for ten cents on the dollar from yokels who hadn't heard of the new deal. The galleries of Congress were full of speculators. In anticipation of assumption, express coaches left for North Carolina, and two sailing vessels were chartered by congressmen who sailed forth to buy cheap bonds. Washington's three secretaries, Humphreys, Jackson and Nelson, joined the speculation lobby.

Madison did not like the looks of this fever and corruption. He was particularly concerned because the soldiers and their families and the common people who had helped finance the war by buying bonds were now being robbed by the financiers. Surely there must be some way by which our new nation could prevent all of the rise in the value of the government paper—from $50 to $1,000—going into the pockets of the new investors. Some of the $950, he thought, should go to the original patriots. He proposed a complicated formula. Hamilton was temporarily blocked.

When the Treasury program was temporarily defeated by two votes, there was great dismay. The aristocrats were now sure that the new government was worse than useless. But the temptation of easy money was soon to corrupt a full majority of Congress. Assumption went through. Victory number one for Hamilton. Victory number one for a planned national economy. Hamilton had established a nationwide financial structure. But the Madison–Jefferson forces were being organized among the poor in the countryside.

The "Solid South" and Tammany Hall were two constant, faithful factors in the Democratic party after Jefferson's botanizing excursion to New York with Madison to make a Virginia–New York alliance with Clinton, as the historians Morison and Commager point out.

The second move around which the forces gathered was the creation of a national bank. Jefferson and Madison opposed the bank. The South had no banks, and to Westerners it was meaningless. The anti-Hamilton group questioned the power of Congress to set up such a banking monopoly. Then did they become strict constructionists in order to block Hamilton. But Hamilton won again by closing the first neat little political deal in our history. At the home of Mrs Bingham, Jefferson agreed to a national bank, on condition that the capital of the United States be moved from Philadelphia to the land of his friend Carroll on the banks of the Potomac. But for this deal Baltimore, Lancaster or Trenton might today be the capital of the United States.

> *Merchants—i.e., gropshop owners—were competing for location of the capital, much as cities today compete for American Legion and other conventions.*

> People from the interior parts of Georgia, South Carolina, North Carolina and Virginia and Kentucky will never patiently repeat their trips to remote New York especially as the Legislative Sessions will be held in the Winter Season.

The national-bank stocks were issued and rose in value. There was a scramble, with more speculation and for more plunder. Members of Congress were again deep in it. A gazette described the financial "maypole" which had been "swollen into a steeple," and suggested, "What goes up must come down—so take care of your head, Brother Jonathan."

President Washington signed the National Bank bill even though his legal adviser, the attorney general, advised him that the bill was unconstitutional.

Point two in our planned economy. Again in the engineering of the program great private profit was made by the already rich. But Jefferson's name became still more popular with the farmers, who were 90 per cent of the population. He was the symbol of the revolt of agricultural interests against the mercantile-financial interests. The historic battle between the Hamiltonian and Jeffersonian concepts of gov-

ernment was on! It continued until the Civil War, each side
trying to get control of the federal government to starve
the other group.

Point three was the tariff act.

Hamilton saw the issue clearly. He urged a tariff as a
bounty to encourage business and relied on the precedent of
previous subsidies to encourage the interstate commerce in
dried and pickled fish and salt meat. He proposed the same
formula as that contained in the Agricultural Adjustment
Act of the Roosevelt regime. He was facing a reverse
economy. To encourage industry a burden was to be put on
agriculture, to be paid out in bounties to manufacturers. By
a proper tariff more boys and girls could be brought into the
mills. England was boasting that four sevenths of the employees in the cotton mills were women and children. To
dress up the act for the farmers, Hamilton took particular
pains to show them how, under a tariff, their wives and children would soon be put to work in the factories of the new
day. A tariff act would help establish manufacturing. Its
main purpose was not revenue. It was to make agriculture
pay for aid to industry. Much of the money derived from
the tariff was to be passed out as subsidies to individual
businessmen to help the development of more and greater
factories. In his truly great report as secretary of the
treasury, Hamilton explained in detail how the grants would
be allocated to the factories. He was not the least concerned
with any constitutional question. In fact, no one arose to
interject the modern bugaboo of interstate commerce or
Congress' inability to select the particular merchants to be
chosen for governmental financial aid. When a glass blower
named Ameling came before Congress in 1791 and asked
for £3,000 to enlarge his factory and tide him over a bad
spell, there was only one point deemed worthy of discussion:
Should we grant this subsidy now or should we wait until
we have looked over all other similar applications?

Hamilton proposed government stimulation of local
manufacture by premium and subsidies. He discussed at
length the equitable disposition of bonuses to manufacturers
in different localities. He decided in favor of bounties based

on volume of sales rather than on profit of owners. In his "Report on Finances" of 1791 Hamilton wrote:

The quantity of business which seems to be going on, is, in a vast number of cases, a very deceitful criterion of the profits which are made; yet it is, perhaps, the best they can have, and it is the one on which they will most naturally rely.

He went further, urging federal inspection of all commodities manufactured, without any mention of whether the goods were to overflow state lines or not. In his report he proposed—

. . . judicious regulations for the inspection of manufactured commodities. This is not among the least important of the means by which the prosperity of manufactures may be promoted. It is, indeed, in many cases, one of the most essential. Contributing to prevent frauds upon consumers at home, and exporters to foreign countries—to improve the quality and preserve the character of the national manufactures, it cannot fail to aid the expeditious and advantageous sale of them, and to serve as a guard against successful competition from other quarters. The reputation of the flour and lumber of some States, and of the potash of others, has been established by an attention to this point.

To these phases of his program there was no disagreement on constitutional grounds. The interstate-commerce clause was not to be narrowly construed until a century later.

> *Until the Third Congress the Senate discussions were secret. In the Third Congress the first member to be expelled was William Blount, who planned to transfer New Orleans from Spain to England. He was a signer of the Constitution. By 1795 the foreign debt was paid off, and by 1835 the domestic debt was entirely repaid.*

Hamilton had agreed with Gorham at the Convention that "the Eastern states have no motive to union but a commercial one." And with this clear vision of economics as the main purpose of the nation he took a group of businessmen and financiers to visit Passaic Falls, where he had selected the site on which American industry was to be located. This proposed national manufacturing center—strongly urged by the national secretary of the treasury—was more than a dreamy plan. A company was actually formed, and the state of New Jersey granted the ancient device of tax exemption for the enterprise. The secretary of the treasury of these United States desired the exemption from New Jersey to aid the industries which would locate there under his aegis. Little did state geographical boundaries deter this financial genius.

For the proposed manufacturing center 700 acres were bought for $8,230. The sum of $160,000 was paid into the treasury of the company. There was a canal which cost $20,000, a weave shop $5,000, a cotton shop $5,000, a print works $10,000, and 50 houses for workers at $250 each. The secretary of the treasury of the United States went to New Jersey to "elucidate anything that may appear obtuse." The secretary of the treasury wanted this to be the commercial capital of the republic.

Providence to New York was a seventeen-hour trip— and twelve hours more to Philadelphia. Niagara Falls honeymoons were startling innovations.

It was only a slight step from his tariff act to his excise act. On that act the issue between Hamilton and Jefferson became clearly apparent to all. With America's great poet-editor, Philip Freneau, attacking Hamilton, the Secretary of the Treasury lost his head. The whisky makers resented the tax. They refused to pay it. Hamilton prepared an army to enforce the excise laws. By the end of September 1794 Washington, his secretary and Hamilton marched off to war on the Whisky Rebellion. The despised poor people were resisting the Hamilton program. He would use force to win while commercial circles discussed the dissolution of the Union. Insurance-company officials met and circulated petitions saying, in brief, we must have a strong government. The riffraff are getting too powerful. Back in the hills the whisky makers became more defiant.

When trouble with France started to brew, Hamilton

found that even with the magic of Washington's name no substantial army could be raised. In fact the deserters from our army were so many that cash rewards were offered for apprehension of each deserter. Hamilton's program required repressive measures to block the opposition.

Washington was inveigled by Hamilton into opposing the formation of any democratic societies and proclaimed that "people in private life have no right to organize for political purposes." Daniel Webster accused Jefferson of treason because he had hinted that Washington had been captured by the aristocrats and monarchists. Toward Edward Livingston, born at luxurious Clermont on the Hudson, Hamilton shouted "Deserter" because that rich young man had joined up with the Jeffersonians. Madison noted that "Bank directors are soliciting subscriptions [for the Hamiltonian cause] like highwaymen with a pistol demanding the purse." Spies opened Jefferson's mail at his home. Hamilton, the job dispenser, insisted that Adams' son-in-law, before receiving an appointment, get a certificate that he hadn't interfered in the New York governmental election. He even rejected the speaker of the House for a position in the army.

Hamilton forgot the first ten amendments to the Constitution. He never was much concerned with human liberty. But the common people had gone too far for Hamilton to respect constitutional guarantees. He insisted that the throttling of Jefferson's uprising was essential. There was only one way, he thought, that it could be accomplished. Under the guise of an attack on the Irish it was proposed to curb all aliens, and by the fourth article of a newly proposed sedition act anyone questioning the constitutionality or justice of an administration measure could be sent to jail. Even Hamilton was later a little ashamed of this measure, but with President Adams' approval and Washington's support a reign of terror started in 1798 and spread like the Ku Klux Klan of later history.

Aedanus Burke, one of the justices of the Supreme Court of South Carolina, wrote that the Society of the Cincinnati was "deeply planned"; it was "an hereditary peerage"; it was "planted in fiery hot ambition, and thirst for power; its branches will end in Tyranny . . . the country will be composed only of two ranks of men, the patricians, or nobles and the rabble."

Many of the clergy supported the Sedition Act. College professors gave it a blessing. Honorary degrees were awarded to the anti-alien Hamiltonians, and many bosses threatened to discharge all workers who opposed Hamilton. Matthew Lyon, a devout Jeffersonian of Vermont, was sent to jail for criticizing the administration. While in jail he was twice elected to office by a popular vote of two to one. The Essex Junto, an organization of wealthy Boston vigilantes, persecuted Thomas Adams, the editor of *The Independent Chronicle*. Famous Sam Adams, then seventy-six years old, went to the jail to pay his respects to Tom Adams. Reckless, intolerant federal judges, like Chase, instructed marshals to exclude Jeffersonian democrats from the juries. Picturesque Duane and many others convicted under the Alien and Sedition Acts, refused the offer of a pardon or release from jails. One Jedediah Peck, supported by Aaron Burr, urging repeal of the Alien and Sedition Acts, marched up and down the country as a revivalist symbol of the breakdown of justice. Up and down the land Jeffersonian (known as Republican) editors were conveniently gotten out of the way by heavy fines or jail sentences. Harvard students favoring these laws in violation of basic civil liberties expressed their approval by breaking more dormitory windows.

But Hamilton continued to use Washington and Adams as an innocent front, while Jefferson quietly was building up his organization in the field. Without the funds available to Hamilton, hounded by Hamiltonian judges, Jefferson had to carry on his work under cover. But he thrived on the Hamiltonian suppressions. Every editor sitting in jail brought more converts to the Jeffersonians.

On May 8, 1794, twenty-eight of the sixty Farmers General who had helped finance our revolution were

executed in France. The vote in the election of 1796
was: Adams 71, Jefferson 68, Pinckney 60. In this year
the first elephant was imported into the United States.

Hamilton soon had a vision of himself at the head of a
great army marching through South America with England
as his ally. Later he brought out a plan for a complete
change of this nation. There was to be a division of states
into smaller states; Connecticut would be cut up into four,
and Virginia into seven. He prepared his seditious unconstitutional plan in great detail:

The continent [should be] divided into ten, fifteen, or twenty countries, to be governed by a Lieutenant or Prefect appointed by the
Executive; certain subaltern appointments should be in his gift. These
Prefects would constitute as proper an upper House for one branch
of the Legislature as could be devised. [The franchise should be] cut
off from all paupers, vagabonds, and outlaws [the poor, the democrats, and] placed in those hands to which it belongs, the proprietors
of the country.

The bitterness, the lawlessness increased. The merchants,
the creditors, the wealthy, the judges were frantically driving Hamilton still further. The intolerance of this group
was not a novelty in our history. For a hundred years these
colonies had imposed the most sadistic of punishments for
every minor infraction of the law. Punishments for criminals
were in proportion to the convict's social peg in society. If
a boss and a worker were jointly accused of theft, the worker
was flogged, while the boss was merely denied the use of the
word "Sir" in front of his name for three months. When
our first internal war was under way, and Tories fought
Whigs, we drove 100,000 Tories from their homes. In
1776, praying for King George was punishable by a fine of
£1,000. Loyal farmers found their cattle painted in fantastic colors. Not until 1784 did South Carolina permit royal-
ists to return. The Pennsylvania Tories were still disenfranchised as late as 1801. Even tolerant Virginia held
the return of confiscated property scarcely worthy of discussion. We took away without compensation at least forty

million dollars' worth of lands, including the Pepperell estate in Maine (then Massachusetts) running thirty miles along the coast, and the Philipse estate of three hundred square miles in New York. Over two hundred farms were carved out of the Morris confiscated estates in New York and sold in small acreage to farmers on easy payment plans. To Nova Scotia 5,800 former peaceful inhabitants of the colonies were driven, including 3,000 Negroes from New York.

Dueling and brutal fist fights were regular pastime in the South. Eye gouging was considered part of the sport.

Not many years before we wrote our guaranties of private liberty contained in the first ten amendments to the Constitution, we had practiced on the loyalists unbelievable cruelties, solely because of their beliefs, not their actions. No Tory was allowed to deal with a Whig doctor or a Whig lawyer. When the Continental currency was valueless, laws were passed that Tories had to pay their debts in good sound money, but on the other hand were compelled to take in payment for their work and commodities the worthless Continental paper money. The very men who urged the Bill of Rights as an essential amendment to the Constitution had, a decade before, violated all the rights thought to be protected therein, and now, in less than a decade after the ratification of the Bill of Rights, they selected new defenceless minorities on whom once more to exercise suppressions.

The extreme rule of censorship practiced by Hamilton, as might be expected historically, was the result of fears and insecurity. The more he drove against Jefferson's awakening of democracy, the further he had to go in his attempt to stifle free speech and a free press. And the further his excesses went, the more the support for Jefferson dared make itself apparent.

One historical distinction between those days and present times must be drawn. The right to bear arms was provided in the Constitution. Arms meant individual firearms. Poison gas and the machine gun were unknown. Power through force in 1790 was not resident in the skill of a few but in the might of the many. The capacity of destruction did not lie in any perfected airplane bombers. In the history of mankind it is now apparent that democracy has always suffered when the right to bear individual arms was impaired. Mainly by force or threats of force have human beings cut down some of the powers of their rulers.

Mrs Emmeline Pankhurst smashes windows in London in 1912. We grant woman suffrage in 1920. January 1, 1936, Miss Christabel Pankhurst is honored by King George.

Hamilton, blind to the rising power of a belligerent disenfranchised people, never saw the hopeless revolution in which he was leading the Tory brigades. Behind him he had the wealth of cities. He held the power. With cunning, he ran campaigns from his law office in Manhattan. The press, though divided, was not yet on a chain-store basis, owned by vast boiler-plate holding companies. Little printshops worked night and day for Jefferson—for the farmers, for the workers.

This struggle for greater liberty for the bulk of the people was articulated in the most fantastic legal phrases. It was termed a battle between States' Rights and National Controls. In simple language this merely meant that the central government was in the hands of the Tories—the Hamiltonians—the mercantile aristocrats. All those, as Madison wrote, who had "great contempt for people who worked in the field or shop" were for Hamilton and hence for a strong central government, at least so long as men like Hamilton held the power. All those like Jefferson who opposed a central controlled government, if run by the Hamiltonians, fought for local home rule, for controls by the states. This was their way of breaking the backbone of aristocracy in America.

Agrarian democracy won the day, but not until Hamilton had planned to prevent a presidential election so that Marshall would become president, which plans were defeated by

Jefferson's request to the governors of Pennsylvania and
Virginia to have troops ready on election day.

The controversy was not really over a theory of politics.
The issue realistically was not one of states' rights. The
great Hamilton–Jefferson warfare—and men did die for
their sides in the battle—was over a point of view toward
life. The one party had faith in the wisdom of the people;
the other never had anything but disdain for the masses.
Jefferson, fearing the rule of property, said:

God forbid! we should ever be twenty years without such a rebellion.
. . . What country can preserve its liberties if their rulers are not
warned from time to time that their people preserve the spirit of resistance? Let them take arms! . . . What signify a few lives lost in
a century or two? The tree of liberty must be refreshed from time to
time with the blood of patriots and tyrants. It is its natural manure.

The first use of the states' rights doctrine came after the
Whisky Rebellion when local organizations were organized
to control the Alien and Sedition Acts. From that time on
throughout our history, all persons and interests not in sympathy with the national administration at any time have
always invoked the theory of states' rights "as a shelter
against federal authority." No political party, no president,
no outstanding public official in our entire history has not
veered from a centralized national philosophy while in
power to a states'-rights theory when out of power. That
the issue was one of basic philosophy of life and economics
and not one of states' rights can best be proven by the violent nationalist steps taken by Jefferson after he became the
war president.

Jefferson's about-face on taking office is the counterpart
of Hoover's shift to states' rights after he was rejected by
the people at the polls in 1932. Jefferson's international war
against the Barbary coast, his tax program and his unconstitutional Louisiana Purchase are samples of his own generous
use of wide national powers. In fact, Quids were organized
in 1804 by those who believed in states' rights as a protest
against Jefferson who advocated a national program. The

name of Quids arose from *tertium quid,* indicating a separation from both of the *national* parties.

But the second revolution—which in many ways was more important than the first—ended on that day in Washington, the new capital of the United States, that city of wind, mud and scant housing, when Jefferson, sitting between John Marshall and Aaron Burr, became president of the United States.

On charges of treason brought by Jefferson, Burr was to be tried before Marshall. Jefferson and Adams were both to die on the same day, July 4, 1826, a half-century after the adoption of the Declaration of Independence.

The monarchists were put out of the saddle. Ex-President Adams sneaked out of town at four in the morning. He saw conspirators all around him. His servants carried munitions by the back way to withstand a siege. Jefferson on taking office shocked many people by refusing to use the president's throne in the well of the House of Representatives. Presidents Washington and Adams had each worn satin coats and silk knee breeches. Jefferson discarded such uniforms of aristocracy. When he entered the White House he found hanging in the great East Room the dirty underlinen of Abigail Adams.

PART V

The Judges Claim the Veto Power

WHEN *the Supreme Court held its first court session the judges wore gowns of black and scarlet, but at Jefferson's request discarded "the monstrous wig which makes the English judges look like rats peeping through bunches of oakum."*

John Marshall, our third chief justice, needed no hairdress to impress the land with his importance. He took part in 1,106 opinions, wrote 519 himself, and dissented in only eight cases. From our earliest days our judges not only resented all encroachments on their province but capitalized their position of temporal advantage. Automatically they were the last to be heard from. Long after Congress has written a law, often decades after the president has signed a measure, in a contest between two litigants—neither one of necessity a state—the court has a chance to speak its piece. In England judges are relatively unimportant because, if they upset acts of Parliament, Parliament can reverse the court early on the morning following the decision. Not so in this land.

Marshall was writing in an era when the mass of people still had some respect for lawyers and legal language. The members of the Bar were the mystics of the day. A Latin phrase, an involved sentence, a hairsplitting bit of reasoning bewildered the public. With the spread of literacy the high-priest status of the attorneys of the land has happily evaporated. Today the leaders of the Bar are with validity cartooned in comic strip and on silver screen. Wholesome it would be if the public tried to read a few Supreme Court decisions from the days of Marshall or even of Hughes. A still greater popular resentment would develop,

223

for most of the decisions on national issues are so involved that not even the lawyers can agree as to what the judges intend to declare the law to be. If judges deliberately tried to create a confused public mind they would have difficulty in finding more confounding words and phrases. Judicial literary production should, though it seldom does, meet the test of a wide public understanding.

Literacy in 1936, 96 per cent; 1787, 25 per cent.

During all of Marshall's term on the highest bench there were only a few decisions of the Court which have had enduring importance. In every such case, however, Marshall tried to induce the public to believe that the judicial process was a simple one. You hold the Constitution in one hand, the new statute in the other—and without turning back your cuffs you can readily see if the statute does or does not conform to the Constitution. But the theory of precision by comparative glances never becomes persuasive. If a simple reading of the Constitution and a contested statute will tell the tale, why do these judges spread their words over reams of paper? Of course you and I will never be able to understand the process, for not even lawyers obtain the knack until the ermine slips over their shoulders. Nor do all judges read the same words in the same way, for judges often disagree.

For many years eminent lawyers, poring through the records of the Constitutional Convention and the later decisions of the judges, have debated whether the convention really intended that the Supreme Court should have the power to veto acts of Congress. Erudite volumes have issued from the pens of students like Louis B. Boudin to prove that no such power was intended. Jefferson, Madison, Hamilton, Randolph and others can be quoted in support of and against the proposition. Presidents Jackson, Lincoln and Theodore Roosevelt are all used as authorities that such power in a few judges was never intended, and that, even if intended, it is high time that we changed out system.

Only one point in the argument is at rest. We can be sure

that there was no unanimous agreement among all the Founding Fathers that the Court had the power to override Congress. When Marshall first stated that the Court had such power he argued, he explained, he reasoned, he advocated as no man sure of his ground and conclusion, acting under a clear mandate, would ever have done. He pleaded a cause; he did not declare he was following instructions of the Founding Fathers.

One other fact is outstanding. From 1787 until 1870 the Supreme Court in only two cases assumed the power to declare acts of Congress void.

Why is it that the judges for our first century of national government found only two acts of Congress which conflicted with the Constitution? Was Congress better behaved then than now? Did those two decisions prevent innumerable other acts which Congress feared to enact because of judicial veto? These two historic cases are of interest not only because they have a direct bearing on the flood of cases of judicial veto in the decades since 1870, but in themselves they are dramatic stories of judicial impropriety and political jobbery.

CHAPTER XVIII

Mr Marbury and Dred Scott

The Most Famous Judicial Decision of Our History

IN THE MIDST of that great political strife—the second American revolution—President Adams, with the aid of his secretary of state, John Marshall, was plotting to defeat the Jefferson–Madison drive for power. A new method of presidential election by a grand committee with six members from each house sitting in secret sessions, with the chief justice of the Supreme Court as chairman, was proposed. This plan had the approval of Marshall, and Chief Justice Ellsworth, himself a candidate for the presidency, agreed to the entire scheme. That Marshall played in with this illegal plot was to be expected because he had never been fully loyal to his chief, Adams. On the side, secretly, he had given indirect aid to Hamilton. That Ellsworth participated in these extralegal maneuvers was not out of tune with the public concept of judicial position in the year 1800. English judges, it was well known, were frequently consulted in difficult and doubtful cases of proposed legislation; and in this nation, in 1800 and even up to the present, judges have often been informal advisers to the president or the members of Congress. But for a future chief justice of the Court to plot an unconstitutional *coup d'état* is happily not usual.

Marshall had been under constant attack as a cheap politician. Was he not handing out all the jobs he could to Federalist printers? The press of the day openly accused him of employing only "aristocratic presses" to publish the federal laws. Political parties had developed.

The election of Jefferson in 1800 destroyed the Federalist party. The country renounced the Hamiltonians. The de-

feat of the aristocrats was so ignominious that President
Adams refused to wait to welcome the new president.

But before Adams left the Capitol, Marshall and Hamilton had arranged that the lame-duck executives would grab
their last patronage. The newly elected representatives of
the people were of the Jeffersonian group. Only the appointed judiciary—holding over in offices for life or long
terms—could continue to circumvent the popular desires of
the day.

In the last month of Adams' term of office he appointed
John Marshall, a youngster of forty-six, chief justice of the
Supreme Court. But Marshall, being a skillful politician and
never mindful of the impartial aspects of judicial office, continued in his office as secretary of state, as well as chief
justice, an act which, if not clearly illegal, was at least un-
dignified.

On the eve of leaving office, this lame-duck president and
his secretary of state sent to the Senate several nominations
for justices of the peace for the District of Columbia. The
legislation authorizing these appointments had been passed
but a few weeks earlier. The nominations bore the names of
President Adams and the seal of Secretary of State John
Marshall. Marshall's party was trying to entrench itself in
the courts after the country had rejected it at the polls.

These nominations for the "midnight judges" included
one William Marbury. When Adams left office he had failed
to deliver to Marbury and the four other new justices their
commissions to hold office as justices.

Madison, the new secretary of state, was commanded by
the incoming president, Jefferson, not to hand the paper to
Marbury nor to any other of the five "midnight appointees."
Marbury sued to force the President, through Secretary of
State Madison, to complete the appointment and to establish his right to the office. In December 1801 the Court
asked Madison why he shouldn't hand over the commission
and told him to reply at the next term of the Court.

Jefferson and Madison, controlling the presidency and
the Congress, were not scared by this interference with the
executive by the Court. Congress promptly repealed the

Judiciary Act under which the Supreme Court held court and adjourned the next session of the Court until February of 1803. Jefferson and Secretary of State Madison then ignored the Court's requests. Jefferson was adamant in his belief that the three departments were to remain independ-ent. Here was the Supreme Court trying to tell the presi-dent what his secretary of state should do.

Everyone knew John Marshall's prejudice. Today we would call it a set-up. The Chief Justice of the Supreme Court was about to pass on a document which he himself had signed as secretary of state. He decided that Marbury had applied to the wrong court. Under the Constitution the Supreme Court could hear such a case only on appeal from a lower court. He threw Marbury out of court. This in-genious escape of the Justice was particularly cute because it left no appeal to Marbury.

P.S. Marbury never got the job.

But Marshall did not stop writing when he decided the issue before him. He wrote a treatise for the record.

The case takes on significance because this chief justice, playing party politics, in deciding the case wrote a tirade against Jefferson and a thesis on the power of the Supreme Court to invalidate acts of Congress. No such message to the people was needed in order to decide the plea of Mar-bury for his job. It must be kept in mind that Marshall had not seen the minutes of the Constitutional Convention. Those precious records kept by Madison were not made public until nearly thirty years later. In 1827, of the then living delegates at the convention of 1787, Madison wrote: "Of the lamps still burning, none can now be far from the socket." A gentle tenderness for the feelings of the surviv-ing delegates caused Madison to withhold publication, and until 1830 no government officials had been allowed to read the records of the convention. Judges had to guess at mean-ings with little but the naked instrument itself before them. But Marshall did know that an act of 1792 directing the secretary of war to make up certain pension lists had been invalidated by the circuit courts and then repealed and passed in amended form by a later Congress.

In the Marbury case he held not only that if two laws conflict with each other the Supreme Court shall decide "on the operation of each," but that if "a law be in opposition to the constitution" in the minds of a majority of the judges, it becomes the Court's judicial duty to veto the law. Otherwise he said judges must close their eyes to the Constitution. He knew that if they open the Constitution at all to look at it they may not be forbidden from looking at all parts of it. He referred to the clause of the Constitution which prevented an "export tax," and queried: What ought judges do if Congress imposed an export duty on cotton or tobacco or flour? As a slap at Jefferson, without any conceivable effect on Mr Marbury, the litigant, the power of judicial veto was written in a Supreme Court decision.

This obiter dictum was to return to plague us later. But while during Marshall's thirty-year term as chief justice many other acts of Congress were attacked in the courts, never again did he try to invalidate any one of them.

Not until a half-century later was our Supreme Court to override another act of Congress. And then in a decision which required a civil war to undo it.

The Marbury decision was a political tract. Its sinister implications were not discerned in 1803 as clearly as they were a century later.

Mr Scott Is Also Shifted to Another Court

Between 1803, the date of the Marbury decision, and 1857 the Supreme Court never once declared an act of Congress unconstitutional, although on many occasions the justices were asked by litigants to do so. Apparently the justices were content to allow the Congress and the president to interpret the conveniently vague phrases of the Constitution.

During this same period the Constitution remained substantially unchanged. After the first ten amendments were enacted in 1791, two other changes followed in quick order —the Eleventh (1794) which cut down the power of the

Supreme Court to hear complaints brought by citizens against states, and the Twelfth (1804) which changed the unworkable machinery for electing the president and vice-president.

All during this period the Court was increasingly resented by the people of the land. The third case brought to the Court was against the state of New York. New York defied the Court and refused to appear to answer the Court's summons. When some time later Georgia was defeated in the Court by one Chisholm, it flatly refused to obey the order and defied the Court. In 1823 Kentucky passed resolutions assailing the Supreme Court decision in the famous case of Green against Biddle, wherein the compact of 1789 between Virginia and Kentucky was interpreted by the Court in favor of Virginia. After the Marshall decision in the case of the Cherokee nations, the state of Georgia once more defied the Court and President Andrew Jackson is reported as saying: "John Marshall has made his decision. Now let him enforce it."

Roger B. Taney, formerly secretary of the treasury and attorney general under President Andrew Jackson, was sitting as chief justice of the Supreme Court in 1857. He was a daring man. He had the nerve to render his opinions in long trousers instead of in knee breeches. While the Court was in session, sitting in the basement of the Capitol, all the judges, without their wives, lived in a communal boarding house near by.

In 1820 Congress had passed the Missouri Compromise Act for the purpose of "insuring domestic tranquillity." In 1819 the admission of Alabama as a state into the Union equalized the number of free and slave states. The admissions of Maine and Missouri continued the parity of strength in the Senate. The Missouri Compromise Act recognized the jurisdiction of Congress over territories. For some years prior to 1857 a Negro slave named Scott was juggled around like a piece of baggage. His owner had taken him into the free state of Illinois from the slave state of Missouri and then into a part of the territory which is now Min-

nesota, which the act of 1820 had declared free territory.
He was then returned to Missouri. Thereupon he sued to
establish his freedom. In the midst of those migrations
black Dred Scott had been sold to one white, Sanford (first
name not used in the lawbooks). The courts of Missouri
naturally held that no taint of freedom could adhere from
Scott's sojourn on free soil either in Illinois or in the Minnesota territory.

To the Supreme Court the case came on appeal. Chief
Justice Taney, with five judges joining him, held that the
Missouri courts had the last word. One judge agreed with
Taney but for different reasons, and two judges disagreed
entirely.

> *In 1856 the Republican party had proposed that Con-*
> *gress prohibit slavery in all territories. Lincoln had*
> *approved. Taney's decision was an intentional slap at*
> *the Republicans.*

Taney, in legal language, held that Scott, a slave, was not
a citizen of Missouri, and his suit for freedom was dismissed for want of jurisdiction of the Supreme Court. That
is all the Court was called on to decide—whether Scott had
come to the right court. But that didn't satisfy Taney. He
went further and declared the act of 1820 unconstitutional.
Unasked, the Court became legislative, thinking its function
was to settle the burning slavery issue. Taney went further
than Marshall. His Court found that the Supreme Court
had the power not only to veto legislation but to settle by
judicial decisions the harmony and general welfare of the
nation.

> *In 1386 in England the chief justice sided with the*
> *Crown against Parliament in several cases. Chief Jus-*
> *tice Tresilian was arrested by Parliament and hanged.*
> *His associates were exiled. Since then the judges have*
> *been judges, not legislators.*

This part of the decision was written solely for political
purposes. One of the judges wanted to be the candidate for
president on the Republican ticket. Two days before the

opinion was delivered, the president, Buchanan, referred to it in his inaugural address. He thought that the Dred Scott decision would settle the slavery question. Taney's decision meant local determination of the issue. Seward, in the Senate, charged a conspiracy between Taney, Douglas, Pierce and Buchanan.

The editor of the conservative New York *Tribune* at that time, Horace Greeley, wrote that the decision deserved no more respect than if it had been made "by a majority of those congregating in any Washington barroom." That great editor said: "This usurpation must be met by revolt."

Lincoln declared:

Somebody has to reverse that decision and we mean to reverse it. If the policy of the Government upon vital questions affecting the whole people is to be irrevocably fixed by decisions of the Supreme Court— in ordinary litigation between parties in personal actions, the people will have ceased to be their own rulers, having to that extent practically resigned their Government into the hands of that eminent tribunal. Why should there not be a patient confidence in the ultimate justice of the people? Is there any better or equal hope in the world?

If the decision had stood, Congress could not have legislated at all on the subject of property rights in slaves. Lincoln seized this decision as his issue. Aligning himself with Jefferson and Jackson, he rejected the idea of a Supreme Court always supreme over Congress and the president. With Jackson he argued that the Supreme Court had not been given a second veto power over Congress. The president had that power, and only Congress could override him.

That the Court guessed wrong was to be made evident by the Civil War, which might have been avoidable but for this decision. But the power to override Congress was further impressed in our judicial mores.

Judge Manton, presiding judge of the Federal Circuit Court, sitting in New York now, says:

It is the judges' belief that the Constitution is the receptacle of their own private economic or social doctrines that makes for doubt of the day and so ominous the future.

The Court had held that Article IV, Section 3 of the Constitution, which gave Congress power over territories, related only to territories held in 1787, when the Constitution was adopted, and that the statute of 1820 was unconstitutional.

Within a decade of the Dred Scott decision a war and three amendments to the Constitution made future Dreds free in Missouri territory and everywhere else in the nation. Lincoln minced no words when he wrote that the Supreme Court had diluted the doctrine of popular sovereignty as "thin as the homeopathic soup that was made by boiling the shadow of a pigeon that had starved to death." And in 1862 Lincoln's Congress overruled the Dred Scott decision by new legislation. The Court made no protest. Black men were free men, but judges still held all men in their ultimate power.

PART VI

From Pine Knot to Candle to Whale Oil to Gas and Electricity

CHAPTER XIX

Times Do Change

THE MOST DEPLORABLE MYTH in our national history is
that our forefathers were rugged individualists. I find nothing in the history of the period to substantiate it. Daring,
adventurous, hardy they were. But in the fight for life and
better living conditions they were co-operative and communal.

The roads were built by ordering all men over eighteen
years of age to share the work. A new settler coming into a
community was accepted on trial, and if he was approved,
all those who could cut lumber with jackknife or home-made
adz helped him erect a home. The erection of a town clock
was often an act of co-operative sacrifice. In many towns
inhabitants jointly subscribed to a newspaper, and no one,
by the law of some districts, was permitted to read the ad-
vertisements until the circulating newspaper had gone to all
the literate folk for perusal of the news. Then the paper
was kept on public file. Farmers banded together to get
fertilizer from dead fish, and then passed ordinances that
every dog in the district during planting season must have
his legs tied, in order to keep the fertilizer underground.
The district watchmen were the forerunners of our federal
weather bureau. Candles were made by all for all. Pasture
lands were not separate plots.

The economic necessities of the early communities were
handled in common. For the luxuries, each one was on his
own, with substantial advantages bestowed on those who
stood high up in the aristocratic scales. On the way to town
meeting the procession walked according to social rank—
military officers, lawyers, doctors, town officers and then

those called Honorable, Esquire, Mister and Sir; just as
Madison's class at Princeton was seated according to social
standing.

Social security for old age and sickness was provided by
church and state, but often supplemented by family treaties.
Two men, the heads of families, would shake hands in agreement to provide for each other's wife and children.

Such a society often survived or perished, depending on
the degree of the united front which was sustained against
weather, soil and hostile Indians.

Economic individualism crept into our society as opportunity for expansion and advancement became more plentiful. Then those who prospered puffed out their chests
to acclaim with a false modesty that anyone with equal
brains and stamina could do likewise. This human con-
ceit was a play for a response: "There are few as capable
as you."

Soon we deserted the practice of joint effort, even for
those things in life most easily produced free of competition. Public libraries, museums, lighthouses, weather bu-
reaus are a few remnants still thoroughly communized,
supported by the general tax budgets for free use by the
public. Roads, at one time private, are now co-operatively
operated.

New sources of power were discovered. The old water
mill could be harnessed by the town, but steam came out of
many and separate kettles. The communities lost their grasp
over power. Power not only destroyed distances as the
steamboats ran in the rivers, but trains, canary-colored, and
with higher-priced seats near the stoves, permitted further
expansion to the west.

From 1820 to 1850 the invitation of our rich soil induced
immigrants from abroad, immigrants as much resented as
they were one hundred years later when we shut down our
gates.

A new life of things came into existence: we first had a
cotton gin in 1793, brushes in 1808, a street light in 1817,
a baby carriage in 1829, a trust company in 1830, a dynamo
in 1831, an anesthetic in 1842, a baseball team in 1846, a

sewing machine in 1846, bloomers in 1848, safety pins in 1849. In 1852 the first compulsory school bill, requiring twelve weeks of school attendance in each year, was passed in Massachusetts.

In 1829 the Workingmen's Party had polled 30 per cent of the New York City vote. By 1833 the workers adopted the British method of trade organization: a strike instead of political action. Ballots were of no avail. Restrictions on voting precluded the possibilities of victory. Each invention disturbed the labor market. On June 8, 1836, the New York *Journal of Commerce* reports, "27,000 persons assembled at City Hall, New York City. They were mostly radicals." In 1837 the panic reduced wages 50 per cent. In these "iron years" salaries were often paid in commodities.

Persistently, ever since, we have lived with sure expectancy of business cycles. The impacts of the depressions were often cushioned by newly discovered national resources. But inevitably new machines sent more men to the scrap heap. Never in a so-called normal period did the owners of the power and the plants pay their workers enough in wages so that the workers could buy back as consumers the goods they created. At times the owners of production searched in other continents and found other workers who could still buy what we produced.

All during these days the wealth of the nation was being concentrated in fewer and fewer hands.

Before the turn of the century "few people denied the need for reform," wrote Henry Adams. The currency system, the tariff, the corruption of the legislature by railroads and oil men and bankers led to a breakdown of business and government. Then we should have known, as a few sagacious critics did, that the Constitution was as antiquated as the Confederation of the Revolutionary War period.

By 1870 the jackknife with which wooden pegs were made in 1787 had been replaced by a steel mill which today has a tower with a worker, and many buttons to press, and a thousand feet away steel nails pouring out by the millions. By 1870 education had been communized. Fire departments which had as a slogan "No money, no squirty" had been taken into the small circle of activity "affected with a public interest."

Labor continued its feeble efforts to get a greater share in the wealth produced each year. Isolated employers, far in advance of their times, realized that the better the working standards, the greater the consumption power of the land. Some few businessmen started to explode the nonsense of overproduction until all human desires were satisfied. Underconsumption was the proper diagnosis of the disease. But these rare dreamers were turned over to the bankruptcy courts of the land.

From 1870 on, Congress under pressure of public protests experimented with legislative solutions. The concentration of wealth and industry was forcing to the wall small independent merchants. In 1929 the three largest automobile companies made 77 per cent of the cars; in 1934 they made 88 per cent. Industry was maiming thousands of destitute workers. The states played with relief measures such as workmen's compensation laws. Persistently judges prevented progress. Theodore Roosevelt, rejecting such judicial stupidities, cried out to the nation:

> I do speak. Let the people recall the decision. The highest right of a free people is the right to make their own laws; and this right does not exist if under the pretense of interpolation an outside body can nullify the laws. I hold that the people should say finally whether these decisions are or are not to stand as the laws of the land.

But just as no employer could fight the stream alone, so no state, by venturing into legislative controls aimed at equal opportunity and production for use, could create anything but a flight of capital and industry across the state lines. The lowest wages, the most insanitary working conditions, the longest hours, the most fraudulent advertising became the highest common denominator for each industry. Only the pressure of organized workers could raise the standards.

Here we are today, the richest country in the world. We have more wheat, coal, oats and lumber than the rest of the nations of the world together. We have nearly half of the cotton and corn and more than a quarter of the oil. But even in 1928, a banner year, we were using only half of our automobile capacity and only two thirds of our agricultural, machine-tool and shoe capacities. What a land of plenty if we could only use our resources and our factory equipment in full!

From 1900 to 1929 our installed horsepower multiplied nine times. But in the latter year one sixth of all families who did not live on farms spent less than a dollar a day for food. In 1933, before the collapse of the banks, 62 out of every 100 families lived on bare-subsistence diets. One quarter of our city people lived in slums. Over one third of the houses in cities and towns have no sanitation or running water today.

The concentration continues. In 1929 nineteen million workers received less than a thousand dollars a year. That means that they could buy less than a thousand dollars' worth of services and things. But thirteen people out of every 10,000 had incomes of more than $25,000. One per cent of the people received 20 per cent of the income.

And still we need more food and houses. In 1929 we could have used, for a decent feeding of the nation, half as many more cows and calves and sheep and citrous fruits.

The government during all the years since the Civil War expanded its functions in many directions. City, state and national taxes rose. And yet in 1929 we paid no more in taxes to city, state and nation for schools, army, navy, roads, prisons, courts, sewage, libraries, water, police and all the other government services than we were paying to the private companies for electricity, telephone, gas, gasoline and oil.

Bread lines besmirched this land of plenty. The government is forced to save the banks, the insurance companies, the farm owners, the home owners.

With disregard for historical background the nation blamed all of the 1929 collapse on the inflation during the Coolidge and Hoover administrations. The bankers had been permitted to inflate to more than twice our present total national debt. But the calumny heaped on the Hoover administration failed to take into account the contribution to the debacle made by the Supreme Court of the United States.

PART VII

Three Leeways

WHEN *the Founding Fathers wrote the Constitution they provided flexibility by the power of amendment; by a check on congressional action through the presidential veto; and by a special provision for interstate treaties where problems affected some, but not all, of the states.*

Before following the long stream of judicial restrictions over congressional action, let us examine what uses have been made of these three pieces of governmental machinery.

CHAPTER XX

The Veto Power

DURING THE CONSTITUTIONAL CONVENTION many of the delegates were concerned with the need of some remedy in case Congress acted unwisely. The grant of veto power to the president was the solution which they found and incorporated in the Constitution. Many delegates wanted this power of the president to be the absolute and last word, but the compromise finally reached provided that, by a two-thirds vote, Congress may override the veto. Although it was urged that the Supreme Court should also have a veto power, the contenders for that plan were defeated in the convention.

During the terms of office of the six presidents who preceded Jackson (1789–1829) the presidential veto power was used only nine times. Jackson made freer use of this power, but principally to refuse appropriations for internal improvements. Not a single veto was overridden until Tyler's presidency (1841–45) and the power was still in relative disuse until the term of Johnson (1865–69). Johnson's presidency was peculiarly uncomfortable and complicated by the adjustments made necessary after the Civil War. He vetoed twenty-one bills, of which fifteen were repassed by Congress. Most of these measures affected admission of new states, reconstruction measures and bills reshuffling suffrage.

Grant used the veto very seldom, and Cleveland, who vetoed over three hundred bills in his first term of office, applied this power principally on measures giving pensions to individuals.

With Theodore Roosevelt the veto power became significant. His veto of the improvement of Muscle Shoals was socially significant, and the strength of congressional independence of the executive was clearly demonstrated by the reversal of the veto.

Taft vetoed the bill admitting New Mexico and Arizona to the Union, and his attempt to prevent tariff reduction resulted in Congress' overriding him on an issue which contributed greatly to his defeat for re-election. The most illuminating veto in our history was Taft's veto of the Webb–Kenyon Liquor Bill. This measure was an effort of Congress to assist the dry states in their efforts to remain dry. President Taft, a successful lawyer and later to be chief justice of the Supreme Court, vetoed the measure because as a lawyer he was convinced that the bill was clearly unconstitutional. Taft followed the presidential rule of Jackson, who declared that the Congress, the president, and the Supreme Court is each entitled to its own opinion of what is constitutional and no department ought take the others' guess too seriously. But Congress, composed of many lawyers, overrode the veto and then, if you please, the United States Supreme Court unanimously held the measure to be valid.

Wilson vetoed thirty-three bills, the most important being the Prohibition Bill of 1919. Congress overrode his veto.

Harding had to cope with the great War Bonus Bill. His veto was undone by the House but allowed to stand by the Senate.

Coolidge pocketed the Muscle Shoals Bill, vetoed a few post-office and pension appropriations, and destroyed the Federal Farm Board Bill, which lacked but four votes of overriding the veto. The Bonus Bill was repassed over his veto.

Hoover vetoed among others the bill for government of the Philippines, and several pension measures. A Bonus Bill was passed over his veto.

Franklin D. Roosevelt's vetoes have been chiefly bills for private relief, save for the Bonus Bill, the only bill on which his veto has not been sustained by the Congress.

The veto power vested in this elected official, the president, is a keen check on a Congress irresponsive to the will of the people. Although the power has been used only rarely on measures of deep social significance, the very existence of the power has deterred Congress on many measures. Many a measure dies scarcely born when it becomes known that the president will veto it, for the proponents know they must be able to gather together two-thirds support to balance off against the president. Unless they are confident, they abandon the program. The power to override the veto also works as a clear check on the president. Not lightly does he run the risk of being overridden.

The comparative use of vetoes by the president and the later action of Congress is shown in this table:

Pres.	Veto	Over-ridden	Pres.	Veto	Over-ridden
Washington	2	0	Johnson	21	15
Adams	0	0	Grant	43	4
Jefferson	0	0	Hayes	12	1
Madison	6	0	Garfield	0	0
Monroe	1	0	Arthur	4	1
Adams	0	0	Cleveland	301	2
Jackson	12	0	Harrison	19	1
Van Buren	0	0	Cleveland	43	3
Harrison	0	0	McKinley	6	0
Tyler	9	1	Roosevelt	41	1
Polk	3	0	Taft	31	1
Taylor	0	0	Wilson	33	5
Fillmore	0	0	Harding	5	0
Pierce	9	5	Coolidge	20	4
Buchanan	8	0	Hoover	21	3
Lincoln	3	0	Roosevelt	113	1

The pocket veto was held valid in 1929 by the Supreme Court. It is a veto effected by the president holding a bill after Congress adjourns. He says neither "yes" nor "no" to the measure, and it dies by pocket veto.

Some critics ask, "Why object to the odd-man—five-to-four—decisions in the Supreme Court when the president—

one person alone—can exercise a veto power?" The analogy is far from apt.

The president is elected for a short term. He is under public control. He can be refused a re-election at the end of four years, and in the meanwhile the people can elect to Congress persons who will by a two-thirds vote override his veto should a negative by the president be objectionable to the people of the land. The Supreme Court judges are set for life. They are not elected. Their appointments do not coincide with the emergence of new issues. They are removed from popular selection. There is no easy relief in case they err. The ninth vote on that bench in those five-to-four decisions carries a fatality to be corrected only by rare and devious later reversals by later Supreme Court judges in later cases or by the cumbersome machinery of amending the Constitution.

CHAPTER XXI

State *versus* State

UNDER THE CONFEDERATION the states had settled their boundary, navigation and commerce disputes by compacts, or in rare instances by suits before the Supreme Court of the Confederation. Under the new Constitution, Wilson of Pennsylvania, on the Committee on Detail, pointed up the language of the old Articles of Confederation in order to make a distinction between treaties with foreign nations on the one hand and compacts between states on the other. State agreements rather than suits were to be encouraged.

Massachusetts and New York had just had a case before Congress, with Rutledge sitting as one of the judges. The court constituted by the Confederation had decided as far back as January 1783 in favor of Pennsylvania in a case against Connecticut. Vermont through its governor had hoped that Congress in 1784 would keep its hands off the New York-Vermont dispute. The Delaware-New Jersey disputes, begun before the Revolution, were not finally put to sleep until 1849. Connecticut had closed her courts to citizens of Massachusetts because her own citizens could not collect their debts in Massachusetts under its Tender Laws. New Jersey contested with Pennsylvania the lands along and under the Delaware River; New York and Massachusetts were fighting over three million acres in western New York. Virginia claimed part of Pennsylvania.

The clause as originally penned made the Supreme Court a complete judge of all matters "which may involve the national peace and harmony." But the delegates wanted no such judicial tyranny, although many people today think that the judges of the Supreme Court are acting as if those

249

broad general powers were granted to the Court by the Constitution. But the Founding Fathers narrowed these powers and defined the Court's jurisdiction. At least they thought they did. And in those powers the emphasis was laid on "controversies between two or more states." This was novel in world history. For the first time, states were bound to obey decisions of a court. Sovereign states would be subject to a summons of a court. According to Jefferson, "this set up a kite to keep the henyard in order."

From 1789 until our times about thirty states have sued other states. There have been about ninety decisions by the Supreme Court. In four cases "armed conflicts between militia and citizens of contending states" accompanied the lawsuits: *New Jersey* v. *New York,* 1820; *Missouri* v. *Iowa,* 1840; *Louisiana* v. *Mississippi,* 1900; *Oklahoma* v. *Texas,* 1920.

In arguing the interstate suits as to rights in the Hudson River the counsel in court in 1824 declared: "Here are three states almost on the eve of war," and New York defiantly and none too politely refused to acknowledge the Court's power, thus unwittingly supporting Calhoun in his development of nullification sentiment. In the Missouri-Iowa dispute 2,600 state troops were actually armed and called into action.

In each of these cases the states were not fighting about the colors to be put on maps in school geographies. It was always a contest of commerce. These battles were miniature Ruhr Valley, Danzig Corridor, Alsace-Lorraine industrial and agricultural controversies. In 1900, in the Texas and Louisiana case, Louisiana objected to the Texas quarantine on yellow fever, claiming the embargo was an excuse for shifting commerce from New Orleans to Galveston. In 1902 Kansas and Colorado were engaged in commercial warfare, Kansas fearful that Colorado's irrigation of its agricultural lands would prevent Kansas farm products from competing in the markets of the nation.

The Louisiana-Mississippi case decided in 1906 involved great financial interests—the oyster fisheries. Each state employed armed patrols during the ten years that the case dragged. Not lightly was oyster commerce to be surrendered. The Washington-Oregon contest of 1909 involved the control of the salmon industry. Fish were shipped throughout the nation from these waters. North Dakota and Minnesota as late as 1923 were in court on Dakota's claim that the Minnesota drainage program had flooded Dakota farms.

These interstate problems were the expected controversies of 1787. The Supreme Court tried to avoid taking these cases because back of each case stood a state army which threatened defiance. At the start it refused to take on boundary cases unless some property rights were involved. Later the Court hesitated even to pass on a state's liability on its outstanding indebtedness. More recently the Court was in doubt whether it could entertain a case where it was clear that the state action against another state was for commercial purposes. Now, however, the Court takes on all these cases, and the number of cases is growing.

But courts are inept in the treatment of these commercial battles. Solutions are never immediate. The cases drag in court year after year:

Missouri-Illinois case, seven years—1900 to 1907.
Maryland-West Virginia, nineteen years—1891 to 1910.
Virginia-West Virginia, twelve years—1906 to 1918.
Wyoming-Colorado, eleven years—1911 to 1922.

These delays, shocking as they appear, have their advantageous aspects. The Supreme Court of course has no power to enforce its decrees. Mr Hughes cannot lead a posse of sheriffs into Colorado or West Virginia or any other territory to collect some money, divide up the salmon in the streams, or fill up some ditches. The interstate cases, starting with troops and great local heat, during the delays of our judicial machinery simmer down, allowing new issues and new local hates to detract public attention from the guesses of the nine judges.

To overcome the expense, delays, and seldom-satisfactory results of litigation, many states have preferred interstate compacts rather than litigation of current issues. Northcutt Ely has figured that there have been over sixty such interstate compacts.

State treaties are attracting much attention at this time. Virginia, Illinois, Pennsylvania, Alabama and West Virginia coal-mine owners have bankrupted each other with cutthroat competition. Thousands of coal miners have been living at starvation levels. No one mine owner, no one district, no one state is able to prevent or even to reduce this interstate warfare. What each state wants to accomplish for itself it can perform only in unison with other states.

When a single state fixes the work conditions and minimum wages of miners, the Supreme Court holds that the law is unconstitutional. When in the federal Congress such a state gets enough support from the representatives of other states to set up those same standards and in addition to protect the consumers on the price of coal, that same court, by a close vote, holds that the coal industry is not sufficiently interstate to permit constitutional regulation by the federal government.

Unless these vetoes by judges of both state and federal legislation are overridden, only two avenues to prevent starvation and industrial warfare are possible. Either we wait until the United Brotherhood of Mine Workers becomes so forceful that it can dictate its own factors of stability, in which event the same judges may hold that such dictation violates the "due process" or some other clause of the Constitution; or those states interested in the sane production and distribution of coal get together on an interstate compact. Many able commentators have favored the latter course.

Interstate industrial compacts are urged by those who fear too much centralization of power in the national government on the one hand, and the total incapacity of any single state to prevent an impending industrial debacle on the other. Commerce, they say, is truly so interlocked that there is no human being who can separate the merchandise that remains within the bounds of a single state from that which flows over the borders of that state. The same railroad or truck or airplane carries both types of goods. The same pick and sweat dig both hunks of coal out of the same pit.

Aside from banking, only in the field of railroad rates has the Supreme Court been helpful. In that case it has held that the power of Congress over interstate rates controls many phases of the intrastate rates along the same route. Where there is an overflow of tracks beyond a state line a state may not disturb the national planning and control. But raw materials and finished products carried on those rails acquire no such relief, although much merchandise is created for ultimate use in another state.

The motive for interstate trade compacts lies in the valid fear of a national bureaucracy. Between 1881 and 1930 the number of our state- and federal-government employees has increased 440 per cent as against 200 per cent increase in Germany and France. At present about one out of every six jobs is a government job. Of the three and a half million persons on the public pay rolls, considerably less than a third are on federal projects. But the executive department of the United States has risen from 6,327 employees in 1816 to 616,837 in 1931.

In the Constitutional Convention the delegates were warned that the president would be too busy to make all the appointments personally. "How can he take time to appoint every tidewaiter" said one delegate. Response: "He will sign appointments in blank."

Such interstate compacts would have to be negotiated between all states similarly affected by the economic situation calling for relief. Except for commodities fixed by nature or climate in definite territories, the compacts would have to be nationwide. Therein is the fallacy of the proposal. Even with milk, a perishable commodity, we find Wisconsin farmers inextricably dependent on New York City consumers. And if New York, New Jersey, Connecticut and Pennsylvania made a milk treaty to protect the farmer and get cheaper milk into the homes, would not

Delaware or Maryland dairies destroy the stability by temporary breaking of the standards established?

Natural resources do not lie necessarily in contiguous states. West Virginia coal is in indirect competition with that dug from Alabama mines. And even if all the coal states were brought into one treaty, the oil of Texas or California could compete the compact out of existence.

New York City dominates the men's clothing market. Baltimore and Chicago also are important factors. Let Illinois, Maryland and New York get together to prevent the sweating of labor, to prevent corrupt unfair competition between the manufacturers, and some antisocial person— a rugged individualist—will bob up in Portland, Maine, Kansas City, Missouri, or some other place to work the laborers longer hours at less wages. Then Missouri and Maine must be added to the pact.

Only dreamers can believe such devices will work at all, even if all the states concerned with coal or ice or bread could be induced to enter into treaties. Hundreds of treaties between each state and other states would be needed to protect the workers, the consumers and the owners. If the treaties were of producing states there would be no adequate concern for the consumers in nontreaty states. Treaties fill a need for bridges, or water supply, or even garbage disposal. But for oil or pants or milk they would spell little save a united front of productive states to gouge the consuming states. Moreover, no one can be sure that the Supreme Court would permit such treaties. Although the Constitution on its face appears to permit interstate trade compacts in case Congress has not covered the field, the Court, nevertheless, if intent on preventing social measures like the minimum-wage legislation, may resent an attempt to get around by treaty what a single state may not do alone.

But if one can't divest these nine men of their power, and if interstate treaties cannot be made effective, it is urged that new overlying states should be created. Our states are haphazard units. The boundaries were not determined by economic factors but only by the whims of distant kings. A

group of gentle persons of great integrity have been pressing for decades to create new regional governments. The
states would continue for municipal and not industrial purposes. New England would be one region, New York and
New Jersey a second, Pennsylvania, Delaware and West
Virginia a third. Other regions would be created out of the
South Atlantic, Northwest, Southwest states, and so on.

All of the objections to interstate commerce compacts
would apply to the creation of such new regions. Such regions would for many purposes have to be contiguous, but
commerce in commodities flows in a nationwide contiguity.
There is no one region of coal or oil or dress consumers.
The nation consumes without regard to state lines, and if
the purpose of production is consumption no production regions can cope with the commerce problem except under a
national plan and national controls.

Wherein lies the danger of congressional instead of regional action? No state is omitted from the rostrum of senators. An examination of the throttling effects of the judicial
vetoes in all fields will indicate that Congress has had a consistently fuller understanding of our industrial dilemma
than have the judges. Representatives and senators, because
they must go back home for re-election, remain better informed of the wishes of the citizens of the nation. They
learn from present life rather than from ancient tomes. Increasingly they learn that men and women will not much
longer tolerate suffering and starvation because five out of
nine judges declare that a desired process to prevent suffering is not what the Founding Fathers had in mind. The people of the land no longer believe that law is sanctified, that
all the wisdom of our day is concentrated in a majority of
these nine men, or that the nine men are even correct in their
estimates of what Madison and Hamilton had in mind.

The debates in Massachusetts on the ratification of the
Constitution have been preserved. There the Constitution
was adopted by the convincing argument that the instrument gave Congress a national control. Mr Dawes, an advocate of the Constitution, observed: "If we wish to *encourage our own manufactures,* to preserve our own commerce,

to raise the value of our own lands, we must give Congs. *the powers* in question." In Connecticut and Rhode Island these sentiments were confirmed. In Pennsylvania, no records being preserved, nothing certain can be said as to what passed in her constitutional convention on this point. In Virginia and North Carolina, the only two states south of Pennsylvania with preserved records, certainly no adverse inferences can be drawn. The two states farthest south viewed "the encouragement of manufacturers" as within the commerce power of Congress.

Whether the dangers of a centralized bureaucracy are exaggerated, whether the evils of such concentration are to be preferred to forty-eight separate conflicting state governments, are matters on which the ninety-six Senators and 435 Congressmen elected from the forty-eight states must be allowed to take their positions, subject to public approval or rejection in their subsequent prayers for re-election. We, the people, through those spokesmen may from time to time say: "Let's try unified controls in coal, in banks, in old-age retirement plans, in the growing and marketing of agricultural produce, in control of stock speculators, in the flow of light and power to homes, factories and farmers." To permit the economics of the nation to be determined by indirection by appointed judges is nothing less than a distrust of the democratic process.

CHAPTER XXII

The Amending Process

Within two years after the adoption of the Constitution, one hundred and eighty-nine proposed amendments were considered by Congress. Within fifteen years twelve had been ratified. The Constitution had been adopted on condition that ten of these changes be promptly made; another followed when the Supreme Court was defied by Georgia; and the twelfth was needed to straighten a presidential election muddle.

From 1804 up to 1913—that is, for over a century—the Constitution was never amended except, as Lord Bryce wrote, "in a revolutionary movement which had dislocated the Union itself."

In the middle of that span the Civil War amendments were jammed through. In 1862 the Corwin amendment to the Constitution prohibiting federal interference with slavery had passed both houses of Congress. But war rewrote the amendment. The Thirteenth, Fourteenth and Fifteenth amendments were ratified in one year and eight months, two years and one month, and two years and eleven months respectively. The Fifteenth passed under military pressure. Ratification having been refused, the Reconstruction Act gave the anti-slavery group the power to wrest the amendment from reluctant Southern state legislatures.

From 1870 to 1913—forty-three years—there was not a single amendment. Four hundred proposals were introduced into Congress between 1870 and 1890. Over one hundred were on the term and method of electing the president. Only four passed even one of the houses of Congress. Another four hundred proposals were pressed from 1889 to

257

1913—many directed at the presidential term of office, some to overcome the dead hand of the Supreme Court, and others to legalize woman suffrage.

From 1913 to date—twenty-three years—there were again over four hundred proposals. Six were ratified.

After two decades of agitation, it took two years to get through the Sixteenth Amendment. Capitalizing a movement of a generation, President Taft stole Bryan's plank and urged the income-tax amendment.

The Seventeenth was needed to hush up scandals in state legislatures and in the United States Senate. By that change the people themselves were to elect their senators. Thus, the Founding Fathers' attempt to keep the people remote from their senators disappeared from our basic law. One more check in the original Constitution was abrogated—after a century of urging.

The Eighteenth was rushed through while we were at war. Forty years of agitation in political form brought the Prohibition Act. The businessmen, under Rockefeller's aegis, wanting sober workers, joined with the Methodist Church and pointed to the need of grain conservation for the military machine abroad.

Within fourteen years the Twenty-first Amendment repealed the Eighteenth Amendment, but the repeal was accepted as a crime-preventive measure and as a plan for raising taxes.

The woman-suffrage amendment, the Nineteenth, was the fruit of a century of progress in the unslaving of women. Militant window breaking was needed to get some action out of the male rulers.

The Twentieth was another long battle to prevent the people being bilked by their discredited officials. It brought the date of inauguration of elected officials nearer to the dates of their elections. It closed up the gap during which defeated officials still ran the country. From the start of the nation lame-duck congressmen, senators and presidents took their last licks in pique and bitterness. Adams and Marshall slipped over, as appointments for judges, men who at the previous election had been rejected by the people. Check up through Hoover and you will find the same cheap last-minute perversion of popular will. The lame-duck amendment was needed in 1933 much more than in 1787. One hundred and fifty years ago the time between election day and the inauguration was consumed in great part by the necessities of tortoise-like travel. Trains, airplanes and passable roads lessened the time gap.

Let us summarize: Fourteen amendments were the result of revolutionary movements; two were for the sole purpose of overruling the Supreme Court; one was to hush up scandals; two to restore to the people the control of their elected servants.

There is one clause in the Constitution, however, that is amendable only on unanimous consent: "No state shall without its consent be deprived of its equal suffrage in the Senate." This section prevents a full-flung democracy. But its very lack of faith in popular power makes it doubly safe to trust to Congress that no section of the nation can be destroyed to the advantage of another.

In our entire one hundred and fifty years the peaceful, lawful machinery proposed by the Founding Fathers for a national constitutional convention for consideration of amendments has not been tried. On the application of the legislatures of two thirds of the states such a convention for proposing amendments shall be called by Congress. That clause has interesting possibilities in these days when so many hundreds of proposals for amendments are being thrown into the hopper. Without such a clause in the Articles of Confederation our present constitution was created in 1787 by just such a process.

Delegate Morris knew that the instrument ought not be frozen:

If we cannot agree on a rule that will be just in all times to come, surely those who come after us will judge better of things present than we can of things future.

If we, in 1936, would keep faith with the 1787 attitude toward change we would move from the economic pocket in which the Supreme Court has caged us. Law should conform to modern living. The amending process is not equipped to adapt our government to piecemeal necessary improvements. In a world stepped up to violent revolutionary changes we require a far more flexible apparatus for fulfilling in legislative action the clear demands of the citizens.

PART VIII

The Court Vetoes Congress

FROM *1787 until 1865, a period of nearly eighty years, the judiciary claimed the right to veto acts of Congress on only two occasions. Since then on sixty-seven occasions the Supreme Court judges have nullified the acts of Congress. Many of these sixty-seven statutes were voided by close votes of the Court. After reading the same briefs and hearing the same arguments, Judge Roberts declared the AAA unconstitutional while Judge Stone found it well within the Constitution. Both men are considered able lawyers! Forty-two of these voided laws were passed by Congresses in control of the Republican party, twenty when under the leadership of the Democratic party, and five when the Congress was divided between the two parties or when the vote was truly nonpartisan. In nearly every case judges sitting in other courts had upheld the statutes which the Supreme Court threw out as void.*

Since 1920 the Court has vetoed more acts of Congress than in the previous hundred and thirty years. Moreover, in more than three hundred cases where the highest courts of the separate states found nothing objectionable in state legislation, the Supreme Court would not allow the acts to stand. More than one hundred separate attempts have been made by the states to correct what they thought to be economic evils, only to find that the Supreme Court said: You can't do that. It relates to commerce among the states, and Congress alone is supreme in interstate trade. In only eight states of the Union do we find that the state supreme courts have consistently guessed the same way the Supreme Court of the United States eventually guessed. In these eight states

261

the state courts have never been reversed on points of constitutionality by the Supreme Court at Washington.

These more than three hundred judicial vetoes of state and sixty-seven of congressional legislation are no doubt one of the main causes of our economic depression. The Court has enforced continued inequality of opportunity among our people and prevented practically every attempt to reduce the miseries of unemployment, old age, disease and accident. It has put its foot down on industrial nationalism. It has not allowed the governmental machinery to be brought up to date, to be in tune with the new industrialism. It compels employers to destroy each other, the better man's victory being clearly Pyrrhic. It condemns the nation to a laissez-faire policy never intended by the vital Founding Fathers.

Eminent critics exclaim: How can these few cases be so important? Congress passes thousands of bills each decade, but the judges have vetoed on an average only a few each year since the Civil War.

The answer must be obvious. Each time the judges kill a particular bill they in effect say to Congress, or to the states: The evil you are trying to remedy cannot be touched by you.

Let us take one example. The textile mills of the North were winding up in a trail of bankruptcies. After the Civil War, if you held a map of the United States flat in your hand, spread some sand (representing industrial organizations) on the New England edge of the map, and then tilted that edge slightly upward, the result would have given a picture of what was actually happening: the industrial organizations of New England were gradually sliding down into the Carolinas and other Southern states. Down there labor was cheaper, cost of living was lower, and in addition children from six years up were working in the mills. Hamilton's prophecy had proven true. But we saw New England unable to compete on such terms.

The elected representatives of all the states sitting in Congress were concerned about the general welfare of the nation. Interstate commerce, they believed, was being

*affected by child labor. In 1918 the states, acting through
Congress, prohibited goods made by child labor from flowing in interstate commerce. By a vote of five to four the Supreme Court declared that the Founding Fathers intended
the states to regulate the hours of child labor and that Congress could have nothing to do with it, no matter what
effects simple congressmen saw on interstate commerce as
a result of child labor. Usually our elected officials give up
after one such rebuff. But four years later the Court had
another opportunity to slap down another congressional
attempt to control child labor. This time Congress used its
taxing power and placed a tax on goods in interstate commerce made by child labor. By eight to one the judges held
that the tax was a penalty and could not be applied. After
that, Congress asked, What's the use?—although it found
it hard to believe that the liquor-tax legislation had never
contained the least suggestion of being a "penalty" on too
much tippling!*

*What happened to the mandates of the Founding
Fathers? What did we do with the congressional powers to
coin money, regulate interstate and foreign commerce, levy
taxes, and all the other instruments placed by the states in
the hands of their representatives at Washington? Did Congress use these powers in due time? Did the Supreme Court
interfere? Where has the Court left us in this muddle?*

CHAPTER XXIII

The Weasel Words of the Constitution

DURING THE LAST FIFTY YEARS the fundamental clauses set forth in the Constitution have been modified or whittled away by the Supreme Court. The extent to which the judges have made themselves the ultimate legislators will be apparent by tracing the use of the separate powers.

Treaty Powers

The treaty power set forth by the Founding Fathers was supposed by them to be one of the most important commercial powers vested in Congress.

Without direct signed treaties Congress has always regulated our imports to and exports from foreign lands. By means of the tariff it determines just what foreign commodities may enter our shores. By high tariff protection we have encouraged the development of selected new industries. By import duties we have been able to benefit the city folk at the expense of the agricultural portions of the nation. Tariffs are truly unilateral treaties, for any tariff against the goods of any foreign nation inevitably induces separate reciprocal tariff walls at the other end of the flow of commerce. Recently these international trade adjustments are being more frankly inserted in treaties with foreign nations. Whether the Court will permit such treaties has not been decided.

The Court has done little to interfere with this treaty power, but one very odd situation has arisen which may make our judicial department appear quite inconsistent if not ludicrous. In order to prevent the undue killing of birds and the preservation of bird life, a treaty was entered into

265

between the United States and Canada. The treaty set up certain closed seasons. By an act of Congress in 1918 the United States prohibited the killing, capturing or selling of migratory birds except as permitted by regulations of the Department of Agriculture under the treaty. The state of Missouri protested. It claimed that birds were not engaged in interstate commerce and that Congress could not do under the treaty power what it might not do by ordinary statute.

The high judges found:

Here a national interest of very nearly the first magnitude is involved. It can be protected by national action in concert with that of another power.

A national economy in bird life is lawful.

We ought to find a pet among the nations. What if Panama or Costa Rica made a treaty with us for minimum wages, hours of labor and unemployment insurance? Maybe the Court would hesitate before invalidating a treaty. Maybe there are no limits on the treaty-making power. Certainly the mere competence or incompetence of the state to act is not a limitation. Will the treaty power cover a bird's wing but omit a child's health?

Due Process

New York State, after many years of political debate, enacted a law declaring that ten hours a day were the most that any man should work as a baker. The Supreme Court of the United States (five-to-four vote) declared the act void. It held that it violated the due-process clause of the Constitution. This case of 1905 has been followed, distinguished and overlooked but never directly reversed.

What is that clause which condemned men to work limitless hours and later permitted states to limit the working hours of women?

After the Civil War three amendments to the Constitution were passed by Congress and ratified by the states. These amendments were intended to subdue the Southern states and to assure Negroes their new freedom. The Thirteenth abolished slavery and the Fifteenth was intended to give civil rights to Negroes. The Fourteenth, adopted under military pressure, is our longest amendment. Added in 1868, it contains five sections. One abolished the rule of the Founding Fathers that five Negroes equal three whites politically. Another disqualified all Confederates from holding office unless Congress removed the disability. Another voided the debts of the Confederate states. Another established the principle that no state shall abridge the privileges of citizens, nor "deprive any person of life, liberty, or property without due process of law."

This last clause, smuggled into a long amendment, controls today the length of hours we work, the pay we get, the railroad rates we pay, our use of ice and bread and milk.

The average citizen reading the entire Fourteenth Amendment might reasonably entertain a belief that it was written to protect the newly freed Negroes. Our Constitution in the Fifth Amendment contained a similar "due-process" phrase. It will be recalled that the Fifth Amendment was part of the Bill of Rights—those first ten amendments which were added to the Constitution promptly after its original adoption. This certainly was intended to refer to civil liberties, and in fact these words, "due process," in the Fifth Amendment, prior to the use of the same words in the Fourteenth Amendment were never given any meaning by the courts other than one that related to court procedure. Not until 1886 did the Court void any act of Congress because of the "due process" words in the Fifth Amendment.

The first test case as to the meaning of "due process" under the Fourteenth Amendment did not concern either Negroes or due process. It had nothing to do with what you or I would think of when we mention due process. No one attacked the fairness of a trial, the right to get counsel, the amount of bail or the absence of a jury trial. Rather did it concern the freedom of Southern whites from the oppression of Northern carpetbaggers.

The Louisiana legislature had set up a corporation to run a slaughterhouse in New Orleans and decreed that no animals could be slaughtered except by that corporation. Local butchers protested. They were being put out of business. They claimed that they were losing their businesses "without due process of law." By a vote of five to four the Supreme Court of the United States rejected the claim of the local butchers and held that their property was not being taken "without due process of law" as mentioned in Section 1 of the Fourteenth Amendment. In the decision on this case, known as the Slaughter House Case, the Supreme Court said that the federal government has only limited power as to what goes on in a state. This was in 1873. The judges declared that due process "has never been supposed to have any bearing upon or inhibit laws that indirectly work harm and loss to individuals." In that decision the judges pooh-poohed the idea of the due-process clause being used to protect the private butchers of New Orleans.

Nor was the amendment held to be of any real use to the civil liberties of the Negroes. Congress believed that under the new amendments giving the Negroes the rights of free persons, no hotel or train or theater should be allowed to discriminate on the ground of color. Congress enacted several anti-Jim Crow laws. But the courts by a vote of eight to one in 1883 said: No—those amendments are directed only against states, and hence employers and railroads and innkeepers cannot be forced to treat all citizens equally. Thus for a time the due-process clause was without significance industrially and inadequate to help the Negro socially.

But within a few years these same vague words were used by the same judges to argue that no state might regulate the prices charged by grain elevators. This, though all the judges must have known that eight of the thirteen colonies in 1787 regulated many commodities by fixing the retail prices thereon.

Gradually these vague procedural words were twisted and turned so that the interpretation of the Slaughter House Case was entirely forgotten. Every important move of every state impinging on the health of workers, the happiness of its citizens, the security of old age, the spread of plenty was attacked as being in violation of due process.

The Supreme Court judges in a short time became the supreme legislators of the nation. They drew the lines for social legislation.

We may regulate our milk business but not our ice. We may regulate our ice business if we get ice over wires into our refrigerators, but not if brought into the homes by trucks. That milk is valueless for babies unless it is cool, is not important when construing the words "due process." We may prevent mine owners from working their miners underground more than eight hours a day, but bakers' days may not be limited to ten hours. We may regulate dentists, but we cannot provide honest standard sizes for loaves of bread. Barbershops may be closed on Sundays, but do not try to regulate the trade of horseshoeing.

We may regulate the insurance business without bumping into due process, but theater-ticket speculators must be permitted their constitutional rights to scalp the public. Cotton ginning may be regulated, but private employment agencies have a constitutional right to charge a fee to the unemployed job hunter rather than to the boss who intends to hire him. We may regulate fortunetellers, but we may not fix minimum wages for women and children in industry. We may injure chain stores and trading-stamp companies, but only if the legislators go at it with certain special techniques.

Bear in mind that such cases come to the Supreme Court of the United States for interpretation under the due-process clause only after the elected state officials have enacted the needed legislation. Some of the legislation is thought wise for health reasons. Ten hours at a baker's oven were deemed by the people of New York the limit of healthy working hours. But the judges, turned medicos, disagreed. Nor did they say that the limit was eleven or fifteen or seventeen hours a day. For miners they thought eight hours enough. Would they say five or six or seven hours in a mine might also be the legal limit?

Since so many of these laws have been vetoed or sustained on the ground of health, perhaps we would be better off if some of the judges of the future were appointed from the

medical instead of from the legal profession. So long as
these appointed officials have the final power to fix hours
of labor it is difficult to find any distinction between legislative and judicial review. The citizens of the land are naturally bewildered. Will the judges think fourteen hours too
much for a bridge builder, five hours for a peanut vendor,
sixteen hours for a manicurist? Is not such mathematical
determination the function of legislators?

Then again, when states wish to regulate fields of business such as coal or ice or bread or milk, the final choice of
businesses to be subjected to orderly competition and proper
distribution methods rests with the majority of the nine
judges. Even a Brandeis says the Court has the right to prevent a state experiment. All of the judges hold they must
strike down any law that is "arbitrary, capricious or unreasonable." These are the judicial illegitimate relatives of
"due process." And yet in every divided opinion of the Supreme Court some judges are judicially determining that the
other judges who do not make up the majority are also
"arbitrary, capricious and unreasonable." Slight solace to
congressmen!

The judges hold that a "state cannot by legislative fiat
convert a business into a public utility." They say it violates
due process. But why should our elected representatives not
say: this business concerns our general welfare so keenly
that it may no longer ride random over the public? Why
should judges have the power to convert by fiat a public
utility into a private business?

Fee-charging employment agencies are examined by a
state legislature. The legislature determines to regulate that
type of business. On a referendum to the people of the state
the regulation is approved by an overwhelming vote. All
the lower courts sustain the legislation. No longer may such
agencies place their charges on the unemployed—those least
able to pay.

Then the Supreme Court declares the regulation in violation of the Fourteenth Amendment.

A railroad objects to local taxes. The Supreme Court
looks at the taxes, the rates, the earnings of the railroad

and orders the taxes to be reduced. No wonder that lawyers have suggested that the proper address to the Court should be: Mr Tax Commissioner Hughes.

My electric-light bill is too high. I complain. My state commission orders the company to reduce the rate. I am a fool if delighted; for, years later, a decision comes down that my legislature, my public-service commission, my state courts were all in error. The new rate, says the Supreme Court of the United States, violates the due-process clause. The company is entitled to a greater return to its stock-holders.

The importance of the due-process clause is not that the Supreme Court has allowed 8 per cent return on utility investments instead of 7 or 6 or 9 per cent. The fact that states may not determine the fair return, select the industries to be regulated, protect the health and happiness of workers by shorter hours, prevent cutthroat competition in ice or coal or bread, reduce the misery of underpaid women and children in industry—this frustration of the states is the crux of our national bankruptcy.

Each veto by the Supreme Court is taken to mean that no other legislation of similar content would pass the nine men. Why try to protect steel workers if legislation to protect bakers cannot get by? And, mind you, we would be just as badly off if the Supreme Court had validated the New York law protecting bakers and invalidated the Utah law for miners.

"Due process" has come to mean, "What kind of a society do the judges want to see in this land?" for miners or bakers, women or children. Under this clause the Court is now "the censor of our social and economic policies."

Taxation

We have seen how the power to tax was thought essential in 1787. The power to tax vested in Congress by the Constitution was one of the features of the Constitution which distinguished it from the Articles of Confederation.

In 1791 the federal government had set up a national

bank. The charter ran for twenty-five years. The War of
1812 had strained the credit of the land. State banks were
organized in the East and in the fast-spreading Western
development. By 1816 there were nearly 250 state banks
with great quantities of notes outstanding. In the crash
most of them closed their doors. The Second Federal Bank
—chartered in 1816—started to press for payment on all
notes which it held. The bank was poorly managed—no
worse than the state institutions had been, but local interests made political capital out of the chaos. Laws were
passed to prevent the Federal Bank doing business in various states. The method of exclusion was a high annual tax.
In Maryland the tax was to be $15,000 per annum.

James McCulloch in 1819 was a cashier of the Federal
Bank. He was sued for $15,000 by Maryland. The state
judges said McCulloch must pay that sum. On appeal to the
Supreme Court, Marshall said otherwise. Marshall and his
Court said that, although Congress had not been given by
the Constitution the power to organize a bank, it was nevertheless within the Constitution because, after enumerating
certain powers granted to Congress, the Constitution said to
Congress: You may enact "all laws which shall be necessary and proper" for carrying into effect the listed powers
and all others vested by this Constitution in the government
of the United States. This case was argued before the Supreme Court for nine days by six lawyers. In 1936 the
judges listen to brief arguments only and refuse to hear
many of the persons vitally and directly affected by their
decisions.

For a long time this decision made sense. Marshall
meant: The Founding Fathers listed up all the specific jobs
they could think of that Congress ought to do, and then said
in effect: Do whatever else you think necessary to carry out
these jobs or any other jobs under the Constitution, which
you think will help the general welfare.

But the public was outraged at the decision. Marshall
took the stump to defend himself. In Ohio the state officers
broke open a national bank and took the money demanded
as a tax. Even though President Jackson, twenty years later,

was to tell the public he intended to disregard this decision, Marshall's banking theory has been accepted by the nation, as evidenced by a host of banking institutions set up by the federal government—the RFC created by President Hoover, farm loan banks, the federal reserve system, et cetera. But Marshall, of the facile pen, was seldom content with merely deciding the issue. In this case he went on to say that if the federal government can run such a bank, no state may tax it. Then he dropped that subtly poisonous phrase: "The power to tax involves the power to destroy." That idle phrase was later tortured to mean that no state could tax certain federal employees' salaries, and the reverse soon followed—a state official could not be subjected to the federal income tax. On the strength of that phrase there are now exempt from federal or state taxes thousands of citizens.

The first power set forth in the Constitution is that of taxation. Taxation was permitted for three purposes: to pay debts, to provide defence, and to provide for the general welfare of the United States. There was only one restriction—the taxes must be uniform throughout the nation.

Taxes were laid from our earliest days right up to the present to accomplish more than the raising of money for salaries of federal employees. Roads, museums, colleges were created and supported by taxes. When we wanted to stop the quantity of liquor drinking or the use of tobacco we put taxes on those articles. A one-cent tax on a package of cigarettes limits the output of the manufacturers. In 1936 we pay fifteen cents for a package of cigarettes; six cents go for taxes. Take off the tax and the cigarette industry would make further gains. Congress has always selected certain commodities for social punishment. The manufacture of automobile tires, furs, platinum jewelry, rouge and lipstick at various times have been singled out for taxation. The general welfare, so Congress said, would be helped by special burdens on those luxuries, or on guns and whisky, which people ought not to use too freely. By taxes their use was to be reduced. In time the increase in deaths of mothers at childbirth disturbed our congressmen. They taxed all of us to prevent that increasing mortality. They divided the money among the states which would aid in this welfare campaign against death. Similar grants were given to states in many other co-operative campaigns for the general welfare.

Ever since the time of Hamilton the national government controlled by taxes the life and death of industries. The tariff, used as an implement to protect new industries, was necessarily an industrial control. The manufacturer of pots and pans would continue or cease doing business dependent solely on a tariff which kept out or let in foreign competitive goods. Sugar would be grown only if Congress used its taxing power to impose a high tariff. By the use of this power at various times Congress decided to have ships or sealing wax made in this land or abroad.

The shrinkage of farm income compared to city income led Congress to employ this same tax power to boost the farmer's income so that the farmer could buy from the city worker.

When Congress taxed the users of ham and bread in the cities for the benefit of the farmers, the Court, by a vote of six to three, said that the Founding Fathers had not intended such a tax power. But when the farmers were taxed indirectly on the cost of their clothing and shoes and harness and rope by a tariff boosting the American manufacturers' prices, the judges said that was entirely valid.

The judges by a vote of six to three did not declare the AAA tax in itself unlawful. They disapproved the use to which the tax process was to be put and then repeated that hypnotic shibboleth, "The power to tax is the power to destroy." The Constitution merely said "that public funds shall be spent for a defined purpose, the promotion of the general welfare." The Court said it would hereafter check up on the purposes which Congress selected. Seeds for farmers, money to sufferers of earthquakes, vocational rehabilitation, elimination of the boll weevil, financing of farmers through the RFC—all these activities were approved by the Court. But if Congress in the spending of money induces standards of treatment of the soil to prevent sterilization of the land, to control non-coöperative farmers who destroy their markets as well as our acres, then the taxing power has been abused. One dissenting justice in this case wrote to his brethren on the bench words to this effect: You must have forgotten that Congress is the ultimate guardian of the welfare of the people in quite as great a degree as you are!

How these tax words of the Constitution have been tortured is also demonstrated in the lawsuits involving our income-tax laws.

During the Civil War we had a national income tax. It was never interfered with by the courts. A new income-tax law was enacted about thirty years later. In 1894 the High Judges by a vote of five to four, after hearing Joseph Choate, the leader of the American Bar, argue that an income tax was communism, declared the act unconstitutional. Judge Field held that the law "discriminates between those who receive an income of $4,000 and those who do not . . . whenever such a distinction is made and the law imposes a tax under it, it is class legislation." This was a real blow to popular congressional economic policy. It took us two decades before we passed an amendment to overcome this decision, an amendment to the Constitution which was pressed through Congress by a conservative Republican president, William Howard Taft.

The amendment gave to Congress the power to tax "incomes from whatever source derived." Everyone thought "whatever source derived" meant what it said. But the Court said Congress could not, even under the amendment, tax income from city or state bonds. Billions of such bonds are outstanding. All tax exempt. I have asked innumerable people to read the amendment and to suggest what broader language we could have used to express a desire for a tax on *all* income. But the judges took these simple words and twisted them into a meaning never to be understood by the average American. No wonder we must despair of writing any new amendments. Should we have said: "Congress shall have power to tax income from whatever source derived, *and we mean whatever!*"?

The question is not whether we should again amend the tax amendment, the question isn't whether Congress has acted wisely in the AAA (although by senatorial representation eighty million people were for that measure and only thirty million against it), but rather whether we intend to let the judges decide which taxes may be levied. The Constitutional Convention is now presumed to have said: Tax— but only for purposes the judges approve.

Coinage

The power of Congress to coin and regulate the money of the land has been the subject of three important lawsuits.

Once more a member of the president's cabinet had become the chief justice of the Supreme Court. In 1862, while Salmon P. Chase was secretary of the treasury, he had approved an act of Congress whereby the government issued some demand notes, which pieces of paper could be used to pay debts anywhere in the land. These notes were legal tender. They were thought essential by Congress after the state bank notes had become worthless and after gold was no longer being paid out on the notes issued by the state banks. After the war, creditors started to insist on gold payment on these notes of the government. Sixteen state courts had held the legal-tender acts of Congress constitutional. Several times the highest court was called in to decide the issue but avoided giving an answer. Finally, in the Hepburn case, Chase, no longer treasurer of the United States, now judge, declared Congress could issue such notes but that these notes were not legal tender. The Court by a majority of one said that Congress had no power to make them legal tender. Nowhere could Chase find that the Founding Fathers had in the enumerated powers referred to the issue of such legal tender. Again we have a political twist to the decision. Chase had let it be known that he wanted to be president. He was a candidate acceptable to the creditors of the land—to the rich. Chase's court at that time had only seven judges (there were two vacancies). The decision was by a vote of four to three. By one judicial vote, the action of Congress, passed with Chase's original approval, was vetoed by the Court.

Other cases testing this same law were pending in the courts. On the same morning when Chase's decision was handed down, President Grant filled the two vacancies existing on the bench. Grant is quoted as saying:

They have struck down the Legal Tender Act giving character to the greenbacks with which you won the war. Acquiesce? Never, I will reconstitute the court.

The two new judges had been the attorneys for railroads and other large companies heavily in debt, unable to pay their creditors in specie and anxious to have the new legal-tender notes declared lawful. Grant was accused of packing the bench. And why not? Packing means only that the president nominates persons who agree with his philosophy of government. What else should a president do?

The Hepburn decision was promptly reversed by a vote of five to four. The notes became legal tender once more. Thus only for a very short interval did this judicial veto of legislation survive. Only because opportune vacancies existed was the Court pulled out of its disgraceful dilemma. A decade later the Supreme Court, when other monetary legislation came before it, refused to invalidate acts of Congress; and finally, in 1935, the Supreme Court in the gold case upheld the Roosevelt policy by which contracts calling for payment in gold were amended by congressional action. After the legal-tender case of 1871, lenders of money insisted that their contracts should specifically provide that the debt be repaid in gold. But when under Hoover the 120 million people of the land all wanted gold for their bills, there wasn't enough gold to go around. We had inflated so that with only four billions of gold we had promised to pay out ten billions of gold. Congress then said: You can't get gold even though the bill or note or contract you hold says the United States or some railroad will pay in gold. This time the Court said Congress could abrogate those contracts. That is the effect of the decision, at least. You can't get what was promised.

It continues to be a highly speculative game to guess in advance what the Supreme Court will do in these money cases. So speculative that vast market operations on the stock exchanges have been predicated, not on crops or human toil or ingenuity of producers and inventors, but on the turns the judges may give to the 1787 concepts of coinage.

In rendering the dissent in the 1935 gold case Judge McReynolds dramatically bemoaned the passing of the Constitution. If he couldn't have the Constitution interpreted as he saw it, "the Constitution" was "gone forever."

Bankruptcy

The Constitution gave Congress the power "to establish . . . uniform laws on the subject of bankruptcies throughout the United States." Congress was thus enabled to relieve interstate and intrastate debtors from the burden of paying their bills. No one at the convention of 1787 believed that contracts were entirely sacred. All contracts must be subject to cancellation under congressional sanction. Contracts to pay money or perform services or deliver goods were to be "impaired" by Congress in spite of the clause in the Constitution that no contracts shall be impaired by any state. And Congress thought it wise to relieve debtors, provided that all the money and goods which a debtor had left be equally and fairly divided among his creditors. Under this act practically every railroad and most of our large industrial companies have at times canceled their contracts with creditors, bondholders and stockholders. Later Congress had to give still further relief to debtors. Even if you have enough money to pay every one off in time, if two thirds of your creditors agree to take less than you promised to pay, the other one third are bound to cut their loans to you by the same amounts. This is a democratic impairment of contracts. This bankruptcy power cuts deep gashes into the sanctity of contracts. Interstate commerce could not survive on any other basis.

In 1787 the separate states had bankruptcy laws also, but at a very early stage of our national development the state bankruptcy power was limited and restricted by the Supreme Court. Bankruptcy in the main was to be an interstate, a national, process. No state, only the nation, was permitted really to interfere with interstate commerce by bankruptcy legislation.

At the time of the framing of the Constitution the states were bankrupt. Special provision was made to take care of their distress. The nation was to take care of their debts. One hundred and fifty years later—in 1936—the cities and states were to appeal once more for help. They pointed to the words of the Founders, Article 1, Section 8: "The Congress shall have power to establish . . . uniform laws on the subject of bankruptcies throughout the United States." The cities and states said to Congress: "Help us. We want extension of time to pay. We want equitable reductions of interest rates. We don't want the bankers to take over our towns. The federal courts should supervise whatever we do in settling our debts." But the Supreme Court read an exception into this Section 8, paragraph 3. After the words "throughout the United States" they inserted "except cities and states." Not all of the nine judges wanted to make that addition to the Constitution. One judge, however, started to tear out the entire clause and seemed to doubt that there was any power in Congress over any bankruptcies, for he spoke of *the supposed power* of the federal government incident to bankruptcy."

Cities and states must muddle along, with great suffering to their creditors, or continue to pay interest on their bonds by closing down schools and health departments.

Contracts

The delegates at the Convention were afraid of the paper-money agitation, inflation and Dan Shays' Rebellion. In Article 1, Section 10, they wrote: "No state shall . . . pass any . . . law impairing the obligation of contracts."

This was intended to prevent relief of debtors by the various states, although Congress was not to be restrained from impairing contracts.

Up in New Hampshire stood Dartmouth College, chartered in 1769 by a grant from the royal governor, establishing a corporation, "The Trustees of Dartmouth College." The trustees divided into two camps, the dominant group being Federalist-Congregationalist, the minority group Republican with non-Congregationalist members. When the state went Republican the legislature amended the charter of the college and put over the heads of the trustees a group of overseers.

The old majority (Federalists—the party of Marshall) took the matter to court. The highest court of the state said that the legislature's act had been entirely lawful, that Dartmouth was a public institution, and that the federal constitution's clause about contracts could not apply because there never was any intent to have the states, in their control over their colleges and public officers, limited by the Supreme Court of the United States. It said that the charter wasn't a contract in the ordinary sense.

An appeal was taken to the Supreme Court of the United States. Brilliant Daniel Webster, as attorney for the ousted trustees, put on a swell act, bringing the judges to tears by his sentimental elocutionary peroration: "It is a small college, and yet there are those who love it." Neither the argument nor the decision was much commented on at the time. The Court held that a college charter was a contract and that a state could not change it. Little did even Marshall appreciate that in 1935 one of our smallest states in one year would grant five thousand charters. After that decision, state legislatures freely gave charters, only to find their hands tied by the Dartmouth case. But Marshall acted with consistency. Previously he had held that the Yazoo land grants in Georgia might reek with fraud, but that Georgia could do nothing about them. A contract was a contract, at least to four of the five judges on the bench. We shall see how later judges reversed these cases and decided that certain contracts could be lawfully impaired. Not all judges read the Constitution in the same way.

One of the earliest decisions of Marshall's successor, Roger Taney, in 1837 carved a large piece out of the Marshall logic of contracts. Massachusetts had granted the right to put a bridge over the Charles River. Thereafter it gave a similar right for another bridge over the same waters. The first beneficiary of the state claimed his business would be hurt. But the Court said: No, in dealing with the state, you get nothing by implication. If the state hasn't said you have an exclusive bridge it can let out the right to put one on each side of you. This reversal of Marshall was even extended after the Civil War so that all contracts with a state are now subject "to regulations for the protection of public health, public morals and public safety." None of the last phrase is in the Constitution. It is judge-made law; and so just when a regulation protects "health, morals or safety" is no longer for elected legislators to decide but for appointed judges to determine.

In college charters the contracts stand. In public bridges the contract is affected with a public interest and can be impaired. If you own a dry-goods store and enter into a contract with the electric-light company to give you light and power for five years at an agreed-upon price, the state public service commission can tear up the contract and raise the rate you are paying to the public utility company. Thus the judges permit the breach of contracts between individuals if they think "health, morals or safety" warrant it.

If you are a farmer and Congress grants you a three-year extension for the payment of your mortgage because it thought it reasonable to give farmers such extensions, you do not get the relief unless a majority of the Supreme Court judges also think that Congress was "reasonable." The banks were permitted to disregard their agreements to pay on demand. This was gaily called a "holiday." The insurance companies refused to meet their contracts. Your policy said you could borrow on it, but after the banking holiday of 1933 that clause was temporarily disregarded. The courts said that was excusable. Minnesota tried something different to help the farmers. It gave farmers up to two years to redeem foreclosed farms, and the Supreme Court permitted that change because it happened to agree with the Minnesota legislature's, appraisal of the need and because it believed the conditions imposed for the extension were reasonable.

Just when a contract is impaired is no longer the question. The problem is for Congress and the states to guess just what kind or amount of impairment the judges will stand for. It is not easy guessing when the votes stand five to four. The Court controls the extent of the breach of contracts. It must not seem unreasonable to the Court. Had the courts stood by Marshall in the Dartmouth College case they might today have made a clear issue. Marshall refused to condone any change in a contract. But since the Charles River bridge case, the courts have said some impairments are lawful and others are not. It depends on public interest as appraised by the judges. The question that confronts the American people is not whether we want to stick to the words of the Constitution. No one will argue that contracts shall never be impaired. Now the issue is: shall Congress decide what kind and degree of breaches of contracts are necessary for the general welfare of the nation, or shall the judges of the Supreme Court continue to have the power to declare the amounts and kinds of impairment? Who are better equipped to appraise the relief the public needs at times from existing contracts—the elected officials or the appointed judges? If a railroad has promised by contract to pay in gold, the Court says Congress can cross out the word *gold*. Certainly an impairment.

To most laymen the issue seems to be: either no impairment should ever be allowed or, if impairment (aside from the great lawful impairment of bankruptcy) is ever allowed, Congress should be permitted to use its discretion without a veto power in the judges. As matters now stand, Congress may legislate as to contracts "for the general welfare," as those words are defined by nine men—the Supreme Court. It is as if the Constitutional Convention had written the clause: No state shall pass any law impairing the obligation of contracts *except as the Supreme Court thinks wise for the nation or for any particular group of creditors or debtors.* (ITALICS NOT BY THE FOUNDERS, BUT BY LATER JUDGES.)

Interstate Commerce

John Marshall, who wrote the Marbury decision, was also to write what has been called the "Emancipation Proclamation of American Commerce."

Two entrepreneurs, Robert Fulton and Robert Livingston, had capitalized the steamboat invention of John Fitch. New York State granted them a monopoly to run the new steamboats in its waters. A man named Ogden who held a permit from Fulton became irritated at one Gibbons a Jerseyite, who held a license from Congress but none from New York. Ogden tried to keep Gibbons out of the New York waters. He took Gibbons to court. The New York courts said that the state of New York had a right to grant the monopoly and Gibbons could not enter its waters. At that time new interstate commercial reprisals were being inaugurated up and down the coast. Masters of New York vessels were excluded from Ohio and Connecticut streams. Gibbons appealed to the Supreme Court in Washington. Daniel Webster, arguing for Gibbons, won another important victory when Marshall reversed that much overestimated New York jurist, Chancellor Kent. Marshall was quite cowardly once more. He decided that Gibbons could sail lawfully in the New York waters solely because he held a congressional permit. But one of Marshall's associates on the bench was more forthright in holding that even if Gibbons held no license from Congress, the state of New York could not ban his boats because the "ruling object" of the Constitution was "to keep commercial intercourse among the states free from all invidious restraints."

The Southern states were promptly troubled by this decision. What of those laws which had forbidden the entry of free Negroes into their states? Would the same national economy be applied to override such local state restraints? While riding circuit, soon after the Gibbons case decision,

the Supreme Court had to face that very problem. Marshall
ducked the real issue once more, but the Court as a whole
held that no state could prevent the entry of free Negroes—
a good decision in the light of the 1787 convention debates,
but openly and consistently violated by every Southern state
until after the Civil War. Despite the Supreme Court's decision Negroes were prevented from crossing state lines.

From these early days until after the Civil War the
Supreme Court was busily engaged in preventing state interference with the free flow of commerce. The court vetoed
Alabama's steamboat-registration law, Louisiana's bankruptcy law, New York's bank tax, Massachusetts' tax on
alien passengers, Nevada's travel tax, California's tax on
vessels and North Carolina's railroad tax. In odd merchandise like dead game, green lemons and water running from
streams, the Court said the states might prevent exports.
But in most important fields, whenever a state took steps
which interrupted the national pattern of commerce, the
Court declared the state statutes unconstitutional.

Near the turn of the century, when our industrial society
was getting into full swing, the Court was faced with the
other side of the economic medallion. If states were not
allowed to interfere with interstate commerce, then Congress must have the right to regulate and control it.

Around 1890 the national regulation of railroads was declared valid. In that same period the Court said Congress
could control price-fixing agreements. The regulation of
prices of commodities, if reached by agreements of manufacturers or merchants, was well within the commerce power
of Congress. Congress had the right—said the Court—to
prevent certain kinds of price fixing in oil or coal or sugar.
Even toothpaste or chewing gum was subject to certain
federal controls. Unfair trade competition, misbranding of
articles, deceptive advertising came within the right to regulate interstate commerce. These minor frustrations of
national commerce could be regulated by Congress.

The congressional power was permitted by the Court to
destroy entirely the business of interstate lotteries. Lotteries,
which during the 1787 convention were considered not only

proper and moral but inherently a lawful undertaking for churches and schools, were prevented in their interstate flow. The States' Rights group objected, but the Court said that Congress could stem the flow of these pieces of paper across state lines. Likewise seditious or obscene literature was included by the courts within the periphery of interstate commerce, despite the Bill of Rights which presumably guaranteed freedom of the press and the free spread of ideas. Congress went on and regulated the interstate business in food and drugs. Only pure food was to cross state lines. Congress laid down standards for determining the word *pure*. Prostitutes carried across state lines were held to be in interstate commerce. Oleomargarine was likewise held to be subject to regulation by Congress.

In 1916 Congress found that many states had tried to prevent the unhealthy commercial competition that resulted from allowing children to work in the mines and mills. It decided that no separate state could accomplish enough alone. Congress wrote a law: No goods are to be shipped in interstate commerce out of a state if children have been employed thereon. Congress left each state entirely free to work children, even babies, at the looms or sewing machines within the state if the goods they made were sold within the state.

The Supreme Court took up the case. In effect it held that the Founding Fathers meant those words, "interstate commerce," to include printed lottery tickets, oil securities, impure tomatoes, sexually inciting literature, prostitutes— but not the products of child labor. The impurity of child labor was distinguished from the defects in ketchup.

Judge Holmes in his dissenting opinion wrote:

Congress is given power to regulate interstate commerce in unqualified terms. It would not be argued today that the power to regulate does not include the power to prohibit.

He wrote that there was no room for doubt on the subject. He analogized the power to control oleomargarine shipments and the products of child labor.

But the Court held that child labor may not be thus reduced and that the act meddled in intrastate affairs even though under the act each state could have continued to work children in the factories. Only the exporting of goods across state lines was to be curtailed.

But Congress continued to regulate interstate commerce in other fields more remote from economic welfare and wide human comfort. It regulated the shipment of stolen automobiles and the kidnaping of human beings for ransom. To such the Court gave its approval. Congress regulated the shipments of prison-made goods and aided the states in punishing people who sold prison-made goods imported from another state. The Court said that the Constitution gave such power to Congress.

Finally the National Industrial Recovery Act test case came before the Court. A short time before this case arose, certain workers in the live-poultry industry, including the teamsters, had refused to load and unload poultry in New York City for shipment in and out of the state. The Supreme Court said that this effort of the teamsters affected interstate commerce and ordered the teamsters to stop their obstructions to the flow of interstate commerce.

But in the NRA case the same Court held that the same poultry business did not affect interstate commerce. Then the jurists further drew the line between direct and indirect effects on interstate commerce. When the coal miners strike for higher wages and better working conditions, we are told that this action directly affects interstate commerce; but when Congress tries to prevent strikes of the workers by setting up boards to regulate coal prices and wages, the Court by a close vote holds coal mining is not such interstate activity as to permit congressional regulation.

Congress set up a retirement plan for railroad employees. The business of railroads for fifty years has been held to be interstate commerce under the Constitution. But the Court held that Congress does not have the power to require railroads to pay pensions to retired employees. Five judges drew that fine line, although Chief Justice Hughes and three others disagreed.

The net result of these decisions means that no longer is

the power in Congress to determine what is and what is not interstate business. That line the Court alone intends to draw. No longer may Congress determine what kind of treatment interstate commerce requires. That is for the Court to decide. Whether pensions or compulsory safety devices or child labor are to be allowed will in each case be decided by appointed judges and not by elected legislators.

Back of this situation there lies a grave problem of government engineering. Do we want the 531 members of Congress to control the hours of labor and working conditions in every nook and cranny of the land? Since nearly every farmer and every factory ships some of its product across some state lines, is every farm and every factory to be regulated from Washington? Will this not produce a giant government, unwieldy, incompetent and corrupt? How far the people of this land want such centralization to proceed is a problem of great moment. Just when does the public need for coal or oil become as nationally significant to our happiness as is the running of the railroads, or the shipping of oleomargarine or stolen automobiles? If we have decided that the running of telegraph wires across the land is interstate commerce, who shall determine that the news flowing on such wires is to be regulated by the separate states only?

But the issue now before the American people is not whether the production and sale of coal or oil or food or news are interstate activities subject to congressional control or local problems to be handled by the separate states for the common welfare, but rather which department of our government shall decide which industrial sores need national treatment as opposed to state treatment. Shall the Congress have the power to say child labor in the cotton mills of all states is as much a nationwide problem as the shipment of three hundred firkins of butter from Wisconsin to Delaware? That the business of lotteries is no less interstate commerce than the shipment of coal? That the proper marketing of Western beef in the Eastern states is just as much of interstate concern as the shipping of Joyce's *Ulysses* across the state lines? Is the oil industry incapable of

national regulation while the fraudulent oil stocks have long
been held to be touched with interstate importance?

We are now in an economic No Man's Land. To most
laymen it appears that Judge Roberts, in the Agricultural
Adjustment Act case, on behalf of the majority of the Court,
said: There is no power to regulate agriculture. Congress
cannot do it constitutionally and the states are incapable of
doing it practically. . . . Neither state nor nation has the
realistic power to regulate ice or coal or minimum wages.
From the decision of the Supreme Court judges there is no
ready appeal. What are we to do when the Court flouts
Judge Holmes's decision that: "Congress is given power to
regulate interstate commerce in unqualified terms"? What
but chaos can come in a society wherein the judges are the
final arbiters as to whether coal or ice or bread is of interstate concern? Is our Congress to regulate commerce to such
extent and in such a manner as seems to be vital for interstate harmony—or are the nine judges, usually with wide
disagreement among themselves, to be the final arbiters?

CHAPTER XXIV

Bringing It Home

These DISTORTIONS of the Constitution do hit into the home.

A man forty-six years of age is thrown out of work. He goes to hunt new work. From a private employment agency he is sent to a job. The agency charges him a fee, but he's down and out. He says: Why not charge the boss the fee? It isn't fair to charge the man who has nothing.

A state legislature hears his story and provides by law that a private employment agency may charge fees only to the employers. The people of the state, on a referendum, vote for this social change. The state courts say: That's fine. The United States Supreme Court says: It's shocking. The Constitution will not allow it.

This man's wife gets a job working at night in a hotel at $9.00 a week. She can't keep the home going; she can barely keep herself alive. Congress enacts a law fixing a minimum wage at which women may be worked in hotels. The woman is to get $11.50 a week. She is delighted. Her congressman has done well for her. Forty-five judges of state and federal courts consider this type of law. Thirty-five say it is good— only ten say it is bad. Again the Supreme Court pushes her back nearer to starvation. It's unconstitutional by five to three, one justice not voting.

When this couple get on their feet, they finally climb into the brackets of the rich. Jointly they have earned $5,000 in one year. Only four men out of every hundred in the United States earn that much. The government tax collector comes around. They file their income-tax return. One day they learn that J. P. Morgan, America's richest banker, paid less tax than they did. They go to see the congressman. He says:

Sorry, but the Supreme Court has decided for Mr Morgan. The Court says none of the money he gets as interest on the bonds he holds of cities and states can be taxed by the United States. His stock dividends are not income. The Supreme Court says the Constitution protects Mr Morgan.

This average American has a brother who for years worked on the railroads. He is now close to seventy. Shouldn't he get a pension? The congressman says: Sure. Five of the judges say: Don't be capricious—you are as arbitrary as the four other judges on this bench. Don't you realize Congress may not fix up such a pension system? That this is not the kind of regulation of interstate commerce which the Founding Fathers had in mind?

His state tries to establish a system of workmen's compensation. This merely means that all consumers pay, in the cost of each article they buy, for the doctor and hospital bills of those workers who have been injured in the manufacture of the goods so purchased. The merchants go to the capital to protest. To the nearest state they will move. Local factories declare that they cannot compete against competitors in other states, for elsewhere no such burden must be added to the cost of goods. The employers prefer to hire lawyers to prove that every accident is the fault of the worker. Thus the cost of the controversy (that is, the cost of the courts and judges) is borne mostly by the taxpayers.

The legislature wasn't scared at all. Our typical worker was overjoyed. The fear of starvation through accident was off his mind. But the high court of his state threw out this act. Ex-President Theodore Roosevelt in 1911 wrote about this episode in New York:

It is out of the question that the courts should be permitted permanently to shackle our hands as they would shackle them by such decisions as this, as the decision by the same Court many years ago in the tenement-house cigar factory cases, and the decision of the bakeshop cases shackled them. Such decisions are profoundly antisocial, are against the interests of humanity, and tell for the degradation of a very large proportion of our community; and, above all, they work to establish as an immutable principle the doctrine that the rights of property are supreme over the rights of humanity, and that this free people, this American people, is not only forbidden to better the conditions of mankind, but cannot even strive to do the elementary justice that, among even the monarchies of the Old World, has already been done by other great industrial nations.

For several years the courts deprived thousands of human beings of workmen's-compensation insurance. An amendment to the state constitution reversed the state court. At last the court acquiesced.

This man—in every hamlet, on every farm, in every shop —finds himself of necessity relying on only one hope. The best inventions of men elected to office are nullified by the judges. Force of union organization is the only avenue open for relief. If the force can be strong enough, even judges appointed for life will respect it. Maybe the burning of bridges and roughhousing of sheriffs by Western farmers crept into the subconscious of the judges and directed the pens which gave some creditors relief.

Congress has enacted a law intended to give the workers an equal opportunity to bargain with the bosses. In the Senate of the United States the popular vote on this legislation, the Wagner-Connery Act, was:

In favor	90,476,084
Against	8,295,115
Not voting	22,712,162

How far the courts will let this legislation stand is now being contested. If the Supreme Court limits the Congress on this law, the drive for unionization will grow at an unparalleled pace. Nine men will decide whether we have peace or violence. What type of men will write this chapter of the United States? And will they write it in blood or in ink?

PART IX

The Seventy-six Economic Gods of 150 Years

CHAPTER XXV

The Interpreters

Who were these judicial witch doctors sitting in costumes far different from the overalls of the workers of the land? Where did they come from? Were they educated? Were they rich; were they poor? Why did these few have powers to negate what hundreds of congressmen, senators, legislators and other judges thought wise and proper? Why do they so often get out of step with their times? Why do they so often disagree among themselves?

Lord Bryce once wrote:

The Supreme Court has changed its color, i.e., its temper and tendencies, from time to time, according to the political proclivities of the men who composed it. . . . Their action flowed naturally from the habits of thought they had formed before their accession to the Bench and from the sympathy they could but feel for the doctrines on whose behalf they contended.

In the early days it was not easy to get men to sit as judges. The Supreme Court was a stepchild department, located in cellars or off wings of government buildings. It had no dignity. Men were appointed and declined designation. Others accepted only to resign and accept higher offices, such as judgeships of state courts (then considered higher) or members of local state legislatures. There was little work to do, tedious traveling on circuit and constant recrimination from Bar and layman.

There have been seventy-six of these judges in a hundred and fifty years. Practically all came from the Eastern seaboard. Even though you cannot determine human character by the points of the compass, let it be known that New York and Massachusetts account for nearly one fourth of the total number. Twenty-one states have never had one of their lawyers on the bench.

Here is the geographical distribution:

2	Alabama	1	Minnesota
2	California	1	Mississippi
2	Connecticut	1	New Hampshire
3	Georgia	3	New Jersey
2	Illinois	10	New York
1	Iowa	2	North Carolina
1	Kansas	7	Ohio
3	Kentucky	6	Pennsylvania
1	Louisiana	2	South Carolina
1	Maine	5	Tennessee
5	Maryland	1	Utah
7	Massachusetts	5	Virginia
1	Michigan	1	Wyoming

Their educational identification with our leading institutions speaks for the best training we can offer:

Harvard Law	6	Columbia	2
Columbia Law	2	Dartmouth	2
Yale Law	3	Western Reserve	2
Cincinnati Law	4	Kenyon	2
		Michigan	2
Harvard	8	Dickinson	2
Yale	8	Transylvania	2
Princeton	8	Union	2
William and Mary	4	University of Virginia	2
Temple	2	Other colleges	28

No college, 8

We must remember these men are lawyers. They belong to a profession which has always been basically dishonest. Most lawyers see nothing uncomfortable in arguing causes they do not believe. They sign their names to clients' briefs even though they know the causes are antisocial. Judges, as lawyers, were of necessity double dealers. Being leading

lawyers before they went on the bench, they naturally represented the wealthy merchants and individuals of their day.
Poor folk cannot pay big fees. Workers seldom have enough
money to contest their rights in the courts, a long and expensive process.

As lawyers these men were taught to look behind rather
than ahead. The precedent made by other judges in other
cases determines the best argument for the next case.
Whether or not society ought to prevent children, at tender
ages, from selling the newspapers of the land is not to be
judged from the social effect of such labor. Rather do
lawyers see what a Blackstone or a Marshall said in some
ancient tome about the legal right of parents to use their
offspring for profit. A federal judge in a recent case in New
York, more honest than most jurists, declared from his
bench, "Economics has no place in the courtroom," and a
federal appellate court judge petulantly said in another case,
"Don't bother us with the social implications of this case.
They have naught to do with the law."

Even though the judges of the Supreme Court have
always been members of the Bar, there is nothing in the
Constitution to prevent the president and Congress placing
a layman on the bench. At least one of our states has found
it most salutary to have nonlawyers sit in its highest court.
But these lawyer-judges, who have made so many more
errors than have our congressmen, have surprisingly enough
admitted the errors of preceding judges. Thousands of
Americans have had the satisfaction of learning that they
have lived in misery or want or were condemned to jail un-
constitutionally. Unfortunately, there is no way by which the
Court, when it does want to admit its error, can properly
apologize to all those citizens it has destroyed in the meanwhile.

In the main our Supreme Court judges have been men of
strong physique. Perhaps being appointed to a life job with
a sure income has some effect on the full flow of man's blood
stream. But there have been exceptions so striking that the
judges could not finally keep the public in the dark. At least

one out of every ten of the Supreme Court judges has held office while quite incompetent. Baldwin was undoubtedly insane in his last years; Duvall was compelled to resign because he couldn't hear; Jackson suffered for years from tuberculosis; Rutledge was totally deranged at times; and Hunt had a paralytic stroke but refused to give up his job until a bill was passed by Congress giving him a full-pay pension.

The United States, unlike any nation in the world, has been run by lawyers. In our Congress, as many as a third of the members have been lawyers. This explains in part the great length and intricate language of our laws. This explains why our simplest statutes are set forth in cumbersome, lengthy accumulations of words unintelligible to the general public.

Many of the judges had been in Congress previous to their promotions. As a senator, a lawyer's vote counts for only one out of ninety-six, but as soon as he sits on the Supreme Court bench he is one of nine and may even be the ninth judge who, in those five-to-four decisions, determines the happiness of millions of lives.

Most of the judges had been in politics. Judges are chosen of necessity from among those who are popularly known— and the forum of governmental positions is the loudest legal sounding board in our society. Many of the appointees had previously been rejected by the people for elected offices.

Here is a digest of the judges' previous political experience:

State legislature	19	Other courts	10
President	1	City, state attorney	11
Governor, lieut. governor	6	U. S. attorney general,	
Congress and Senate	20	solicitor general	11
State supreme court	22	Cabinet	20

We picture Supreme Court judges as being very old. Although that has been the case during the past twenty-five years, when the average age of appointment of justices reached over fifty-nine, yet in the first few decades the average was only about forty-five. But young or old they usually sit until they die. The average term in office of a Supreme Court judge is sixteen years.

Here are the ages at appointment, arranged by decades:

Terms		Average age	Terms		Average age
1789–	99	49	1859–	69	51
1799–	1809	43	1869–	79	56
1809–	19	45	1879–	89	58
1819–	29	52	1889–	99	56
1829–	39	51	1899–	1909	53
1839–	49	54	1909–	19	59
1849–	59	46	1919–	29	58
			1929 to date		59

Nearly all of them have been well-to-do. Their legal careers have been spectacular in part because they represented the large utilities, as was the case with Charles Evans Hughes; the railroads, as did Butler; trust companies, as did Roberts. I intend no implication by making this point other than the obvious conclusion that any lawyer who has been the advocate, with great success, for the corporate interests of the land is often unaware of the problems of life confronting the poor and the weak.

Those judges who started with little personal wealth seem to be more unmindful of the threats of unemployment, penniless old age and the perils of industrial accident and disease than do those of secure family wealth, like Oliver Wendell Holmes.

This is no place for even brief profiles of these seventy-six rulers of our land.

Attractive vibrant characters many of them were. Jay, steadfast loyalist until 1773; Rutledge with his twenty-six slaves; Cushing, the only lawyer in Lincoln County; Wilson, a fugitive from arrest because of land speculations; Blair with his 100,000-acre estate; Harrison, who declined to sit; Washington, a favorite nephew of George Washington; Story, with his income of over $10,000 a year from legal writings; Curtis, who took in over a half million dollars in his law practice: such were the men who held the seats up to 1857, the time of the Dred Scott decision. From that period until the 1870s we find men like Swayne, counsel for railways; Miller, who died penniless; Davis, who left two million dollars at his death in 1886; and Strong, who resigned to practice law in Pennsylvania.

During the industrial era we run across Matthews, who resigned because the salary was too small; Shiras, who was counsel in practically every important lawsuit in western Pennsylvania in his day; McKenna, the personal attorney for Leland Stanford, the richest man in the West; Holmes, who died with an estate of close to half a million dollars; Taft, who left a similar amount; Gray, with only a quarter of a million; and Day and Brewer, with no personal estates.

There is no need for any outsiders trying to guess about these men called judges. Justice Samuel Miller, who sat on the bench for twenty-eight years, from the time he was forty-six, when he was appointed by Lincoln, until he died penniless in 1890, wrote in 1875:

I have for thirteen years given all my energies and my intellect to the duties of my office, and to the effort to make and keep our court what it should be. . . . But I feel like taking it easy now. I can't make a silk purse out of a sow's ear. I can't make a great Chief Justice out of a small man. I can't make Clifford and Swayne, who are too old, resign, nor keep the Chief Justice from giving them cases to write opinions in which their garrulity is often mixed with mischief. I can't hinder Davis from governing every act of his life by his hope of the Presidency, though I admit him to be as honest a man as I ever knew. But the best of us cannot prevent ardent wishes from coloring and warping our inner judgment. It is in vain to contend with judges who have been at the bar the advocates for forty years of railroad companies, and all the forms of associated capital, when they are called upon to decide cases where such interests are in contest. All their training, all their feelings are from the start in favor of those who need no such influence.

Many articles and books have given appraisals of the present nine justices. As a group they are consistent at least in one respect: they consistently disagree with each other on important issues. Such divisions of opinion are implicit in their backgrounds and previous records. Read in the light of Justice Miller's statement just quoted, these thumbnail sketches may take on real meaning.

Thumbnail Sketches of the Nine Justices

CHARLES EVANS HUGHES, born in 1862, after a faithful clerkship became a member of a law firm which represented life insurance, railroad and banking companies. An able lawyer, keen investigator, who rode to governorship on a spectacular job as counsel in an investigation of insurance companies. But he touched only the surface of the insurance problem, uncovered vast corruption but apparently was unaware of or unconcerned with the deeper implications of insurance—its influence on farm, railroad and housing problems.

In 1910 he was appointed to the Supreme Court by President Taft and for six years supported minimum-wage legislation, helped the Court reverse its previous disapproval of federal-employers-liability-insurance acts, dissented in the Leo Frank civil-liberty case and rejected the yellow-dog labor contracts.

In 1916 he ran and was rejected by the people for president, later joining the Harding cabinet. Responsible for gagging Karolyi, former president of Hungary, on a visit to our shores, he himself kept silent all through the Daugherty-Fall corruption era when noncabinet citizens seemed to be aware of the filth at the cabinet table.

In 1932 he went back on the bench on Hoover's appointment after years of representing the richest and largest corporations of the land.

Senator Borah joined with twenty senators in opposing his appointment solely because of Judge Hughes's reactionary point of view. Senator Norris wisely warned us, "No man in public life so exemplifies the influence of powerful combinations in the political and financial world as Mr Hughes." Even Senator Carter Glass opposed the appointment. Judge Hughes's administration of the Court will go down in history as one which has done much to confuse the public. He is aware of this reputation, and it obviously worries him. To the amazement of many he defended the Railway Retirement Act, the regulation of milk by New York State, and some other social legislation.

WILLIS VAN DEVANTER, born in 1859 in Indiana, son of a successful attorney father. He held local political jobs and at the age of thirty became chief justice of the Wyoming Supreme Court. Resigned after only one year to represent railroads, cattle and land companies. In 1897 he became an assistant attorney general, to be appointed in 1903 a district judge by President Theodore Roosevelt. In that position he decided an important case against the Standard Oil Company and two cases in favor of his former client, the Union Pacific Railroad. President Taft sent his name to the Senate for appointment to the Supreme Court. William Jennings Bryan shouted, "This is the man who held that two railroads running parallel to each other for two thousand miles were not competing lines," one of the roads being the Union Pacific. In practically every case involving railroads his interpretation of the Constitution agreed with that of the railroad's attorney; and in nearly every case involving civil liberties he has found no effective protections in our Bill of Rights. He is an expert on legal forms and procedure.

JAMES CLARK MCREYNOLDS, born in 1862, spent his early years of practice in Tennessee. Defeated for Congress in 1896. After several years in the United States attorney general's office, he joined the New York law firm headed by Paul D. Cravath, still one of the leading law offices of the country representing undeviating resistance to any planned economy. Later attorney general under Wilson, but soon a trouble maker in the cabinet, and promptly put on the Supreme Court on the first possible occasion. Forthright, not wheedling, reactionary. Intolerant of modern ideas such as preventing child labor and providing minimum wages. Favors gag laws and jailing of those who carry red flags. Once supported human liberty under the Bill of Rights to permit advertising of baby farms for mothers of unwelcome children. He is isolated on the bench. To him a contract is still immutable. He is comfortable while people starve.

Louis D. Brandeis, born in Kentucky, 1856. Successful Boston attorney advocating laws limiting hours of labor and minimum-wage legislation long before the issues were popular. His appointment to the Supreme Court was bitterly fought by the leaders of the American Bar, but President Wilson stuck to his guns. Brandeis soon lined up with Oliver Wendell Holmes on the bench, favoring wide latitudes of state experimentation and preserving free speech and free press except during the World War, when the Civil War bullets in Judge Holmes's body brought both judges to limit the First Amendment. He never mentions the profit motive in his opinions, but hammers away at the dangers of bigness. He made an outstanding contribution to our jurisprudence by starting a new type of factual briefing for the education of the judiciary. Law to him is not remote from life. He once wrote: "There is no reason why five gentlemen of the Supreme Court should know better what public policy demands than five gentlemen of Congress."

George Sutherland was born in England in 1862. Not eminent at his profession, law, he went into local politics, ending in the United States Senate. He fought progressives such as Senior Senator Robert La Follette, Senator Beveridge and President Woodrow Wilson. One of the dominant bosses of the Republican party, he attached himself to the Harding campaign headquarters.

At one time he was president of the American Bar Association. Practically all of our modern legislation was opposed by Sutherland during his political days. Having done well by himself in the game of living, he fails to appreciate any of the reasons why uncontrolled society destroys the ambitious and able as well as the incompetent and phlegmatic.

Pierce Butler, born in 1866 of poor parents. Became a locally noted wrestler. Soon after admission to the Bar he became identified as attorney for railroads, opposing lower rates and urging higher valuations. Rejected by the people in 1906 for state senatorship on the Democratic ticket, he joined the office of the United States attorney general, losing his two most important cases, one against the meat trust and the other to enforce the Pure Food and Drug Act.

When President Harding nominated him for justice of the Supreme Court, several senators opposed the confirmation. The City Council of his own city sent in a protest against confirmation. Attorney General Daugherty's strong endorsement of Butler was needed to assure the Senate confirmation. When the Senate acceded to the appointment it was generally understood that the Justice would not sit on railroad cases.

HARLAN FISKE STONE, born in 1872 in New Hampshire, though always closely associated with the very rich and, before his accession to the bench, frequently appearing as their lawyer, spent his legal energies in the main at Columbia University until in 1924 he was appointed United States attorney general. In 1925 he was advanced to be a justice of the Supreme Court. Lining up with Cardozo and Brandeis on most issues, his opinions have neither the gracious style of Cardozo nor the analytical factual background material of Brandeis, but they carry a sting which clearly indicates the wide breach on the bench and a vitality and directness that speak an excitement for the future. His disdain for the "stuffed shirts" of the legal profession, his inward fear of acting up to the role of one of the nine legal dictators, are evident at every oral argument and in each opinion he writes. Probably more deeply troubled by conflict between elected and appointed rulers of the nation than any of his brethren on the bench. If he does not resign in disgust we may some day address him as chief justice.

OWEN J. ROBERTS, born in Philadelphia in 1875. A brilliant mind, great powers of concentration and a Macaulay-like memory of printed words brought him prompt advance both as a teacher of law and as a practicing attorney. While practicing he clearly indicated abhorrence for co-operative governmental activities, coupling the creation of quasi-judicial bodies with the threat of Communism. When President Coolidge was forced to move in the oil scandals he selected Roberts as one of the government counsel. Later Senator Walsh, who had inspired and conducted the investigation of the great Coolidge-era oil frauds, Senator La Follette and other senators opposed his appointment to the Supreme Court. The Senate had just rejected the nomination of Judge Parker and in comparative retrospect might now admit they erred. For a time Judge Roberts was considered the deciding justice, but he now falls in line with Van Devanter, Butler and Sutherland in cutting down the power of Congress.

BENJAMIN CARDOZO, born 1870, in New York City. Remote aesthete, his legal ability soon was recognized by the New York Bar. He was a lawyer's lawyer. As chief justice of the Court of Appeals of New York, he repeatedly led that court to reverse opinions of previous decades. His writings have a grace which invite laymen as well as lawyers to read the current law reports. Reluctant to leave his New York court, he now probably regrets leaving to accept President Hoover's nomination for the Supreme Court. By instinct or intuition he reaches the conclusions which Judge Brandeis reaches through economic slide rules, Judge Stone through disciplined scholasticism, and which Holmes attained by leading a full rich life.

In ability, erudition and tenacity these nine jurists clearly surpass the highest bench of any state court and are collectively superior to any group of men ever sitting on the Supreme Court bench during the century and a half of its existence.

PART X

How to Curb the Judges

JAMES MADISON *had proposed a periodic review of the Constitution. Pennsylvania had long had such a procedure. Much
can be said for a constitutional system under which, each
decade, the people take stock to see what portions of their
basic laws are out of date and what new additions would be
helpful.*

*Today the great munition manufacturers—the Du Ponts
—are the leaders in a movement to resist any such reconsideration. They have inveigled Alfred E. Smith, former
governor of New York, now a bank president and realtor,
to become their standard bearer. The bitterness of William
Randolph Hearst is acceptable to them. They have been
grateful for Walter Lippmann's assistance. They have the
support of many organizations such as the Union League
Club of New York, whose committee, including United
States Senator Barbour, Republican of New Jersey, and
Congressman Bacon, Republican of New York, has clearly
stated the conservative position on change:—*

They [being anyone who wants a change] are seeking either to in-
timidate, overawe or undermine the Supreme Court, or to limit its
powers, and some have indulged in suggestions even more sinister
and lacking in character and responsibility, such, for instance, as an
increase in the number of judges, such additional judges to be appointed from those who it is known in advance will be subservient
to the will of the executive appointing them.

*The Du Pont-Smith-Hearst-Liberty League group is
solidified. Within their ranks there are no divisions. But as
must be expected, those who advocate a change are split into
innumerable factions.*

More than seventy different amendments aimed at the veto power of the courts are pending in Congress. But Senator Logan from Kentucky does not see eye to eye with Senator Schwellenbach from Washington, although both want a sufficient national power to prevent economic chaos. Newton Baker, former secretary of war and now the legal adviser to the utility companies in their struggle against government competition, announced: "Of course the Constitution should be amended," adding: "I have a couple of amendments myself." His proposals will not coincide with those of Senator Norris or of John L. Lewis or of Congressman Marcantonio. From the law schools we find the professors writing drafts of proposed changes. General Hugh S. Johnson thunders against "judicial anarchy" and asks for legislation to prevent the bewilderment that has come over the land because of "judicial frustration of popular mandates." Labor organizations have repeatedly asked for clarification, and change. Social workers resolve at their meetings that an amendment is needed for the health of the nation. Lawyers don't budge.

There exists a profit-making entity, the American Institute of Public Opinion. Its function is to poll groups of people on questions of public interest. In August 1935 it announced answers indicating in general the following:

"Do you favor curbing the power of the Supreme Court?

"Yes   41%
"No   59%"

"Would you favor an amendment to the Constitution to increase federal government control over wages, hours, working conditions and business practices in all lines of industry?

"Yes   48%
"No   52%"

In November 1935 it announced a new poll allowing for an answer, "No opinion" on the question, "As a general principle would you favor limiting the power of the Supreme

Court to declare acts of Congress unconstitutional?" The tally showed:

"For   31%
"Against   53%
"No opinion   16%"

Whether or not this organization in its appraisal of public sentiment included in proper proportions the men in the mines, factories and farms as well as those who ride in Pullmans or sail fast sloops, the cry for change shown in the answers is so striking that it cannot be disregarded. Moreover, in valuing this public expression, bear in mind that since November 1935, the date of the last poll, the Supreme Court has vetoed the stabilization of the coal industry, the granting of pensions to railway workers and the fixing of minimum wages for women in any state of the Union.

Sixteen different senators and forty-seven different members of the House of Representatives—elected from thirty-one different states—offered resolutions in the last Congress asking for amendments to the Constitution.

The only reason the popular demand for a change has not crystallized is that in the diversity of proposed remedies no leadership has developed to bring about an agreement on a common program. In the absence of such an agreement the laissez faire group, symbolized by the Liberty League, can hold its fort.

CHAPTER XXVI

Suggestions

THE ADVOCATES OF CHANGE fall into three primary camps. There are those who claim that relief from the judicial congestion of a national program can be obtained without a statute of Congress or amendment to the Constitution; those who desire some statutory changes; and those who seek new amendments.

Without a Statute or Amendment

In deploring a recent decision of the Supreme Court of the United States, one of our smoothest critics wrote: "Somehow and sometime, the decision will be reversed." True enough, the High Court has the capacity to reverse itself. To the credit of the judges it must be said that the Court has quite often admitted its errors. But seldom has the Court said frankly: We were wrong in Smith against Jones. We take it all back. More often does the Court turn a neat corner, take a slight wiggle and distinguish a new case from its old-time decision. Few men, including judges, are willing frankly to admit errors. In the midst of such wiggling even lawyers cannot chart a course.

In 1851 the High Court abjectly declared that it had erred in a decision of 1825. During the intervening years many citizens suffered by that early faulty guess—or maybe the later guess was wrong. For some years foreign corporations were deemed ineligible to sue in the federal courts, but in 1844 the Court changed its mind and opened its doors. Until 1852 the Supreme Court said it had no power to hear cases arising on the Great Lakes. Then for the first time the

311

judges re-read the law. Just how they knew in 1852, and not before, that the delegates of 1787 meant the Court to take jurisdiction over the Great Lakes is not disclosed in the opinion. A decision of 1903 was corrected after twenty-seven years, and one of 1895 was set straight in 1904.

In the field of taxes the Court has been most versatile and fickle. Contracts are another field where the Court has often adjusted its ideas. Slowly, to be sure, the courts have bent the constitutional phrase about not impairing a contract. Each set of judges has given the clause a little different twist. For a time the judges held that Congress could not touch monopolies among manufacturers, since manufacture is not interstate commerce. On that occasion the *American Law Review* said: "The Sugar decision counterbalances all the good the Court has done in seventy years and inflicts a wound on the rights of the American people." Within a few years the Court reversed its position. After the first legal-tender cases, on which the New York *Times* commented: "The first legal-tender decision, if it stands, strips the nation of one of its means of warfare and defense," we find a flat reversal.

From a score or more of such reversals, all listed by Justice Brandeis in a recent decision, some people reach the conclusion that our present dilemma can be resolved by patiently waiting for the Court to change its mind.

The embarrassment of that position lies in the fact that the reversals usually come only after a change in personnel on the bench. The plea realistically is for reversal by death. But not even death brings results soon enough for a hungry people. Some of the important swings of the Court had to be induced through open defiance by states or large groups of citizens. Oftentimes decisions of the Court have lain dormant for decades for the simple reason that, after the Court has spoken its last word, it becomes legally difficult, if not impossible, to bring another case before it. The very finality of the decision removes the opportunities for correction.

But even if we could rely on the Court itself to correct all its errors, the pace of present economic and social change permits no such fortuitous and lazy national jurisprudence.

In an integrated economic structure such as the world enjoys today each decision has the inevitable capacity to bring immediate unemployment, disease and misery.

The best that can be said for the many generous reversals is that they prove the absence of science in the law. The nine men do not always claim to possess a divining rod for testing the pure mind of the Constitution. Increasingly often the decisions must be rendered without any opportunity to test the statute against the results of actual experience and operation. Cases arise by accident, parties juggle for favorable facts, and by pressure, in a welter of briefs, we develop our legal "system of delusive exactness."

To urge a continuation of correction by reversal is merely admitting that the law is uncertain, so uncertain as to lose the respect of the people. In days of increasing dictatorship, uncertainty in the law encourages the forces of Fascism.

Reform by Statute

Those who urge reform by congressional act without amendment suggest three different devices: take from the Court the right to hear appeals on constitutional questions; add more judges to the bench; or prevent decisions on constitutional questions by bare majorities.

Let us examine these three courses.

1. *Take away the right to hear appeals*. The Supreme Court is today a constitutional convention sitting in perpetual session with no readily available check left in the people. Can we arrange to have the Court act only as a court without being a constitutional convention of nine?

The Founding Fathers provided that the Supreme Court's jurisdiction was definite in only two respects: (1) cases involving ambassadors and (2) cases involving states.

In those cases the jurisdiction is original. A state or an ambassador may go directly to the Supreme Court. In all other cases the Supreme Court may hear appeals from lower courts, but only if Congress says it wants the Court to hear such appeals. Bear in mind that all of the lower federal courts from which such appeals may come can be discontinued entirely by an act of Congress. They are not constitutional courts.

Two years after the Civil War was over a rebel editor—McCardle—was arrested by federal military officials in Mississippi for publishing "incendiary" articles. McCardle pointed to the First Amendment to the Constitution and from his jail asked, "What about freedom of the press?" Congress wanted to keep him in jail and did not want the Supreme Court to have any say in its reconstruction program in the South. McCardle fought the case up to the Supreme Court. That Court decided in great haste that it would hear his argument for freedom. The case was set down on the court calendar for March 1868. Congress, alarmed at the possible interference by the Court with its program, rushed through a law specifically aimed at Mc-Cardle. Congress said to the Court: The Constitution says you Supreme Court judges can hear appeals only under our "regulations and exceptions." We now regulate you and make an exception. You shall not hear any appeal from any decision on the law under which McCardle is in jail. Johnson was president; he vetoed the bill. Congress passed it over the veto.

The Court took pause. It said that McCardle's right of free press affected "millions of our fellow citizens" and that the country had "a right to expect" the Court's attention. But unanimously it declared: "It is quite clear therefore that this court cannot proceed to pronounce judgment in this case, for it has no longer jurisdiction of the appeal."

On these words many Americans who want a unified industrial nation pin some idle hopes. They suggest we repeat the formula and allow no appeals on constitutional issues. They forget that not many years after the McCardle decision the same Chief Justice Chase took much of it back. He said: Even though Congress may "under imperious public exigency" pass legislation like that used to oust the Court in the McCardle case, the Court need not always agree with Congress as to whether an "imperious public exigency" exists.

It is true that Congress has limited the jurisdiction of

the federal courts in many directions. No longer may federal courts grant labor injunctions as they did from 1870 to 1932. You cannot sue a citizen of another state for money in the federal court unless the amount involved is at least the sum Congress has fixed. But let Congress try the McCardle plan over again with the Supreme Court, and it is most doubtful that the judges will meekly submit. They will find no "public exigency." They can find many words in the Constitution to befuddle the issue. That instrument, in referring to the Supreme Court, talks of *cases* in one clause and *controversies* in another. What a heyday the legal mind, remote from mine and farm, can have with that! And if that isn't enough, explore this: When does a case or controversy arise? Is it not when someone questions a law, and isn't the Constitution also a law, or did the Founding Fathers distinguish between law—statute and constitutional?

This indirect approach to the problem would leave us in decades of doubts. Not until the Supreme Court had been approached with an avalanche of cases would we know whether or not the judges would accede to the regulation imposed by Congress. Maybe they would declare the regulation aimed at shutting their mouths unconstitutional. Maybe their vote on that question would be by five judges to four!

In aid of this approach some people have suggested that we establish a new court like our Court of Claims to which all appeals on constitutional points will flow, taking from the Supreme Court all appellate jurisdiction. Only in rare cases would the Supreme Court then, it is urged, get constitutional cases under its original jurisdictional powers.

Such a course will either confuse the public still further or create another machine which in time will try to curb our Congress. The public will never understand such a flank attack. It would satisfy only a few lawyers in the community.

2. *Increase the number of judges.* Early in our history the Supreme Court was reduced to five members—to prevent, said the Republicans, the appointment of one of their party to the nation's highest tribunal. During the Civil War, in 1863, the number of Supreme Court judges had been increased to ten. But after Johnson became president, Con-

gress became antagonistic both toward him and the Court
and reduced it to eight, which it became on the death of
Judge Wayne in 1867. Since much of the distrust felt for
the Court disappeared with the election of Grant, a new
statute was passed in 1869 providing for a bench of nine,
and there have been nine judges ever since. There is no
constitutional limitation on the number of judges. It is
urged that Congress should provide, in a joint program with
the president, that all the United States senators shall sit
on the bench in addition to the present nine judges, thus
approximating the British system. There is only one qualification—the judges, under the Constitution, must be appointed for life so provision would have to be made that the
senators retire from the bench if not re-elected to the Senate.
Under this program the nine non-senator judges would still
have the power to veto statutes, but only those passed by a
majority of less than five in the Senate of the United
States.

To add all of the senators has many attractive features.
Of course the senators need not sit actively as judges. The
effect of their addition would merely be that the judges
would be aware that they had nine votes out of a total of
(96 plus 9) 105 on constitutional questions. But what if
senators refused to resign from the bench? What if their
resignations in advance were held unconstitutional by the
present bench of nine?

Others urge: If we cannot add all the senators to the
bench, why not add one or two judges as we have done in
the past? This proposal seems to me to be one of cringing
desperation. It might bring temporary relief but certainly
has no enduring benefits. To dig the Supreme Court out of
a hole we filled vacancies in the '70s, but aside from the
reversal of the one opinion in the legal-tender case there
was no visible enduring benefit.

Jefferson's and Madison's appointees did not sustain their
acts but joined with Marshall. Jackson's appointees opposed
his policies soon after appointment.

Then again, who would be added? Wilson put McRey-

nolds on the bench to be relieved from the embarrassments
of McReynolds as an attorney general. Hughes went on the
bench from 1910 to 1916 and voted as a liberal; but after
sixteen years as private attorney for large financial interests
and as cabinet officer, and even after twenty-one United
States senators warned the public of his unsocial attitudes,
he went back to the Court to line up fairly consistently with
those who veto the popular mandates. Then again Hoover
puts a Cardozo on the bench and Coolidge appoints a Stone.
These perversities of selection should give the proponents
of this approach considerable pause.

3. *No more five-to-four decisions.* Here again a change
is proposed that is said to require no amendment. The shock
of the odd god ruling the land leads to many proposals for
an act of Congress providing that: "No statute may be declared unconstitutional except by a greater vote of the justices than the present five-to-four majority vote." Some
—among others Senator James A. Reed—want it to be six
to three; others seven to two. Senator Borah at one time
strongly urged such an amendment, quoting Webster and
Clay in his support. Others say, to veto an act the Court
should be unanimous.

Whether the judges will agree that such statute is a
"regulation" or whether they will set aside such "regulation" as being antagonistic to the republican form of government guaranteed by the Constitution is truly an open
question. But even if the judges chanted "Amen," little will
have been accomplished other than to create a triad, quartet
or ninesome of gods not subject to election or recall. The
essence of allowing a civilized people to act through their
currently elected servants will not have been obtained.

Constitutional Amendment by Change of Vocabulary

If a mere act of Congress will not satisfactorily enlarge
the bench or destroy the slim majority rule of reaching decisions or remove the Court from constitutional questions,
these same controls could be set forth in the form of amendments to the Constitution. But if we are going through the

effort and stir of an amendment, why not seek a more direct and enduring approach to the problem?

Those who urge amendments fall into two main classes. Some want to redefine words like taxation, interstate commerce, due process, contracts and general welfare. Others want to address an amendment to the power of the Court to override the Congress.

I have examined no less than a hundred separate drafts of amendments. Many are pending in Congress. I find a variety of suggestions: to limit the jurisdiction of the Court to revenue acts; to provide that constitutional cases may not be brought by individuals but only by states; to declare that a judge loses his office if he votes to invalidate an act. Some would extend the federal power over interstate commerce to include practically all enterprise. Others would extend the federal power to cover practically all legislation regarded as desirable to promote the general welfare.

Many proposals seem simple and clear on first reading. If any of us could learn in advance how the judges would interpret the words employed, the agreement on many of these drafts would be a simple matter.

Charlton Ogburn, the able counsel for the American Federation of Labor, proposes an amendment to circumvent the judicial destruction of economic and social legislation. His aim is to give Congress power to legislate in any field of "general welfare" and to provide that no defence may be set up by any person on the basis of contract violation or lack of due process:

The Congress shall have power to pass laws concerning matters affecting the general welfare of the people. This power shall be superior to the police power of the several states, and defenses invoking deprivation of property without due process of law and the obligation of private contracts shall not be imposed to any suit brought under any law made under this power.

Lloyd Garrison, formerly chairman of the National Labor Relations Board, suggests:

Congress shall have power to promote the economic welfare of the United States by such laws as in its judgment are appropriate, and to delegate such power in whole or in part to the states. Existing state powers are not affected by this Article, except as Congress may occupy a particular field.

Several senators propose amendments on the lines of the above but refer specifically to wages, hours, industrial practices and agriculture.

Congressman Lewis proposes no longer to allow corporations to complain if the due-process clause hurts them. His amendment reads:

The provisions of Section 1 of the Fourteenth Amendment to the Constitution of the United States shall be held to apply only to natural persons and not to corporate or other artificial persons created by law.

Senator Ashurst has a seven-word amendment:

"The Congress shall have power to make laws *to regulate agriculture, commerce, industry and labor.*"

Congressman Marcantonio suggested:

The Congress shall have power to establish uniform laws through the United States to regulate, limit and prohibit the labor of persons under eighteen years of age; to limit the work time and establish minimum compensation of wage earners; to provide for the relief of the aged, invalided, sick, and unemployed wage earners and employees in the form of periodical grants, pensions, benefits, compensation, or indemnities from the Public Treasury, from contributions of employers, wage earners and employees, or from one or more of such sources; to establish and take over natural resources, properties, and enterprises in manufacture, mining, commerce, transportation, banking, public utilities, and other business to be owned and operated by the Government of the United States or agencies thereof for the benefit of the people, and generally for the social and economic welfare of the workers, farmers and the consumers.

These are samples of the attempts to grant to Congress unmolested power over certain of our economic problems.

To all these and similar proposals the objection is made that Congress is irresponsible: it may yield to temporary pressures. Of course this may be true, but our choice is simple. Do we want a responsive government, one which acts upon public demand (called by the Liberty League "yielding to group pressure") or do we want the present judicial blockades? If a group of nine men is all that preserves our liberties, then we are lost in any event.

Another objection raised is that the states will be utterly submerged. If our Senate were set up on a basis of a majority of the popular vote on democratic lines there might be some danger of a bare majority of the population overriding the wishes of the balance of the people. But not so in our congressional structure, where little Nevada can balance New York in the Senate, New York can override, with five votes to spare, eighteen states in the House, and Pennsylvania and Indiana can override New York.

Of course the basic danger of any such amendment, no matter how worded, arises from the historical proof that the judges will again whittle away any new words we may select. Try as we will to give Congress more power, what guarantee is there that the Court will not say: Yes, Congress has those powers, but not if they run counter to the due-process or contract clauses, or if in the use of such power the taxing power is improperly employed. . . . These judges who have blocked our progress will not surrender like cowards. They have faith in an unregulated economy. By what proof from their past acts do we justify a belief that they will run away?

The reason why no new weasel words will do the trick is to be seen from the old words so often fought over in the past.

Due process, for example. Nine lawyers sit on the bench. They all agree that the act of Congress must stand unless it appears to be "arbitrary" in its violation of due process. Arbitrary is the word they use. Five say Congress was arbitrary. Four say no, Congress was reasonable. The five judges call the other four arbitrary. Q. E. D. The act falls.

And before we try to write new legalisms, let us bear in mind what the judges did with that simple phrase: "incomes, from whatever source derived." Years of struggle to procure the Sixteenth Amendment to the Constitution with those concise words have brought a stream of decisions that *whatever* means all except certain sources of income. Other decisions of the Court in turn chiseled down the word *incomes*. If two words like *incomes* and *whatever* can be contracted or expanded by the judges at pleasure, what hope is there that *economic welfare* will stand up as the authors may now hope for it? What a party the Court will have with any such phrases! Don't forget that due process today means, not 5 or 6 or 6½ per cent return on capital, but such exact per cent of return on such computation of base capital as the judges from time to time think reasonable. Words of necessity have changing contents. Whose content do we wish applied? Appointed judges or elected representatives?

CHAPTER XXVII

An Amendment Toward Democracy

DURING OUR CENTURY AND A HALF of national existence we find a constant but slow tendency toward democracy. We have moved a long way from the limited rights to vote which existed in 1787. No longer do property qualifications leave the voting power in the very wealthy. By three separate amendments the people have obtained greater powers of the franchise. Women vote, Negroes have the right to vote and we elect our senators by direct election rather than through our local legislatures.

Aside from state representation in the Senate, the only two nonresponsive devices in our machine of government still in existence reside in the right of a president to remain in power after the popular mandate of the people has rejected his program and the right of appointed judges to veto the popular desires of the people. As to the presidential situation, the lame-duck amendment recently enacted absorbed part of that social lag, and the provision for overriding of the presidential veto by two thirds of the Congress considerably reduces the peril of an executive out of tune with the times.

But we are still living with a Court devised for a population of only 25 per cent literacy, when the worker was thought disqualified to express an opinion as to the type of government he desired.

It is high time we amended our constitution so that Congress has the power to override any decision of the Supreme Court. This is the English system. But today our Supreme Court is both a Parliament and a House of Lords. The Court is not controlled by the Constitution, because the words of the Constitution seldom dictate any one ineluctable decision. The Court at times reverses its own precedents, and although it prefers to follow its own former decisions, it is not bound to do so, any more than is the British House of Lords.

If we followed the British system by an amendment to the Constitution the Court could not declare a law unconstitutional but could, of course, decide that a law reached only certain persons or situations. Congress then, if it desired, might enact a new law to comprehend the facts which the judges had held untouched by the previous one.

For example, the Supreme Court declared that stock dividends were not income under the income-tax law passed under the income-tax amendment. Under a British system Congress would enact a new law saying: Stock dividends are to be deemed taxable income. Thus would that issue be put to rest. Under our present system, if we want to tax stock dividends, or tax city or state bonds or judges' salaries or the many other items of income excluded by judicial decrees, we have only one recourse, additional amendments to the Constitution.

If we do not care to go so far as Great Britain toward a forthright complete democratic control, we might at least follow one of the dramatic proposals of the delegates at the Constitutional Convention.

Madison repeatedly urged that the Supreme Court be put on a parity with the president in the veto power. He advocated: if the Court declares an act unconstitutional, Congress should have the power to override the decision by a two-thirds vote of both houses.

This suggestion has all of the authenticity of wide support of many of the Founding Fathers. It contains that degree of pause and delay which permits coagulation of public opinion. A law passed in 1936 would not reach the Court until 1937 or 1938; if declared void, the Congress of 1938 or 1939 could override the veto, but the public would have had several years of debate on the value of the law in the meanwhile, and many new congressmen would be holding office in 1939 who were not sitting in 1936.

The Madison plan was proposed when there were only a

dozen or so states in sight. With our forty-eight states it
has an enhanced advantage over the cumbersome machinery
of amendment by states. It calls for an impersonal consideration of political issues not possible in the suggestion of
Popular Recall of Judges or Judicial Decisions, devices
urged by President Theodore Roosevelt, Alfred M. Landon and others around 1912.

If we called a constitutional convention to review the entire instrument we would probably have at the convention
none other than our senators and congressmen; and any
new constitution so written would in turn have to face the
fundamental question: Should not our people be permitted
to determine their national destiny by the votes of states
represented in the Senate and of people represented in the
House, rather than by divergent opinions of fortuitously
appointed judges, sitting for life, not subject to recall or
disapproval?

Madison had proposed that in case both the president
and the Supreme Court veto an act, a three-fourths vote of
Congress would be required to override these dual vetoes.
Such a high vote, in view of the historical record of presidential vetoes—a record not available to Madison in 1787
—now seems unnecessary.

The Madison suggestion if adopted would in time enhance the stature of the Court. The Supreme Court in
vetoing an act of Congress would be inspired to build up
enough popular support for its decision to cause Congress
to hesitate about overriding it. Such a machinery of necessity will make the judges wary of taking positions which
Congress will certainly override. On the other hand, judicial
opinions from the highest bench would then be read with
wide public interest, and the Congress in turn would be less
than impetuous in slapping down a Supreme Court decree,
particularly if it were unanimous. The Supreme Court would
establish a continuity of integrity—but only if it deserved
it. Its valid sanctity would rest on a broad base. It would
once more be a court and not a constitutional convention.

State legislation would still be reviewable by the Supreme
Court. In 1925, for example, whereas 34 out of 309 cases

in the Supreme Court of the United States raised constitutional issues, in New York State only 9 out of 480, in Wisconsin only 8 out of 288, and in Colorado only 5 out of 271
arguments in the highest courts of those states required an
examination of constitutional questions. State acts could
still be voided by the Supreme Court, but under this machinery Congress, by appropriate legislation, might take
into the federal control the gist of such state legislation. For
example: the Court declares state minimum-wage legislation unconstitutional as being in violation of due process.
Unless Congress acted further in that field the Court's
decision would be the last word. But Congress could by a
two-thirds vote override this opinion by passing a minimum-
wage law nationally or permissive for states.

If Congress were permitted to override the Court, there
would be territorial trades in Congress. Oklahoma would
urge the right to regulate ice; Pennsylvania, the right to
stabilize coal; New York, the right to prevent loss-leader
merchandising; or Oregon, the privilege to control private
employment agencies. There would be give-and-take. But so
would there have to be similar give-and-take on any legislation adopted under any one of the other proposed amendments, which change only words rather than basic popular
controls. But such exchanges are of the essence of the democratic process.

To reshape our nation by writing new constitutional
definitions is but a grammarian's chimera. To select, by new
definitions of *general welfare* or *commerce* or *due process,*
areas for congressional control and regions for continued
judicial domination is only bequeathing to our children the
repetition of our dilemmas. To segregate certain areas for
democratic controls to be left in Congress and others to
remain in the Court is but to say we fear democracy.

In our land the democratic process has never been given
full sway. All through our history our heroes—Jefferson,
Jackson, Lincoln, Theodore Roosevelt—have spoken in
burning terms of this frustration of democracy by the Supreme Court.

If we move toward the Madison amendment, if we

restore to Congress the power of legislation, if we overcome the judicial veto by giving Congress the power to override the Court as it can the president, we can call to the support of our cause none other than John Marshall. As if in penance for his Marbury dictum, he declared in 1804, when Congress threatened to remove a federal judge from office:

A reversal of those legal opinions deemed unsound by the legislature would certainly better comport with the mildness of our character than the removal of the Judge who has rendered them unknowing of his fault.

Democracy in a complex society can persist only if the ultimate power of government flows without hindrance from the people to their elected responsive officials. The frustration of congressional action by judicial interpretation requires Congress to choose between surrender and leadership.

THE END

INDEX

INDEX

Abolitionist literature, in 1835, 196.

Adams, Abigail Smith, wife of John Adams, 108.

Adams, Henry, on reform, 239.

Adams, James Truslow, 111.

Adams, John, library of, 20; writes of division in Second Continental Congress, 49–50; radical member of committee, 50; peace negotiator, 57; fights for protective trade clause in treaty, 64; worried by commercial backwardness of states, 8; on democracy, 70; profile sketch of, 108–9; royalist plans of, 165; receives thirty-four electoral votes for president against Washington's sixty-nine, 187; approves Sedition Act, 216; as ex-president, leaves Washington at 4 a.m. the day Jefferson is inaugurated, 222; dies on same day as Jefferson, 222; wore satin coats and knee breeches, 222; plots to defeat Jefferson–Madison drive for power, 227; appoints Marshall chief justice, 228.

Adams, Samuel, not at Constitutional Convention, 7; pays $2,000 in depreciated currency for suit of clothes, 16; a wealthy radical, 38; organizes secret movement in 1774, 47; suggests that America declare herself free, 50; introduces man to negotiate union with Canada, 55; on the function of the Confederation, 58; profile sketch of, 109–10; favors ratification, 180; pays respects to Tom Adams, 217.

Adams, Thomas, 217.

Age of Reason, The, by Thomas Paine, 115–16.

Agricultural Adjustment Act, underlying philosophy of, appreciated by Madison, 68–9; formula same as that contained in Hamilton's tariff plan, 213; Court's decision on, 288.

Alabama, admitted to Union in 1819, 231.

Albany Convention, in 1754, 9, 45.

Alleghany Mountains, effect on nation, 44.

Allen, Ethan, takes Fort Ticonderoga, 48.

Amending process, method of, affected by ignorance of Western development 133–34; dictated by compromises of Constitutional Convention, 173–74; in other governments, 174.

Amendments to Constitution, relating to election of vice-president, 164; of higher validity than original sections, 194; first ten ratified, 194; due-process clause of Fifth repeated in Fourteenth, 194; the First, 194–95; the Second, 197–98; the Third, 198; the Fourth, 198–99; the Fifth, 199–201; the Sixth, 201; the Seventh, 201; the Eighth, 202; the Ninth, 203; the Tenth, 203; the Eleventh cuts down power of Court, 172, 230–31; the Twelfth, 231; the Thirteenth, 257; the Fourteenth, 257; the Fifteenth, 257; the Sixteenth, 258; the Seventeenth, 258; the Eighteenth and Twenty-first, 258; the Nineteenth, 258; the Twentieth, 258; the three following the Civil War, 266–67; more than seventy now pending, 308–09; discussion of those now pending, 317–21.

Ameling, glass-blower, asks subsidy from Congress, 213.

American Institute of Public Opinion, 308–09.

Americanisms of 1787, 125–26.

Anesthetic, first used in 1842, 238.

Annapolis, the Deauville of early America, 34; convention meeting place, 70.

Arkwright, water frame of, 44.

Army, pay in 1780s, 17; pay and pensions of, 52–3; unpaid soldiers form a mutinous bonus army in 1783, 55.

Articles of Confederation, powerless to control commerce, inflation, etc., 17–18; sent to states for ratification in 1777, 53; necessity for revision

329

The

New York to Philadelphia
= 48 Hours
= 2 Hours
= ½ Hour